Women and Missions: Past and Present

Anthropological and Historical Perceptions

Cross-Cultural Perspectives on Women

General Editors: Shirley Ardener and Jackie Waldren, for The Centre for Cross-Cultural Research on Women, University of Oxford

CROSS-CULTURAL PERSPECTIVES ON WOMEN | VOLUME 11

Women and Missions: Past and Present

Anthropological and Historical Perceptions

EDITED BY

*Fiona Bowie, Deborah Kirkwood
and Shirley Ardener*

BERG
Providence/Oxford

First published in 1993 by

Berg Publishers

Editorial offices:
221 Waterman Street, Providence, RI 02906, USA
150 Cowley Road, Oxford, OX4 1JJ, UK

Library of Congress Cataloging-in-Publication Data
Women and missions: past and present: anthropological and historical
   perceptions / edited by Fiona Bowie, Deborah Kirkwood, and Shirley Ardener.
      J. ca. -- (Cross-cultural perspectives on women)
     Includes bibliographical references (p.   ) and index.
     ISBN 0-85496-738-9 (Cloth) 0-85496-872 5 (paper)
  1. Women in missionary work. 2. Missions--Africa. Sub-Saharan.
  I. Bowie, Fiona. II. Kirkwood, Deborah. III. Ardener, Shirley.
  IV. Series.
BV2610. W618 1993   92-15997
269'.2'082--dc20   CIP

British Library Cataloguing in Publication Data
A CIP catalogue record for this book is available from the British Library.

ISBN 0 85496 738 9 (hb)
     0 85496 872 5 (pb)

Photographs by courtesy of Studio Edmark, Oxford; Professor E. Kirkwood;
Langham School, Zimbabwe; Borneo Mission Association; and the Bodleian
Library, Oxford.

Printed in the United States by Edwards Brothers, Ann Arbor, MI.

Contents

Acknowledgements

The editors gratefully acknowledge the support given to this project by the Economic and Social Research Council.

Adrian Hastings' paper 'Were Women a Special Case?', first delivered at the Centre's Workshop on the Past and Present Impact of Missionary Activity on Women, at the Cherwell Centre, Oxford in 1987, has been published in Adrian Hastings, *African Catholicism*, SCM, 1989.

Abbreviations

AIM	Africa Inland Mission
CCK	Christian Council of Kenya
CIM	China Inland Mission
CMS	Church Missionary Society
COCIN	The Church of Christ in Nigeria
CPSA	Church of the Province of South Africa (Anglican)
CSM	Church of Scotland Mission
CSM & AA	Community of St. Michael and All Angels
CWW	Committee for Women's Work (SPG)
DO	District Officer
ECWA	Evangelical Churches of West Africa
EKAN	Ekklisiyar Kristi a Nigeria
EKAS	Ekklisiyar Kristi a Sudan
LMS	London Missionary Society
MHM	Mill Hill Missionaries (The Society of St. Joseph)
PMS	Paris Missionary Society
SIL	Summer Institute of Linguistics
SIM	Sudan Interior Mission
SJ	Society of Jesus (the Jesuits)
SPCK	The Society for Promoting Christian Knowledge
SPG	The Society for the Propagation of the Gospel
SUM	Sudan United Mission
USPG	The United Society for the Propagation of the Gospel
WMA	Women's Mission Association (SPG)
WMMS	Wesleyan Methodist Missionary Society

List of Photographic Plates

List of Maps

Preface

A swift glance at the contents page of this book leaves no doubt as to its diversity. Not only do the essays range over time and space, the contributors themselves bring a variety of skills, experience and insights to the study of women in the context of Christian missionary activity; many issues are explored and topics revealed for further discussion and research.

Given the extent of the field, in terms of both history and geography, selectivity was essential. The relative compactness of the book, which some readers may welcome, has both positive and negative aspects. We regret that we were not able to include essays dealing specifically with women medical missionaries or with the work that women undertook as linguists and as translators of the Bible, hymns and religious works. The impact of the missions on the women in the receiving cultures, manifested in their participation in church-related groups such as the Mothers Union, the YWCA and the well-known Manyano associations in South Africa merit further close attention. The conscientisation of women in the context of liberation theology, notably in South America, is another area where further study must be undertaken.

This volume owes much to earlier work. For example, among many others, the three editors of this book have each, independently and for long, been interested in missionary activity in Africa and in the study of women. We have all published on these topics, as the references to various of the contributions here will indicate. This book conjoins our dual interest and adds to already published work sponsored at Oxford by the Centre for Cross-Cultural Research on Women. Studies of particular relevance include the *The Incorporated Wife* (eds H. Callan and S. Ardener, 1984), which considers examples of the relationships between women and the institutions employing their husbands. The British Colonial Service, the British Council overseas, the military and a transnational oil company, provided examples of the processes whereby the identities and activities of wives are shaped.

At the workshop that preceded the above book, Janice Brownfoot asked Kirkwood why missionary women had not been included in her study of settler wives in Zimbabwe. Kirkwood's first response was 'because they appeared marginal to the social life of the settlers'. The omission was not forgotten and she recalled how her close friendship with a Zimbabwean professional woman had drawn her attention to the impact of a mission education on a particular, if somewhat exceptional, young woman and her family. On her next visit to Zimbabwe in 1983, Kirkwood and her husband visited some of the pioneer mission settlements. In one missionary cemetery they were struck by the contrasting sizes of two headstones (see illustration on p. 30). The larger commemorated a male missionary, the smaller that of his co-worker wife: here was a further prod for the present study.[1]

Ardeners's work on the early history of Cameroon aroused her interest in the mission field. Until 1887 the Baptist Mission Church had an important role in pre-colonial Cameroon. This mission, which was later replaced and augmented by other Christian denominations, still maintains a presence through the Independent Baptist Church in Limbe (formerly Victoria), Cameroon. There had also been many significant female missionaries in West Africa, of whom Mary Slessor of Calabar is one of the more famous; Emily Saker, Gwen Thomas and Anna Rhein-Wuhrman of Cameroon are other examples.[2] Ardener, like Kirkwood, was interested not only in the various roles of the missions, in the influence of particular missionary women, and in the way they contributed to the development if specific settlements and boundaries, but also in how much the national identities of some African nation states owed to them, especially through the life experiences of the elites. This could only be hinted at here, however. Still more work needs to be done.

Other examples of the interest taken by the members of the Centre in colonial contexts is Helen Callaway's acclaimed book *Gender, Culture and Empire* (1987)[3] and the biography which Alison Smith, together with Mary Bull, edited: *Margery Perham and British Rule in Africa*

1. Coincidentally, Cunningham's interest in missions was enhanced when he visited a British cemetery in Calcutta and saw the headstone of Mrs Mary Hill (p. 85).

2. Emily Saker wrote a book about her father Alfred Saker (1909) which provides some glimpses of her own life and that of her mother. For Gwen Thomas, see G., Hawker *An Englishwoman's Twenty-five Years in Tropical Africa* (1911). Anna Rein-Wuhrmann wrote several books in the first quarter of this century, which are valuable sources of ethnographic material on the Kingdom of Bamum. See also S. Ardener *Eye-witnesses to the Annexation of Cameroon 1884–1887* (Government Press, West Cameroon, 1968) for further information on missionary activity in Cameroon.

3. Published by Macmillan Press in 1987, this book was awarded the Amaury Talbot Prize for African Anthropology.

(1991). Another of the Centre's books, *Bilingual Women: anthropological approaches to second language use* (eds. Pauline Burton, Ketaki Kushari Dyson and Shirley Ardener 1993), also deals with the effects on women of culture contacts, as reflected in their language choices, which were often subject to various colonial and missionary policies.

From these and other recent studies and discussions it is clear that colonial and missionary activities must not be treated as though one were merely a branch of the other. Clearly, there was a complex relationship between administrators and missionaries. Sometimes the missionaries identified with the local people and their traditions in opposition to Colonial Office policies; often missionary health and education programmes advanced colonial objectives; sometimes missionaries were criticised for tampering with traditional customs by administrators who wished to preserve them; examples of such cases can be found in the chapters that follow.

There was, of course, a third dimension to be considered, to which Fiona Bowie also draws attention, namely the ability and skill used by peoples among whom both parties worked in accepting, rejecting or transforming the goods and services offered. Indeed, the people selected what they wanted and went their own way when they did not agree with the advice tendered. This volume demonstrates the tenacity of local beliefs, even in some cases after hundreds of years of persuasion, and shows (to any who are still in doubt) that those living in non-Western cultures have certainly not been mere pawns in administrators' and missionaries' games. Indeed, insufficient thought has been given to the transformations brought about in missionary culture itself by those it targeted – of whom some became missionaries or church workers themselves – who have in their turn made an impact on the visitors and through them on their metropolitan institutions.

With this background, in September 1987, the Centre held a workshop, convened by Kirkwood and Ardener, to elicit new material on mission policies, on women missionaries, and perhaps more importantly, on the reaction to their endeavours of women in the receiving communities. The workshop was sponsored by the ESRC and was held at the Cherwell Centre, which, fortuitously, is run by the Sisters of the Holy Child Jesus, a missionary order. We are very grateful to them for their efficient hospitality.

At the end of the sessions there was an immediate demand that we should publish the papers: hence this volume. Not all of the contributions, for various reasons, could be included; there are references in the text to some of those omitted. They include papers by the Reverend Timothy Gorringe, Chaplain of St John's College, Oxford, who opened the workshop with some valuable comments on the history of mission activity, and Bishop Michael Nazir Ali, now General Secretary of the Church Missionary Society in London, who gave the closing address. Professor Kenneth Kirkwood, Dr Iona Mayer and Anne-Marie O'Neill Baker all made valuable contributions, which will be incorporated in their own work elsewhere. At the workshop several biographies of individual missionaries were presented: the Reverend Max Saint (author of *A Flourish for the Bishop*) spoke about three women in Sarawak.[4] Dr Francis Mazhero gave an account of work in progress concerning the life of Barbara Tredgold of Zimbabwe. He is currently working on a full-scale biography, which is nearing completion. Elisabeth Croll and Yongjin Zhang discussed various female missionaries in China; their material, will, no doubt, be published elsewhere. In order to cover a wider range of data here, Professor Aparna Basu, Dr Elizabeth Isichei, Dr Valentine Cunningham, Dr Joan Burke, Modupe Labode, and the Rev. Dr Peter Williams were invited to contribute to this book; we are grateful to them for their co-operation.

The editing of the volume proceeded more slowly than we wished, owing to our other obligations, and we therefore invited one of the contributors, Dr Fiona Bowie, to join us in the task and to write the Introduction. Fiona Bowie had long experience in the mission field, having undertaken fieldwork while living on a station in Cameroon before writing a thesis on her findings entitled 'A Social and Historical Study of Christian Missions among the Bwanga of South West Cameroon', which she is preparing for publication. She has also published work in the field of women's spirituality, and is editor of a journal *Logos: The Welsh Theological Review*.

A working pattern emerged: Kirkwood and Ardener made their editorial comments on the texts, passing them on to Fiona Bowie, who, after adding her own, submitted them to the contributors for their consideration. We would like to thank Fiona Bowie for undertaking these responsibilities, and for the admirable Introduction she has written. The volume was conceived by the two convener-editors and their colleagues at the Centre, but its realisation has been speeded and enhanced by the work of our co-editor Fiona Bowie.

Deborah Kirkwood and Shirley Ardener
March 1992

4. Max Saint was formerly a missionary in Borneo. We are indebted to the Borneo Mission Association for the frontispiece depicting a nativity scene, which delightfully brings into focus and weaves together a multiplicity of cultural strands deriving from Borneo, Europe and the Middle East, and neatly illustrates some of the themes of the book.

Silverware presented to Mr Hill, principal Missionary Clergyman at the Mission Chapel at Berhampore.

The inscription reads: 'At a meeting of the Gentlemen on the 28th of Nov[embe]r 1858, whose families were in the habit of attending THE MISSION CHAPEL AT BERHAMPORE, it was unanimously resolved to subscribe a sum of money to procure THIS ARTICLE OF PLATE TO BE PRESENTED TO MR. HILL, as a mark of their sense of the manner in which he conducted himself during a period of fourteen years that he resided at that Station as the principal Missionary Clergyman. Signed F. W. RUSSEL. Chairman.'

(Photographs by courtesy of Studio Edmark, Oxford)

"Bethleham Tableau" Girls of St Monica's School, Sandkar, British North Borneo. 1926
(From the Archives of the Borneo Mission Association, Bodleian Library, Oxford MSS, Ind. Ocn. v 20 1/10)

1

Introduction: Reclaiming Women's Presence

Fiona Bowie

Making Women Visible

> To be pleasing in his sight, to win his respect and love, to train
> him in childhood, to tend him in manhood, to counsel and con-
> sole, to make his life pleasant and happy, these are the duties of
> woman for all time. (Rousseau)[1]

In being seen as adjuncts to men, rather than as historical protagonists in their own right, women have been systematically written out of historical and anthropological records.[2] Valentine Cunningham, referring to the early work of the London Missionary Society (LMS), notes that: 'missionary work... was clearly perceived as a task performed by men that women merely supplemented. Missionary was a male noun; it denoted a male actor, male action, male spheres of service' (p. 89). Reports from the field to head office commonly began 'Dear Fathers and Brethren', and womanly details were edited out of letters when prepared for publication (ibid.). In many cases we know little of the roles played by women in the mission field. Deborah Kirkwood tells us that although Bishop A. W. Lee dedicated his book *Once Dark Country* to his wife 'Without whom the life portrayed in these pages could not have been lived, nor the pages themselves written', he says virtually nothing about Mrs Lee or what she did (p. 28). Even the gravestone of the Rev. Neville Jones, commemorating his missionary work, is twice the size of

---

1. Quoted in M. Eichler, 'The origin of sex inequality', *Women's Studies International Quarterly* (Vol. 2, No. 3, 1979–343), in Borrowdale, 1989.
2. From the anthropological perspective, see Ardener, 1977a, b.

that of his wife who shared his labours (ibid.). James Hudson Taylor (1832–1905), founder of the interdenominational China Inland Mission, was virtually a lone voice when he wrote to mission candidates: 'Unless you intend your wife to be a true missionary, not merely a wife, home-maker and friend, do not join us' (Williams, p. 64 below).

The invisibility of women in history, scripture, anthropology and other literary sources and academic disciplines has become a common-place, and recent publications, especially from the 1970s onwards, have attempted to rectify this situation.[3] *Women and Missions: Past and Present* is one such contribution to this important task of reclaiming women's history and highlighting women's experience. It brings togeth-er a variety of disciplines (social anthropology, history, religious stud-ies, literature) and of perspectives, with papers looking at both women missionaries and the impact of missionary activity on women. The time-scale stretches from the beginning of the modern missionary movement in the late eighteenth and early nineteenth centuries to the present, and contributors come from both mission-sending and mission-receiving countries.

No attempt has been made in this volume to cover all geographical areas, denominations or periods of time. It should also be made clear that our focus is exclusively on Christian missions. The papers reflect the authors' own expertise, with nineteenth-century Protestant missions and sub-Saharan Africa receiving particularly detailed attention. The dual approach to women as missionaries and the effects of missionary activity upon women, with contributors from both the traditional mis-sion-sending, as well as mission-receiving countries, enables us to draw parallels between Western attitudes to women as missionaries and the attitude of missionaries towards women in the cultures in which they worked. This connection between women's roles at home and abroad is illustrated in Valentine Cunningham's analysis of Charlotte Brontë's novel *Jane Eyre*: '[She] does not have literally to go out east to aid the cause of women's emancipation. That particular eastern missionary work is, metaphorically speaking, required to be done also at home' (p. 100). Questions of power and authority, the contextualisation of the gospel message and of the different nuances in women's experience

3. In anthropology see, for example, the numerous publications of the Centre of Cross-Cultural Research on Women (Queen Elizabeth House, Oxford). In the biblical sphere Elizabeth Schüssler Fiorenza's *In Memory of Her* (1983) has been a seminal work. The recent interest in women's history is testified to by titles such as *Discovering Women's History* (Beddoe, 1987), The *Women's History of the World* (Miles, 1990) or the two volume *A History of their Own* (Anderson and Zinsser, 1990).

according to particular circumstances, are also raised in various ways by all the papers in this volume.

A Liberating Gospel or a Colonial Conspiracy?

When I returned to Britain from conducting fieldwork on missionaries in Cameroon, a frequent question put to me was, 'Well, what's the answer? Is the effect of the missions good or bad?' The question didn't make sense; it was the wrong question. A few sentences could in no way express the experience of being a missionary, their motivation and dedication, the multifaceted effects of missionary activity, or Cameroonian perceptions of their Western visitors. I usually replied by quoting what many Bangwa had said to me on numerous occasions when asked about the effect on their lives of the presence of a mission station.[4] Their rather puzzled answer was invariably, 'We have suffered.' If I asked for elaboration my respondents would add, 'Before the mission came our children died'; 'When we were sick we had to walk for three days to the nearest hospital'; 'Our people were dying of malaria'; 'Our people were left behind because we had no secondary school'; and so on. The benefits of mission education and medicine, the development of craft industries, and also the less material aspects of the missionaries influence – their honesty and their care and concern for individuals were obvious to and appreciated by almost all the people I spoke to. As far as the Bangwa were concerned, any considerations of cultural disruption, clashes with mission power and authority and arguments over ownership of land were outweighed by the improved standards of living and the political recognition which having a permanent mission entailed. On the other hand, Western missions in Africa and elsewhere have been evaluated negatively by recipients of their activity. Ngugi wa Thiong'o, in his essay *Church, Culture and Politics* (1972),[5] for instance, put the case that:

> The European missionary had attacked the primitive rites of our people, had condemned our beautiful African dances, the images of our gods, recoiling from their suggestion of satanic sensuality. The early African convert did the same, often with even greater zeal, for he had to prove how Christian he was through his rejection of his past roots.
>
> So that in Kenya, while the European settler robbed people of their land and the products of their sweat, the missionary robbed people of their soul.

4. The Bangwa, of South West Province in Cameroon, have had a permanent mission station, run by the Focolare Movement, since 1965. I conducted fieldwork in this area in 1980–1.

5. Quoted in Dinwiddy, 1978–439.

Thus was the African, body and soul, bartered for thirty pieces of silver and the promise of a European heaven.

Both perspectives, that of the Bangwa and of Ngugi, are in some sense 'true'. The reactions of different ethnic groups and geographical entities, of various sections of a population (chiefs or commoners, converts or traditionalists, young or old), of women and of men, of missionaries and of their hosts, will often vary. Missionary societies also employ contrasting strategies. The fundamentalist evangelical churches (including, it is sometimes claimed, the Summer Institute of Linguistics – the main translators of the Bible into vernacular languages),[6] which are particularly active at present in South America, adopt a largely negative view of native societies, with considerable emphasis on the spiritual and material values of (Western) Christianity and need for conversion. In this respect they resemble their nineteenth-century predecessors rather more than they do other contemporary missionaries from mainstream Churches. Also in South America, Maryknoll Missionaries from the United States, for example, adopt a more liberal strategy which stresses the need to work with the people, enabling them to reach their own goals, which may not include embracing the Christian faith – an approach influenced by liberation theology.[7]

The same denominations or missionary societies generally change their tactics over time as self-understanding develops and outside influences, such as the Second Vatican Council or the women's movement, make themselves felt.[8] As Schreiter (1985: 150) has made clear, there is a dialectical relationship between the preaching of the gospel and culture. The Church is challenged by, and has to come to terms with, its host culture, which in turn is affected by and must react to and accommodate the changes wrought by Christian preaching. An example of this is the way in which the Aladura healing churches in Nigeria have com-

6. See Jonathan Benthall's interview with William R. Merrifield in *Rain*, December 1982, No. 53, pp. 1–5, and subsequent correspondence from Brian Moser (*Rain*, February 1983, No. 54, pp. 10–11) and Theodore Macdonald, Jr and Robert Armstrong (*Rain*, April 1983, No. 55, pp. 12–13). SIL are also known as the Wycliffe Bible Translators. They are interdenominational but primarily recruit from Protestant Evangelical circles.

7. Cf. Salamone's description (1987) of Dominican Sisters in Nigeria and S. Ardener's account (1968) of early Baptist missionaries in Cameroon for a similar contrast in mission approaches.

8. Some of these changes, as well as the continuities, are documented in Michael Nazir-Ali (1990) and in Bowie (1985).

bined elements of traditional and mission teaching.[9] On the other side of the equation, Stanley (1990: 174) makes the point that:

> Missionary experience has now compelled Western Christians to re-examine their rationalistic presuppositions, and to recognise that non-Western attitudes to such phenomena as spirit possession may be much closer to biblical conceptions than previous missionary generations have been prepared to admit.

One of the strengths of the papers in this volume is their avoidance of over-simplistic generalisation through their attention to detail and to the nuances of particular missionary periods and cultural situations. To return to the question, 'Is the gospel liberating and, in particular, is it liberating both for women missionaries and for women influenced by missionary teaching, or is it oppressive (colonialist/imperialist)?' one must answer that it can be both. It all depends on your standpoint and on whether one wishes to view missionaries within their own cultural context or through the lens of the 1990s. The wealth of data presented in these papers will enable readers to form their own opinion. I will mention here some examples which illustrate the ambiguity of the mission experience in relation to women.

Women as Missionaries

Opportunities for worthwhile careers were limited for middle-class women in Victorian Britain (and America). Marriage and motherhood or genteel but poverty-stricken and indolent spinsterhood were the options open to many women. Swaisland quotes an article in *Frazer's Magazine* from 1860 in which this dilemma is spelled out (p. 71 below):

> ...cramped and depressed in their narrow circle of duties to which they are confined. They are conscious of power and may not exert it; of ambition and must stifle it. The disenchantment of life has fallen upon them, they cannot take refuge in active occupation to forget it.

Protestant missionary societies argued about the desirability of sending out women to 'heathen lands', whether as single women or as wives

---

9. Wessels (1990: 114–15) refers to an essay by J. M. Schoffleers in which Christ as *nganga* (healer) is seen 'as the paradigm *par excellence* for an African Christology'. For Wessels, 'The excitement implicit in the idea of using the *nganga* as model for the image of Christ lies precisely in the fact that the *nganga* or medicine man was viewed by Protestant and Catholic missionaries alike as the adversary of Christ'.

of male missionaries. In either case, it was middle-class women of suitable character, in good physical health and ideally with some training, who were recruited. Speaking of the mid-1800s, Swaisland notes that nine out of ten women who applied to emigration societies, though not necessarily as missionaries, were rejected. For missionary work criteria were certainly strict. A member of the SPG Committee for Women's Work stated: 'Far too large a proportion of people who are seriously pathological, or at least queer are offering' (Kirkwood: 34). For those who were accepted there were opportunities for independent action and challenges which would stretch the woman missionary's abilities. Learning new languages, Bible translation, setting up schools and clinics, establishing women's groups of various kinds, conducting religious services, as well as meeting the challenges of running a home in a new culture and climate, more than occupied their time.

Together with the many women missionaries whose achievements were credited to their husbands or to other male missionary colleagues, a few outstanding individuals have left their names as well as their mark on history. Sider (1987) has written of the remarkable career of Frances Davidson, a Brethren in Christ missionary in central southern Africa between 1897 and 1922.[10] Davidson was a gifted linguist and formidable organiser, involved in Bible translation and in the establishment and running of mission stations with all the numerous duties, calling for courage and stamina, which that entailed. Philip Kulp's mother Christina (b. 1896), a Church of the Brethren missionary wife in Nigeria, was also a linguist and is remembered for her work in translating hymns into vernacular languages and setting them to music, as well as in the development of schools and women's organisations (Kulp: 1987). François Coillard, in his account of missionary life in Central Africa, published in 1902, presents a picture of his wife, Christina, negotiating a safe passage through hostile territory, bartering, teaching, healing, counselling, acting as peacemaker, as well as coping with domestic responsibilities (such as washing and no doubt starching linen in the bush) (Kirkwood: 30). Mary Slessor (b. 1848), Scottish-born like Christina Coillard, was from humbler stock than most nineteenth-century missionary women, but after fifteen years of

10. Sider (1987: 55) gives the following description of the Brethren in Christ Church: 'The Brethren in Christ Church was a small religious group, numbering approximately 3,500 members in 1897. The founders of the church were mainly from Anabaptist-Mennonite backgrounds and had had pietistic conversion experiences in the later 1700s. Their conversions led them to found a new relgious body (first known as River Brethren) in 1780 in Lancaster County, Pennsylvania.' They embarked upon overseas missionary work in the late 1800s.

missionary work in south-eastern Nigeria became the first woman in the British Empire to be appointed a Vice-Consul (Hackett, 1987: 51–2).

There were also a small number of outstanding women remembered as missionaries to their own people, such as Pandita Ramabai (1858–1922), mentioned by Aparna Basu. Ramabai came from a Brahmin family and was unusual in having received an education. As a young widow Ramabai studied in England and became a Christian after sending her daughter to be educated by the Anglican Wantage Sisters. On her return to India, Ramabai concerned herself with the plight of young widows and became a greatly respected social activist and evangelist, earning the title *Pandita* or 'learned'.

If women missionaries and missionary wives did find new and rewarding spheres of activity not open to their sisters at home, the cost was also high. Health was a major problem for both women and men, with women often having the additional burden of pregnancies, more likely to end in miscarriage than would have been the case at home, and of rearing young children without the benefits of medical care or family support. Cunningham looks at correspondence between the London Missionary Society and Mary and Micaiah Hill in India to illustrate some of the hardships endured by the missionary pioneer: 'We are constrained in this climate to live medicinally'; 'My eldest boy has been several times on the verge of the grave'; 'perpetual mortality around us' – these are some of the comments made by the Hills in the 1820s and 1830s. While the LMS published records glossed over such comments, the archival letters reveal:

> a long litany of illness and deaths through epidemics, dysentery, fever, cholera. They tell of ailing children, dying wives, dead missionaries, missionary widows and orphans, as well as the occasional mad woman who has to be shipped home (at great expense, accompanied by costly female attendants, against the will of reluctant ships' captains who increase the fare in consequence of their worries).

Stress was another problem mentioned by missionaries. The sponsoring societies were hungry for success stories of 'heathen conversions' and rapid growth, whereas there was often little to show for the missionary's expenditure of time, health and energy.[11] M. O. Williams (quoted in

---

11. This was particularly the case where missionaries worked in areas such as China or India, which were already dominated by a World Religion (a metacosmic religion or soteriology in Pieris' terms). It is only rarely that conversions take place from one World Religion to another without the use of force:

> ...mass conversions from one soteriology to another are rare, if not impossible, except under military pressure. But a changeover from a tribal religion to a metacosmic soteriology is a spontaneous process in which the former, without sacrificing its own character, provides a popular base for the latter. (Pieris, 1988: 89)

Kulp, 1987: 5) lists among the stresses of missionary life:[12] 'shift in physical environment, adaptation to another culture, working in another language, living in two worlds, facing rapid change, dealing with nationals, relations with fellow missionaries, the possibilities for criticisms to become condemnation, need for recognition and status, engaging in significant work and maintaining family life'. Many of these problems were highlighted for women. Recognition was harder to achieve, as was the freedom to exercise responsibility. Women often felt torn between duties to their children and to their evangelical work, and suffered the pain of parting with older children, as those who survived infancy were usually brought up and educated in their country of origin. But in the nineteenth century, no less than today, it was social attitudes which proved one of the greatest handicaps to women missionaries, wasting talent, time and energy which could surely have been better employed.

The 'Headship of Man': Questions of Female Authority

At the 1888 London Missionary Conference J. N. Murdock argued that 'Women's work in the foreign field must be careful to recognise the headship of man in ordering the affairs of the kingdom of God' (Johnston, 1888, quoted by Williams: 65). This was certainly the opinion of Allan Becher Webb, Bishop of Bloemfontein in southern Africa, who stated in 1883, referring to the sisterhood he had started (Swaisland: 79):

> All Sisterhood work, to be perfect, ought...to be carried on with the real central power vested in the Bishop.... The work must be under his personal control (as representing the Great Head of the Church) and rule; not under the irresponsible rule of any woman.

Frances Davidson was given considerable freedom to exercise her skills in central Africa but was still hampered, and on more than one occasion put in what she felt was an untenable position, by the demand that she subject herself to male authority (Sider, 1987). Bishop Steigerwald, in the early 1900s, instead of recognising her achievements in establishing and running a mission at Macha, on one of his rare visits commanded that: 'she cease to take the place of a man and that she should place herself in "subjection"'. After the bishop's departure Davidson confided to her diary (ibid.: 71):

12. Both Kirkwood and Cunningham mention the socially ambiguous position of the missionary, neither fully part of white colonial society nor of native society. Missionaries were often at odds with the colonial governments but they were viewed by native peoples as one and the same (cf. Kanogo and Bowie).

I cannot yet see that I have been so much out of place if I have had charge and did some of the things which falls to the lot of man. My training before coming to the field was more of a man than a woman. I worked with men as a member of the faculty and was treated as an equal, and no doubt they often gave me the preference because I was a woman. I believe the Lord called me because I had more experience along some lines than many of our people. He wanted someone who was not afraid of obstacles and would be a help in a new country, and so quite unexpectedly to myself He laid hands on me. No doubt because He saw I would listen. Had He wanted a nice modest woman-ly woman, He no doubt would have chosen such.

Davidson did, however, feel obliged to 'submit' and she returned to the United States prematurely as a result of such unresolved tensions.

One of the strongest arguments put forward by women missionaries for more equal treatment was the obvious contradiction between trying to improve the situation of native women while failing to set a good example of male/female relations within the mission community itself. This was the line taken by Miss Gollock, who argued in 1912, quoting a recent report of a special committee of the Conference of Missionary Societies of Great Britain and Ireland, that:

It seems only good that the natives should see the Christian women mission-aries not segregated, not treated as if they must by reason of sex be kept out of authority and responsibility, always subordinate, even the wisest and ablest, to the most callow and tactless young man; but treated by fellow-mis-sionaries as honoured and trusted fellow-workers, fellow-thinkers – able to serve with self-control and with a sacred sense of responsibility which comes not from the commands of man, but the consecration of the Christian to the service of the Master. The women cannot give their best, either in example or precept, till this opportunity is afforded them. (Williams: 66)

The widely-held belief in women's inferiority (or perhaps male fears of their own weaknesses which they felt were challenged by more capa-ble women) continued to contradict women's own experience and knowledge of their capabilities. No doubt many women did not have the strength of character or the opportunities of a Frances Davidson to enable them to exercise the full range of their abilities, and limited their horizons by accepting the subordinate roles assigned to them.[13] Williams (p. 66) concludes his paper with the observation that as long as

13. Salamone (1987: 33) notes that: 'The relationship between religion and repression of women is often greatest in societies in which a myth of male domi-nance prevails in the face of contrary empirical evidence. Such societies are marked by male idealization of their mothers, distrust of their wives and other women in general, and an overvaluation of female purity and male sexual prowess.'

the traditional Protestant societies remained male-dominated they were unlikely to attract the best recruits, which may help to explain why women often shared and accentuated, rather than challenged, the missionary/native dichotomy in the areas in which they worked.

That difficulties concerning male versus female authority are not confined to the past is made clear in an interesting article on Dominican Sisters in Nigeria by Frank Salamone (1987: 34–5), who claims that women's and men's experience of missionary work can differ because of their respective structural positions:

> In a number of ways, men and women missionaries led different lives in Nigeria. Women tended to work on a day-to-day basis while men tended to reproduce the hierarchical structure with which they felt most comfortable. Specifically, they thought in terms of dioceses, parishes, buildings, and laity. Much of their thinking tended to be dichotomous. Conversely, the sisters tended to think of people in need. Their work focused on the church as a process; that is, on a living and changing entity not tied up by rigid laws and divisions. As one sister stated, the men's job was 'to preach and distribute sacraments' while women tended to the real work.

The Dominican Sisters did not arrive in a new area with a panoply of Western resources, but with the traditional greeting (in Yauri), through an interpreter, that 'they had come to enjoy life with them' (Salamone, ibid.: 36). They wanted to befriend the people and learn their customs before overpowering them with schools and hospitals. From his own research Salamone concluded that the sisters have been able to adapt to the post-colonial era in Nigeria better than male missionaries. They were recruited from rural areas and arrived in Nigeria with the requisite skills for missionary work. As they gained confidence in their abilities they worked increasingly with the Nigerian women, furthering their needs, despite the hostility this provoked from 'The male-dominated hierarchy of the Church in Nigeria, Rome, and the United States' (ibid.: 40). The different experience of male and female missionaries is also reflected in the area of expectations (ibid.: 41–2):

> The priests consider their official work to be preaching, teaching, and distributing sacraments. Therefore, it is not surprising that they often wonder whether their lives have been wasted when they see the few converts they have made become Muslims or fail to live up to the precepts they had apparently embraced so fervently. Since the sisters saw their role as one of improving the lives of others as opposed to simple conversion, their success was more easily realized. This position was shared by both career and short term sisters. They were not against conversion, but it was not their primary goal.

The sisters' less authoritarian and hierarchical approach to missionary work, possibly because of their own lack of position and responsibility in the structures of the Catholic Church, has apparently paid dividends. In areas now vacated by expatriate men the women have been asked by the Nigerian Government to return, and they now run rural co-operatives and train people, at their request, in modern farming methods (ibid.: 42).

Mission Impact on Women: Liberating or Enslaving?

Wessels (1990: 14) notes that the New Testament word *paradidomi*, used to describe the apostolic task, has a dual meaning – 'to hand down by tradition' and 'to deliver up or surrender' in the sense of betrayal. Did the apostles, the later Church and the missionaries faithfully transmit the message of Jesus, or did they betray it? asks Wessels. The question suggests that the author adopts a kernel/husk view of religion, that it is somehow possible to pass on a pure form of Christianity separate from the culture in which it is embedded.[14] Experience, however, reveals that missionaries can only transmit their faith from within the context of their own culture and presuppositions. Their awareness of this phenomenon and openness to change will vary, but there is no such thing as one 'true' or basic form of Christianity behind or beyond its social milieux (although Christians may agree on certain credal forms and values).

Western Christianity has been variously received, as noted earlier, and its impact on women is as difficult to evaluate as the missionary vocation for women. In a discussion of polygyny and monogamy, Hastings (p. 118) cites two contrasting examples of African women's reactions to missionary activity. Women rioters at Owerrinta, Nigeria, stated in 1929: 'Our main grievance is that we are not so happy as we were before'; whereas two women from Sierra Leone and South Africa insisted at the All Africa Conference in Lusaka in 1974 that monogamy was the greatest gift that the missionary church had brought to African womanhood. Missionary journals and academic studies by missionaries tend to emphasise the positive sides of missionary activity, whereas a more negative evaluation is common in the writings of those from missionised countries.[15]

There is no doubt that missionaries have held extremely ethnocentric views of non-Western societies, and that 'saving the heathen' was a motivating force throughout much of the modern missionary period.

14. For a discussion of these questions, see Schreiter (1985); Pieris (1988) and *Concilium* (1989). These works all deal, in various ways, with the problems of contextualisation and inculturation, and missionary approaches to these issues.

15. Cf. the articles in *Women Missionaries and Cultural Change* (ed.) Kulp, 1987), which are mostly by academics involved with missionary societies, and see the discussion of African novels in Dinwiddy (1978).

Jeanette Winterson's humorous portrait of Pastor Spratt who 'spent most of his time out in the jungle and in other hot places converting the Heathen' in her novel *Oranges are not the Only Fruit* (1990: 8) conveys the atmosphere of self-sacrifice, conviction and hypocrisy which seemed to fuel the missionary enterprise. Tabitha Kanogo, writing of mission education in Kenya, tells us that (p. 165–6 below):

> The 'otherness' of the African provoked simultaneous revulsion and com-passion; revulsion for the so-called heathen moral depravity and cultural inappropriateness of the African experience, and compassion for a 'fallen' race which must be redeemed from its low estate.

This attitude is illustrated by Bishop Paul Rogan, a Roman Catholic Mill Hill missionary in Cameroon, who wrote to one of his priests in 1941, in typically colourful language (Bowie, 1985: 139):[16]

> ...many of our people are obstinate, self-willed, stiff-necked, careless and independent; but after all, they are only 'black men' as we say. There is no gentlemanly tradition behind them. They know only what we teach them. And do not we say every Friday at Mill Hill 'O that I could penetrate into the most distant (most Bush) parts of the world (the top of Mbo hills) where thy sweet name is yet unknown'.

With a sense of racial and religious superiority the behaviour of most missionaries was patronising and authoritarian, with corporal punish-ment, for both women and men, practised by missionaries as well as by government officers and commercial agents. It is probably only in the decades since most former colonies gained independence that attitudes have begun to change substantially, although, as the papers in this volume reveal, there has often been considerable friendship and goodwill between individual missionaries and the people among whom they worked.

The link between Western cultural values and the missionaries' civil-ising task, as they saw it, is well attested throughout this volume. Mod-upe Labode, for instance, shows (p. 126) how the change from the African 'kraal' with its round huts, to square houses corresponded to spiritual changes. The house became a symbol of civilised, that is West-ern, Christian values. The Church of the Brethren missionaries in Nige-ria in the 1930s expended considerable energy trying to persuade fami-lies to pray and eat together (Bowman, 1987: 17). In 1965 the European family was still being presented as a model for Nigerians, and Bowman (ibid.: 27) reports that:

16. Letter to Father Kerkvliet, 18 August 1941. Mbetta Diocesan and Vicarate General Information Files.

it soon became clear that members of the committee were not able to bridge the cultural gap between western and Nigerian understandings of family life. In Nigeria, men and women simply do not do things together. There was embarrassment as the newly founded Christian Home Family Life Committee tried to plan meetings and programs, such as family planning. The men on the committee did not see that issue as necessary to Christian family life.

Similar missionary attempts to impose Western family values and practices on African social structures are described below by Fiona Bowie, taking case studies from Cameroon. The Roman Catholic Mill Hill Missionaries, for example, tried to force Bangwa and Mbo women to leave their babies at home in a cradle, instead of carrying them on their backs to the fields, to dances, to market, and so on. In this, as in other matters, they were conspicuously unsuccessful (p. 155).

The line between merely imposing inappropriate Western customs on people and exploiting their labour and goodwill was often delicate. Girls in mission schools were usually prepared to be good wives and mothers on a European model, and their education was largely domestic – cooking, cleaning, sewing, laundry work, hygiene, and so on, as well as farming. Labode (p. 136ff.) illustrates the way in which girls who came to a mission for education, expecting to receive an academic education as well as domestic training were sometimes disappointed. It was not always clear whether the girls were being prepared as wives or as domestic servants, and they were certainly used as servants by the missionaries under the guise of training for future life. Kanogo (p. 181) records that in Kenya there was an explicit policy within the Church Missionary Society not to give girls an academic education which would enable them to compete with men for jobs. This attitude was, of course, very similar to that of the British Government between the First and Second World Wars with their concern to keep women at home and thus ease unemployment among returned servicemen. If academic expectations for girls were low in the mission field, the same could equally well be said of their European sisters.

Almost despite the official mission policies, although with a good deal of dedication on the part of some women missionaries in particular, women did receive an education which enabled them to play a part in the future of their countries. Aparna Basu shows how the positive effects of missionary education for women went far beyond their relative insignificance numerically. An educational survey of Bengal in the 1830s found that the only literate women were courtesans or dancing girls, Vaishnavis (followers of Shri Chaitanaya) and women who had to manage their estates who therefore needed to be literate and numerate

(Basu: 190).[17] Gaining access to high caste Hindu and Muslim women was a problem for missionaries, as they were secluded from the outside world and forbidden to attend schools or places of worship. The *zenana* missionaries therefore went to the women in their own homes and became accepted as friends as well as teachers. With Independence there were women in the top echelons of society who had received a Western education and who were poised to share in the government of their country.

It can be claimed with some justification that missionaries have been leading exponents of social reform for women. In India missionaries drew attention to the low status of Hindu women. Basu (p. 189) quotes a Hindu saying: 'A woman's intelligence does not rise higher than her foot', which was interpreted to mean that her rightful place was to serve her family. Child marriage, the plight of child widows, the lack of female education and women's lack of autonomy attracted mission attention, and this in turn influenced Indian reformers such as Rammohin Roy (Basu: 201, below). Mary Slessor, like other female missionaries in Nigeria, confronted the native authorities over what she considered to be the inhuman treatment of women and slaves. She was active in rescuing twins and their mothers, who were commonly ostracised (the twins being regarded as an aberration and often put to death), earning the title 'Eka Kpukpro Owo', 'Mother of all the Peoples' (Hackett, 1987: 51).

Elizabeth Isichei's paper on the Anaguta in Nigeria reveals the ways in which Christianity could be both empowering and disadvantageous for women. Missionary activity here, as elsewhere, favoured patrilineal over matrilineal systems of marriage and inheritance as these were closer to Western models. The Anaguta matrilineal system gave women considerable freedom in choosing whom they would marry and live with. From this point of view Christian teaching has led to a loss of mobility and independence for women. In the traditional religious sphere Anaguta women were excluded from the most important rituals of the tribe. Christianity has enabled women to adopt leadership roles which are more consonant with their economic power, but which were denied them by the traditional elders.

Living in Two Worlds

One theme that emerged from the papers delivered at the workshop on Women and Missions, particularly in those concerned with contempo-

---

17. Attia Hosain, in her novel *Sunlight on a Broken Column*, set in Lucknow in northern India, describes the educated courtesan and the rare entrance of the English governess into the *zenana* enclosure.

rary situations, was that of living in two worlds. The acceptance of Christianity does not mean the adoption of all the values and customs of the missionary, and some sort of accommodation has to be reached between the old system of thought and practice and the new. Schreiter (1985: 151) has noted that although missionaries and church leaders may be aware of and perturbed by the existence of syncretic and dual systems, in which Christianity and some other religious world view are merged or run parallel, for many Christians this is not the case. Schreiter is probably right in saying that one reason why syncretic or dual systems are so hard for mission churches to deal with is that they 'ask some very hard questions, in turn, about the nature of the identity of the older churches', posing a challenge to the cultural contexts which mission Christianity has taken for granted as the norm.

Sarah Skar's paper on Catholic missionaries and Andean women, based on detailed fieldwork in one particular Runa village, examines a situation in which Christianity has been preached for 400 years, but has made only a superficial impact on Quechua culture. Until recently the hegemony of the Roman Catholic Church in Peru was such that a baptismal certificate was necessary before a citizen could acquire official identity papers (p. 244), the population were, therefore, nominally Christian. Skar compares the Runa village, based on reciprocity, with the Church as a hierarchical institution, associated for the Runa villagers with forced labour and external domination. The missionary priests in the town admit that they have made little progress among the mountain Runa, and conclude that Runa religiosity is superficial. But far from having a superficial religion, the Runa live in a sacred world, although not that of Catholic Christianity. *Pachamama*, the fertility goddess of the earth, seems to be linked by the Runa with Santa Rosa, patron saint of the village. The priests are invited to the village to celebrate her feast on 30 August, the time when *Pachamama* is said to be 'open', awaiting the planting of the fields. Through his symbolic actions in celebrating mass, the priest 'makes a contribution to Runa worship of the controlling forces in the landscape, perceived by Runa as crucial to the protection and procreation of the villagers' crops and herds' (p. 243).

The reason for the lack of fit between villagers' and priests' notions of what they are doing lies, according to Skar, in a mismatch between Runa and Catholic notions of gender. As Pieris (1985: 99) has argued: 'No major religion could have travelled beyond its seat of origin and become incarnate in the lives of the masses had it not sent its roots deep into the popular religiousness of each tribe and race.' In Peru these roots have still, it seems, to establish themselves in Quechua soil.

A fascinating account of a dual religious system, this time in Grahamstown in South Africa, was given by Iona Mayer.[18] For the Xhosa, Christianity has functioned as a religion of adjustment, making people employable and consumer-minded and therefore compliant within a modern, Western-style economy. As the adage has it, 'When the whites came here they had the Bible and we had the land. Now they have the land and we have the Bible'. As well as a religion of adjustment the Xhosa also needed 'a religion for resistance and self-assertion – anti-colonial or liberation religion'. To fulfil this need some liberationist strands in mission Christianity or Independent Churches are drawn upon, but also, almost universally, Xhosa ancestor religion. Mayer suggests that among the largely Christian population of Grahamstown participation in Xhosa traditional (ancestor) religion is ubiquitous. Women are highly visible and active participants in church life, so, given that Xhosa ancestor religion is patriarchal in its bias, what can be the attraction for women in maintaining a dual system? asks Mayer. The answer is posited in terms of complementarity:

> A church, viewed as an organisation, is a voluntary association, like a society or club – cutting across the family or kinship ties of individual members. Its locus of activity is outside the home and family. This is no doubt part of the attraction for women – they get away for a while from wearisome domestic cares and relationships. The ancestor religion is complementary in that its locus is domestic and its whole thrust is to mobilise groups of kin and reinforce family ties. Grahamstown women can well do with having both spheres and both kinds of support.

Ancestor religion can give women a positive sense of identity through establishing links with their clan, in the face of a white society in which they are subservient, but it also allows them a prophetic role. Mayer reminds us of Evans Pritchard's words, 'Man speaks to God through the priest, God speaks to man through the prophet'. Both ancestor religion and Christianity reserve the priestly role for men, but women more often than men receive messages from family ancestors in the form of dreams. The prophetic role can also become a vocation in itself, as in some African Independent Churches. Helen Callaway (1980: 331–2) noted that the sister of a Nigerian Anglican bishop was a leading prophetess in the Cherubim and Seraphim Society, a role she could not have achieved in a mainstream Church.

---

18. 'Old Believers: Women and Ancestor Religion in Grahamstown, South Africa'. Unpublished paper presented at the CCCRW Workshop on the Past and Present Impact of Missionary Activity on Women, September 1987, Oxford.

Anne Marie O'Neill Baker,[19] in a paper on elite Nigerian women in Lagos, also examined the coexistence of Christianity and an African traditional religion, and asked what benefits women could derive from participation in a dual religious system. O'Neill-Baker found that most of the young Yoruba women she spoke to expressed a preference for both a Christian and a customary marriage, and were encouraged in this by their parents, who had often had 'double marriages' themselves (p. 13). As in Grahamstown, the Christian and traditional systems each gave partial advantages and were not seen to overlap in their spheres of influence. A Christian marriage was favoured by the women, if possible in church, because the man could then only take one wife. The traditional ceremony ensured that the husband was 'more likely to behave himself in a proper manner because you can then appeal for a family counsel of senior members if things go wrong and they will make him behave'.

My own fieldwork in Cameroon indicated similar lines of argument. Christian marriage is favoured by most young baptised women as an indication of fidelity within a monogamous relationship. It is, for the same reason, often resisted by young men. Traditional marriage with exchange of bridewealth gives women some security as a woman's husband cannot dismiss her without losing his 'investment', and it ensures the participation of a wider network of kin in the relationship. It does not, however, offer any guarantee of monogamy. Among the Bangwa, as in Grahamstown, traditional healers are also universally sought out by Christians and traditionalists alike, as they alone can deal with the underlying causes of disease, be it a relationship with ancestors or witchcraft.[20]

The final paper in this volume, by Joan Burke, deals with a different kind of adaptation, that of a Roman Catholic Sisterhood in Zaire, which has increasingly incorporated Kongo values into a Western Christian structure. The study provides an example of the reciprocal relationship referred to by Schreiter (1985: 150ff), in which the specific cultural context in which Christianity is received affects its understanding in local terms, as well as, through the transformation of institutions, giving a positive contribution to the other 'older churches'. Among the matrilineal Kongo, fertility and motherhood are supremely important values for women. Becoming a religious sister involves a commitment to celibacy, a particularly difficult concept for Kongo women as it contra-

19. 'The Economics of Monogamy amongst the Yoruba in the Nineteenth – Twentieth Centuries'. Unpublished paper presented at the Workshop on The Past and Present Impact of Missionary Activity on Women, Oxford, September 1987.
20. Bowie (1985).

dicts their deepest cultural values. Burke traces the way in which the Zairean sisters have transformed the metaphor of 'sister' to one of 'mother', so that as religious women they have come to be seen as 'mothers for all'. Through their participation in the life of the Sisters of Notre Dame, the Zairean women have also enlarged the understanding of the celibate religious vocation in their Order as a whole.

The papers in *Women and Missions: Past and Present* will undoubtedly raise questions, and certainly do not provide any quick or easy answers for those who want to pigeon-hole women's experience as good or bad, empowering or demeaning. What does become clear is that women have been active participators in the modern missionary movement and that their experience cannot simply be subsumed under that of men. Women and men live in different cultural worlds and this will inevitably manifest itself in missionary life and attitudes. It is also apparent that as recipients of missionary activity women's voices need to be heard. Missionaries treated male and female converts differently, according to their own understandings of proper male and female roles. They encountered societies which also distinguished in various ways between the sexes and worked either to reinforce or to undermine these categories. Although broad patterns do emerge, each context is different. It is in detailed examination of particular missionary encounters that the authentic experience of women is revealed and their presence made visible.

Bibliography

Anderson, B. S. and Zinsser, J. P. (1990) *A History of their Own: Women in Europe from Prehistory to the Present*, 2 vols, Penguin, London

Ardener, E. (1977) 'Belief and the Problem of Women' and 'The "Problem" Revisited', in S. Arderner (ed.), *Perceiving Women*, Dent, London: 1–27

Ardener, S. (1968) *Eye-Witnesses to the Annexation of Cameroon 1883–1887*, Buea Ministry of Primary Education and West Cameroon Antiquities Commission

Armstrong, R. (1983) 'Summer Institute of Linguistics' (Letter), in *Rain: Royal Anthropological Institute News*, April, No. 55: 13

Beddoe, D. (1987) *Discovering Women's History*, Pandora, London

Benthall, J. and Merrifield, W. R. (1982) 'The Summer Institute of Linguistics' (Interview), in *Rain: Royal Anthropological Institute News*, December, No. 53: 1–5

Borrowdale, A. (1989) *A Woman's Work: Changing Christian Attitudes*, SPCK, London

Bowie, F. (1985) *A Social and Historical Study of Christian Missions among the Bangwa of South West Cameroon*, Oxford D.Phil

Bowman, M. (1987) 'The Impact of Women Missionaries in Nigeria: A Look Through the Decades', in P. M. Kulp (ed.), *Women Missionaries and Cultural Change*, Studies in Third World Societies, June, No. 40: 15–29

Callaway, H. (1980) 'Women in Yoruba Tradition and in the Cherubim and Seraphim Society', in O. U. Kalu (ed.), *The History of Christianity in West Africa*, Longman, London

Dinwiddy, H. (1978) 'Missions and Missionaries as Portrayed by English-speaking Writers of Contemporary African Literature', in E. Fasholé-Luke et al. (eds), *Christianity in Independent Africa*, Rex Collings: London 426–42

Hackett, R. I. J. (1987) 'Beyond Afternoon Tea: Images and Roles of Missionary Women in Old Calabar', in P. M. Kulp (ed.), *Women Missionaries and Cultural Change*, Studies in Third World Societies, June, No. 40: 47–54

Hosain, A. (1988) *Sunlight on a Broken Column*, Virago, London

Kulp, P. M. (1987) 'Mothers, Wives and Co-Workers: Women Missionaries of the Church in the Brethren of Northeastern Nigeria', in *Women Missionaries and Cultural Change*, Studies in Third World Societies, June, No. 40: 1–13

Macdonald, T. Jr (1983) 'Summer Institute of Linguistics' (Letter), in *Rain: Royal Anthropological Institute News*, April, No. 55: 12

Mayer, I. (1987) 'Old Believers: Women and Ancestor Religion in Grahamstown, South Africa', unpublished paper

Metz, J.-B. and Schillebeeckx, E. (eds) (1989) *Concilium: World Catechism or Inculturation?*, T. & T. Clark, Edinburgh

Miles, R. (1990) *A Women's History of the World*, Paladin, London

Moser, B. (1983) 'Summer Institute of Linguistics' (Letter), in *Rain: Royal Anthropological Institute News*, February, No. 54: 10–11

Nazir-Ali, M. (1990) *From Everywhere to Everywhere: A World View of Christian Mission*, Collins, London

O'Neill-Baker, A.M. (1987) 'The Economics of Monogamy amongst the Yoruba in the Nineteenth – Twentieth Centuries', unpublished paper.

Pieris, A. (1988) *An Asian Theology of Liberation,* T. & T. Clark, Edingburgh

Salamone, F. A. (1987) 'Feminist Mission Sisters: Nurses, Midwives, and Joans-of-All-Trades. The Dominican Sisters in Nigeria', in P. M. Kulp (ed.), *Women Missionaries and Cultural Change*, Studies in Third World Societies, No. 40: 31–46

Schreiter, R.J. (1985) *Constructing Local Theologies*, SCM, London

Schüssler Fiorenza, E. (1983) *In Memory of Her: A Feminist Theological Reconstruction of Christian Origins*, SCM, London

Sider, E.M. (1987) 'Hannah Frances Davidson: Pioneer Brethren in Christ Missionary', in P.M. Kulp (ed.), *Women Missionaries and Cultural Change*, Studies in Third World Societies, No. 40: 55–76

Stanley, B. (1990) *The Bible and the Flag: Protestant Missions and British Imperialism in the Nineteenth and Twentieth Centuries*, Appollos, Leicester

Wessels, A. (1990) *Images of Jesus: How Jesus is Perceived and Portrayed in Non-European Cultures*, SCM, London

Winterson, J. (1990) *Oranges are not the only Fruit*, Pandora, London

PART 1

WOMEN MISSIONARIES

2

Protestant Missionary Women: Wives and Spinsters

Deborah Kirkwood

Introduction

The instruction to the first apostles was unequivocal: 'Go then to all peoples everywhere and make them My disciples' (Matthew 28, 19). Thus at one level the history of Christianity is the story of mission. Women were active as missionary apostles from the earliest times. St Paul would add messages to workers in the field at the end of his epistles. Thus, in his letter to the Romans, he concluded with greetings to

> Our sister Phoebe who serves the Church at Cenchrae. Receive her in the name of the Lord and give her any help she may need from you . . . and to Priscilla and Aquila,[1] my fellow workers in the service of Jesus Christ. (Romans 16, 1–3)

Priscilla and Aquila appear to be early examples of husband and wife engaged in missionary activity together. Throughout the Middle Ages, the Renaissance and beyond, missionaries were being despatched throughout Europe and even further afield to bring Christian enlightenment to those perceived as pagans. In 596 Pope Gregory the Great sent St Augustine of Canterbury to lead a mission of thirty monks to evangelise the Anglo-Saxons. Augustine frequently despaired of the latter as receivers of the gospel but in due course many became missionaries themselves. Countless women were involved in this work, frequently, as members of religious orders. An early British example was Lioba, 'born of a Wessex noble family' (*Oxford Dictionary of Saints* 1978: 246) who was invited by Pope Boniface in 748, along with other women from the Abbey of Wimborne, to help in the evangelisation of Saxony through the establishment of convents. Whether such women as Lioba could be

---

1. Aquila, a tentmaker like St Paul, and his wife Priscilla are referred to five times in the New Testament and seem to have played a significant role in the missionary work of the young Church.

regarded as true missionaries might be questioned, but in an article entitled *Missiologie Antifeministe* (1951) Father Pierre Charles, SJ, writes that there is clear and irrefutable evidence, though the documentation is rare and spasmodic, that in the early Church women played a very significant role in the work of converting the pagans, and that they were regarded as true bearers of the Christian message.

In the course of time, and no doubt for a variety of reasons, women became increasingly marginalised in the Church, both at home and in the missionary situation. Fr Charles identifies two factors which he believes to have been significant. First, when they were included in missionary enterprises they were strictly confined to the cloister and their chief role was to educate the daughters of European colonists, despite the desperate need for workers in the field among the indigenous women. He quotes Cardinal Brancanti who, writing in 1682, declared that the unique function of missionaries is to preach the Word of God (a role forbidden to women) and thus according to this definition, and in conformity with the marginal role of women in the Church, the latter could never be regarded as true missionaries. Secondly, and perhaps more importantly, they were perceived as taking a prominent role in some of the notorious heretical sects of the twelfth, thirteenth and fourteenth centuries and were thus not to be trusted to deliver the 'true' message. This view was later reinforced when, during the period of the Inquisition, women were deemed to have a propensity for the practice of witchcraft, being potential friends of the powers of darkness and likely to play the role of a 'fifth column' in the missionary battle against heathenism among the pagan peoples of Africa, Asia and America. On the basis of his extensive research, he argues that this latter belief was a major factor in the virtual exclusion of Catholic women from true missionary work until the late nineteenth century.

From the seventeenth century onwards, the process of change embodied in the Reformation, and in particular the abolition (in Protestantism) of the requirement that the clergy remain celibate, indirectly led to a different involvement of women in the church as wives, daughters and members of the extended family. Meanwhile European expansion overseas during and after the seventeenth century provided the circumstances for the foundation of the great Protestant missionary societies – The Society for Promoting Christian Knowledge (SPCK), 1698, The Society for the Propagation of the Gospel[2] (SPG), 1701, the London

2. The Society for the Propagation of the Gospel joined with the Universities Mission to Central Africa in 1963 to become the United Society for the Propagation of the Gospel.

Missionary Society (LMS), 1795, the Church Missionary Society (CMS), 1799, the Paris Missionary Society, 1828, and many others.

In this essay the main focus will be on Protestant missions in South Central Africa during the past 200 years. There was tacit, if not explicit, understanding that these missions would not compete for converts outside their own agreed and designated geographical areas of work. Soon after work began it was recognised that unless direct contact was established with the women in the receiving communities only one half of the population might be reached; who better to make this contact than women working as missionaries? This view was reiterated as missionary work expanded to include more remote and culturally diverse overseas territories. In due course other reasons emerged for including women in missionary enterprise.

There were few Protestant religious orders for women and initially they entered the mission field through marriage and the extended family, as daughters, sisters and nieces. By then it was not unusual for wives to accompany husbands who worked abroad as sea captains or soldiers and, of course, the presence of women was implicit in the enterprise of pioneer settlement (Kirkwood, *The Incorporated Wife*: 143). Single women became missionaries in their own right later during the latter part of the nineteenth century in response to a belief that they had been 'called' to this work. It would be inaccurate to make too sharp a distinction between marriage and vocation as alternative routes to missionary work. Many of the wives of earlier missionaries were deeply religious women who chose, or were chosen as, marriage partners on the basis of a shared commitment to propagating the gospel among the 'heathen' in distant and possibly dangerous countries (see Cunningham, p. 85ff below).

Wives

The wives of missionaries filled the traditional roles as providers of conjugal comfort and as homemakers. David Livingstone, married to Mary the daughter of Robert and Mary Moffat, was conscious of the importance of a wife for both these functions. In 1858 he advised his brother-in-law, John Smith Moffat, recently married to Emily and about to travel to the High Veld in the northern Cape Province in South Africa,

> If I recollect aright you might be out in March; as you will have snow in winter you will be fain to lie close to keep each other warm. (*Matabele Mission* 1945: 3, letter dated 14 January 1858, ed. Wallis)

However, a few months later when Livingstone discovered that his own wife was pregnant he grumbled in his diary,

This is a great trial to me for had she come with us she might have proved of essential service to the Expedition in cases of sickness and otherwise, but it may all turn out for the best. (Livingstone, 1956: 3)

Missionaries were encouraged to take their wives with them for a variety of other reasons. Their presence could be interpreted by the host society as an indicator of peaceful intention and this gave the missionaries hope that they would be received as friends. Groves, writing of Mary accompanying David Livingstone on his travels in southern Africa, observed:

Sebituane gave Livingstone a warm welcome and deeply appreciated the confidence shown by the presence of Mrs Livingstone and the children, for in Africa men travelled alone when doubtful of public security. (Groves, 1945: 125)

Secondly, it was believed that wives would serve as models of female behaviour, and with their husbands demonstrate the merits and virtues of the monogamous family. But Oliver, writing of East Africa, expresses reservations about the relevance of the model in some cases:

Protestant missionaries lived in comfortable villas . . . their wives and daughters necessitated large domestic staffs . . . . They presented an example of Christian family life, but in an economic setting which was far beyond anything to which an African minister could aspire, and in a family and racial privacy which only the domestic servants could penetrate. (Oliver, 1952: 242)

But here perhaps he failed to take account of the many missionary families who lived in great poverty and simplicity with few comforts, let alone luxuries. A further consideration was the belief that the presence of his wife would reduce the risk of sexual temptation to which a single man might be subject. Wallis, in his introduction to the *Matabeleland Mission of J. S. and E. Moffat* and in the context of a description of the disastrous Linyanti expedition[3], wrote: 'The untended deaths and agonies of women and children were a heavy price to pay for masculine frailty' (*Matabeleland Mission*: xvii).

Though Emily Moffat had been disappointed that she and her husband had not been included in the Linyanti party, she wrote in a letter home after she had been in the field some years:

3. It had been one of David Livingstone's plans to establish a Mission at Linyanti among the Makololo people just north of the Upper Zambezi River. A party of three mission families set out in March 1860; only four members of the party survived. Travelling during the dry season they encountered hostility from the Makololo people and suffered from lack of water. It seems those who died suffered from fever and general deprivation, though it was suggested that they might have been murdered.

I am almost an advocate, in such raw missions as this, remote from help in time of need, for a *bachelor* commencement. I thank God for the privilege of coming here and I like to think He sent me with my husband, but I think wiser human plans might have been devised. (*Matabeleland Mission*: 164)

It seemed important to missionaries and to the steadily increasing numbers of pioneer settlers and white administrators that indigenous women should be taught traditional Western domestic skills, including cooking, sewing and laundry and this was another task that it was thought could best be undertaken by missionary women. Mrs Broderick, wife of the Rev. George Broderick of Bonda Mission in Southern Rhodesia, gave classes in general housekeeping,

With the general result in increased cleanliness and more decency in clothing . . . these girls were saved from a lapse into heathenism or being taken by the RC's, who have a large staff of sisters at the mission nearby. (USPG, *Mashonaland Quarterly Journal* 13 December 1912)

While from the Rev. H. R. Quin, a bachelor, came a *cri-de-coeur* for women workers, not necessarily wives, in his letter home to the Mashonaland Association: 'I was never very good with girls . . . I have tried to teach them sewing, but am no good at it. I think I was teaching them to sew backwards' (ibid. 1 May 1908).

Contact with, and the instruction of, the women was seen as a key to the consolidation of the gains made in the conversion of the men, though in some cases it was reported that women came forward more readily for baptism and religious instruction. In fact it had to be recognised that,

Notwithstanding the contempt in which heathen women were held, their influence in the household was boundless – unless it could be secured for Christ there could be no such thing as family regeneration . . . even in a degraded woman a neighbour and a sister could be discerned. (Douglas, *CMS Papers* , 1888)

In effect, missionary wives were not only 'married to the job' but they were often married for the job; when a young missionary wife died her widower would seek a replacement, very often from within the wider family circle of missionaries. Roger Price, whose wife died on the Linyanti expedition, soon travelled south to Kuruman and married Elizabeth Moffat, daughter of Robert and Mary. And William Sykes, whose wife and baby died of fever,

realised the need of a helpmate if he were to carry on his work and journeyed to the Cape in search of a bride . . . he married the sister of the Rev. F. W. Kolbe, the Society's missionary at Paarl. 'She is 30 years of age' wrote Sykes, 'healthy, strong and willing'. (Clinton, 1959: 39)

Norman Goodall wrote in the Introduction to his authoritative history of the London Missionary Society,

> In some societies, particularly those of North America, wives hold independent appointments alongside their husbands and the work they do receives official recognition. This has never been practised in the LMS. When a single woman missionary already holding an appointment in her own right marries another missionary, intending to share his work, she is required to resign her position as a missionary. This does not betoken ingratitude on the part of the Society; far from it, it registers the fact that the continuing service which she may render is offered by her without any contractual obligation. The volume and nature of this service is incalculable. Apart from all that a wife's companionship means in a man's work, apart from the distinctive contribution in Christian witness which a missionary's home offers, there has always been rendered by missionaries' wives an immense volume of work in schools, dispensaries and cottage industries, in translation and literary work, in the training of women workers, and in experiments that bear the stamp of a creative originality. To have attempted a record of this work, or even to have named all the outstanding illustrations of it would have been too large an undertaking. With all its inadequacy this single salute to a company which included in many cases the real heroes of the story must be all that can be offered. (Goodall, 1954: 13)

The relative 'invisibility' of missionary wives poses a problem for researchers. The more forceful personalities, such as Christina Coillard (see p. 29 below) and Mary Moffat, and those who sent their own reports and letters to the various missionary society journals are easy to locate. But many who no doubt worked effectively but unobtrusively are lost from view. Bishop A. W. Lee in his book *Once Dark Country*, while dedicating this to his wife 'Without whom the life portrayed in these pages could not have been lived, nor the pages themselves written', tells us virtually nothing about Mrs Lee or what she did. Headstones in a missionary graveyard tell their own story; that commemorating the life of the Rev. Neville Jones is of the same design, but exactly twice the size of that over Mrs Jones's grave where she lies alongside her husband. In the monthly journal of the Society for the Propagation of the Gospel, *The Mission Field*,[4] reports on Women's Work always occupy the last few pages of each number. Lobengula expressed his own views on missionary wives, or rather on their absence:

> The Roman Catholics tried to force their way in, but were sent south. Lobengula asked them where their wives were. They told him that they did not believe in wives. He then asked them where were their mothers, and they are

4. *The Mission Field* was the monthly journal of the SPG and included reports of the work and workers of the Society from all over the world.

said to have given some answer to the same effect. His reply was, 'I do not wish anyone to teach my people who does not believe in mothers and wives'. (Pascoe, 1901:362a)

Christina Coillard: Missionary Wife and Partner

Christina Coillard was an outstanding example of a nineteenth-century woman, a committed Christian, who, attracted to mission following a youthful encounter with Robert Moffat, realised her vocation through marriage. She was born in Scotland in 1829 into a Baptist family, and had received an excellent education in Edinburgh. On a visit in Paris in 1857 she met the Rev. François Coillard who was about to leave for Basutoland to work for the Paris Mission;[5] they became engaged by letter and were married in Capetown on 26 February 1861. It was 'a marriage of true minds' and for thirty years they worked together to further the spread of Christianity in central Africa. In his story of their life and work, *On the Threshold of Central Africa* (1902), François Coillard refers constantly to Christina and his dependence on her in every sphere; she was a woman of strong character and keen intelligence. It was a matter of grief to them that they had no children, but they were joined early on by François's niece Elise.[6] After some years in Basutoland they ventured north of the Limpopo River in an attempt to convert the Banyai (Shona) people and establish a mission among them. In this they were unsuccessful and indeed found themselves in considerable danger:

> Threatened by attack from Chief Masonda my wife and niece sat down under a tree to sew . . . our position became more critical every instant. My wife on her side was doing her own work; she had assembled the wives and children of the evangelists [African members of their party] round her to besiege the Throne of Grace and gather strength in calmness and prayer. Masonda had been plotting to throw our ladies down from the crag we had been climbing. (Coillard,1902: 28)

Later during the same journey they were obliged to negotiate with Lobengula to ensure a safe passage over his territory. Little progress was being made and Coillard asked his wife to mediate: 'With her habit-

---

5. French Protestant missionary societies were not allowed to work in French colonial territories, which were reserved for the Roman Catholics; thus François Coillard went to British Basutoland.

6. Elise married M. Jeanmairet, a fellow missionary, in November 1885. In due course this young family was to suffer the loss of at least one child.

Plate 2.1 Gravestones in the Missionary Cemetery at Hope Fountain Mission, Zimbabwe

ual calm and charm of manner she recounted our journey and the object of it and our experience among the Banyai. Not once did he interrupt her. He was conquered.' (ibid.: 340).

In 1884, the Coillards embarked on a new and ambitious project – to find their way to the Barotse people on the Upper Zambezi and to establish a mission there. This had been an aim of Livingstone, and the Linyanti expedition twenty years earlier had formed part of this project. Describing the journey north Coillard wrote:

> Every day we have to congratulate ourselves upon having my wife and niece with us. The complications their presence occasions are nothing in comparison with the benefit it brings us all. My wife has taken her place as mother and hospital nurse among us and she is often our providence . . . We left my wife and niece to rid themselves as best they could of a nightmare which had haunted them ever since leaving Mangwato – the washing . . . And think what an accumulation of linen! (Ibid.: 131)

In order to obtain food on their journey the missionaries were obliged to purchase their necessities by barter, usually of cloth and beads in exchange for grain and, occasionally, meat or poultry. This was another responsibility for 'Madame Coillard':

> And so it falls on my dear wife to bargain with these noisy and sometimes impertinent gangs. She has to answer quietly, buy with prudence, and explain gently in order to send them away satisfied. It is hard drudgery and

Levi and Joel [catechists] who had at first willingly accepted the office of helping 'their mother' soon saw that and backed out of it leaving her to manage alone. (ibid: 143)

These responsibilities were additional to the more usual tasks of a missionary's wife: she also taught the women and girls: 'many came for help and instruction with sewing. Others had confidences to make and advice to ask from the *missis wife* – a mother on whose discretion they could depend' (ibid.: 333).

Having been persuaded to start a school for the boys in the Barotse royal household the Coillards soon found that they had the nucleus of a girls' school as well and found themselves 'over-run',

future consorts for Lewanika's sons were sent to the school – little girls whom we now have to shape and polish up. Our house will soon be crammed. These good people cannot understand that a missionary's wife can be crushed beneath so much work and so many cares. (Ibid.: 340)

One gains the impression that Coillard was only too ready to leave some of the more challenging tasks to Christina, while referring many times to his concern for her health: 'my poor wife is utterly worn out with fatigue' (p. 277), and a little later, 'my poor wife is always ill and can bear the strain no longer (p. 360), 'She is the least robust of us and has the hardest and most active life' (p. 231). She died at their mission home in Sefula on 28 October 1891 after thirty years of marriage, nearly all spent in active missionary endeavour. Her niece Catherine Mackintosh, wrote of their partnership,

Every crisis to him was a spiritual crisis. 'People do not know the apprehensions, the inward trembling that I know.' She was the heroine, if you like, she never knew fear . . . he lacked self confidence and dreaded having to assert himself. (Mackintosh, 1907: 286)

Paying tribute to her life and character after her death Mackintosh wrote:

Madame Coillard's character was a vey powerful one. She had strong likes and dislikes which her intense sincerity did not allow her to disguise . . . She had great influence with the natives; more, strange to say, with the men than with the women. The Basutos stood rather in awe of her, but the sufferings and miseries of the Barotsi drew out all her compassion and forebearance. (ibid.: 378)

Spinsters

As the extent of family tragedies involving the deaths of young mothers and children from illness and adversity, especially in tropical Africa, became more widely publicised, the official attitude regarding the presence of wives in the field came under increasing scrutiny. At the same time there was growing awareness and interest in mission and missionaries. *Sunday at Home*[7] was typical of magazines and periodicals which were read in Christian households which always included stories of missionaries and their work in foreign countries. More to the point, overseas missionary work began to appear as a real possibility to young women wishing to move out of the limited domestic sphere into more interesting employment which might involve travel and excitement, as well as religious fulfilment. At the same time educational opportunities for girls were increasing (see Swaisland, this volume). Meanwhile, in the missionary societies there was growing awareness that specialised and more professional expertise, especially in education and medical work, were required, as well as evangelistic enthusiasm and the traditional wifely domestic skills.

However, it was not until the second half of the century that the engagement of unmarried women for missionary service overseas was seriously considered. In 1866 a Ladies Association was formed under the auspices of the SPG with the following objectives:

1. To provide female teachers for native females and to select suitable candidates.
2. To assist female schools by providing suitable clothing and school materials and maintenance for boarders.
3. To employ any other methods which may be suggested for promoting female education.
4. To assist generally in keeping up an interest in the work of the Society.

Here it is timely to recall the work of the home-based associations and home workers generally. They were of vital importance in raising funds and generating missionary interest. Mrs Knight-Bruce, wife of Bishop George Wyndham Knight-Bruce, who pioneered Anglican missionary work in Mashonaland (then part of Southern Rhodesia) in the 1890s, established the Mashonaland Association in England. She edited the *Mashonaland Quarterly Journal* for several years, even after the untimely death of the Bishop from blackwater fever in 1896. The *Journal* provided an important link between field workers and supporters at home. The Association raised money for the Mission by subscription and donation; it might not have survived without this financial help, as is made clear by correspondence between the Bishop and the SPG in

---

7. *Sunday at Home* was a monthly journal for family reading.

London. David Footman, in *Dead Yesterday: An Edwardian Childhood*, recalls life in England in the early years of this century:

> In pre-cinema and pre-radio days missionary activity played quite a part in rural England. In hundreds of villages groups of serious ladies enjoyed the social get-together of making knickerbockers for little boys in darkest Africa. And about twice a year, in every village a small party from one or other missionary society would arrive to stage a 'do'. There was an address . . . a tea, stalls and a display of posters. (Footman, 1974: 72)

The first single woman missionary to be sent abroad by the SPG was a Miss Lawrence, who went to Mauritius in 1867 and then to Madagascar. She was invalided home in 1899 and died in 1914.

In 1904 the Ladies Association became an integral part of the SPG and was designated the Committee for Women's Work (CWW) under a standing committee of the Society. The members included the wife of the then Archbishop of Canterbury, Mrs Edith Davidson, wives of other senior churchmen, one or two of the clergy and some members of Anglican sisterhoods. The function of the CWW was to find, train and send out women missionaries for the Society. By 1915 there were 333 women engaged in education, medical work and evangelism. A brief survey of the correspondence between members of the CWW and the SPG suggested that many were turned down or recommended for home work on grounds of health, lack of appropriate skills or temperamental unsuitability. The following qualities were listed in an SPG pamphlet entitled *What Sort of Women do we Need*? (SPG Records 1915):

1. Women who are 'mission hearted'.
2. While women of all classes may be suitable on grounds of character the special skills required mean in practice women from 'higher' social classes.
3. Women who have received a good general education.
4. Professional qualifications are desirable, especially in medicine, nursing and teaching.
5. In the work of evangelism women are needed abroad not only as district visitors, but as *friends* – the importance of friendship with educated women must be emphasised, especially in China, Japan, India, etc. All require imagination, sympathy and adaptability.
6. Candidates should be willing to go anywhere, and should readily accept preparatory training.

A word of caution was included: 'Many earnest women in the mission field have confessed that their greatest trial has been in connection with life in a household of very earnest women of different temperament'. We are here reminded of St Paul's entreaty in his letter to the Phillipians:

> Euodia and Syntyche, I beg you to try to agree as sisters in the Lord . . . and I want you my faithful partners to help these women for they have worked with me to spread the Gospel. (Phillipians 4, 20)

Temperamental suitability seemed to be an overriding consideration: 'Far too large a proportion of people who are seriously pathological, or at least queer are offering' wrote one member of the CWW. Among women especially it was felt that missionary work was taken up as an escape. In a memorandum to the Committee in 1924 the Rev. K. MacPherson wrote:

> The life of many women missionaries is unhappy because they have an inward conflict. Many young women missionaries experience contact with men of their own age for the first time when they go into the field. A new gaiety and colour and spontaneity enters their lives . . . the natural and wholly right instinct of mating emerges into consciousness and is stimulated by the conditions . . . . This can produce conflict and strain . . . . Inner conflict leads to nervous breakdown. Unless a woman can bring her sexual life into a state of balance she ought not to be subject to the strain of religious life abroad – the conditions will not give her a chance. (SPG CWW, 1924)

Another Committee member wrote:

> Women are constitutionally, though there are exceptions, more emotional and less controlled, more anxious minded, more easily 'worried', more given to overtax their strength . . . more sensitive to spiritual and moral atmosphere surrounding them . . . more depressed by heathenism. (SPG CWW, 1924)

Training colleges for women missionaries were established at various centres, including Wantage, Warminster, Truro and Winchester. Later, the SPG founded the College of the Ascension at Selly Oak in Birmingham, where it formed part of a complex of denominational missionary training centres. Fiancées were also encouraged to undergo a period of training for missionary life.

In the Church Missionary Society (CMS) there was a similar early reluctance to engage single women as missionaries, although the work of women as 'wives, sisters, daughters and female members of missionaries' families' was greatly valued, especially for the purpose of furthering female instruction. In 1815 the Society received the first offers of service from single women but these were declined. In 1830 the CMS Bishop Wilson, while appealing for money for the instruction of women and for mission households to take in girls and teach, feed, and clothe them turned down emphatically 'one single lady who wished to come [to China]. "No! the lady will not do. I object on principle to single ladies coming out to so distant a place with the almost certainty of marrying within a month of their arrival'" (Stock, Vol. I:316). Nevertheless, between 1820 and 1886 103 women, unmarried or widows of missionaries, were working in the field. In due course a Ladies Committee was formed and during the 1880s 'a new race of CMS women missionaries' appeared. Volunteers were accepted for East Africa, China and Japan. An advertisement appeared in the mission press, 'Wanted immediately, 3 ladies for East Africa. Must be whole-hearted missionaries, physically strong' (Stock, Vol. III: 368). There was a quick response. A further appeal for women to work in Palestine resulted in seventeen volunteers coming forward, of whom ten went at their own expense and thanks were offered to

the Lord Himself . . . for leading the Society along a path marked out by His own Providence . . . and so He raised Christian Ladies with private means as the pioneers of perhaps the most important development of the work in recent years. (Stock, Vol. III: 368)

Various training homes for women were established and it was noted that the increase in the number of women missionaries enlivened the valedictory meetings. In 1890 the Society's laws were revised to cover cases of female candidates received by the Ladies Committee.

Education and medical work provided early career opportunities for women abroad as well as at home. Missionary medical work began with the informal first aid and home nursing help and advice offered by wives; this sometimes served as a first point of friendly contact between them and the hoped-for converts and adherents. It progressed gradually to the establishment of clinics and well-equipped hospitals, staffed by missionary doctors and nurses and offering some measure of professional training to local recruits. Full certificated nursing and medical qualifications usually required the resources and facilities that could only be provided by government-funded hospitals. This area of missionary work is of great consequence and requires a separate paper (but see Pat Holden, 1991).

Education is implicit in the concept of mission and all missionaries were educators, in the first instance by example and precept. As soon as it seemed feasible schools were established to provide more formal education, usually initially for boys. For example, St Augustine's Industrial Native College for boys was set up as a memorial to Bishop Knight-Bruce on the site of his original mission at Penhalonga[8] in 1897. In 1916

8. St Augustine's College developed into an academic High School. In due course it became co-educational and the old St Monica's was used as the girls' boarding house. It is still one of the most prestigious schools in Zimbabwe numbering several of the leading politicians and professional men and women among its alumni.

Mrs Elaine Lloyd,[9] the wife of the Rev. Edgar Lloyd, wrote about St Monica's school for girls, built on the same site in 1903: 'the boys then sought teaching for their women and St Monica's sprung up under the shadow of St Augustine's to meet the needs of the womenfolk' (*Mashonaland Quarterly Journal*: 9 May 1916).

Spinsters did not replace missionary wives but helped to further work among women. Catherine Langham and Mabel Shaw were two spinsters who made distinctive contributions to the education of women in Southern Rhodesia (Zimbabwe) and North East Rhodesia (Zambia). An early reference to Langham appeared in *The Mission Field* (October 1906: 317):

> Catherine Langham is not yet going out as a missionary but is proceeding to St Peter's Grahamstown with a view to further training; a Cape Government Cookery Certificate . . . will enable her to take up industrial work at some mission after a time.

The next reference to her is in the *Mashonaland Quarterly Journal* in 1915 where she is reported as having given an interesting talk on 'Laundry' at St Monica's school. After nearly thirty years working under the auspices of the SPG at a variety of mission schools throughout Southern Rhodesia she recognised a specific need for a school where African women could be prepared for marriage with men from the emerging elite who had received a Western-style education and who were working as professional men, teachers, priests and government clerks. Her friendship with Freda Tully, a wealthy and generous English woman, enabled her to achieve her aim independently of the Diocesan authorities. This independence was regarded with some suspicion by the Bishop and their initiative was not welcomed. However, a sympathetic white farmer offered them the use of some land and the Langham Homecraft Village opened in 1943; later it was to become a model for similar schools with the Church's belated approval. The Langham Homecraft School clearly met a real need. News of it spread and within a few years they were receiving several hundred applications for the 200 places, mostly from men who wanted this 'finishing school' education for their fiancées. Young wives and mothers were also welcomed, and babies provided useful models for the teaching of infant care. After Langham

9. Mrs Lloyd was the wife of the Revd Edgar Lloyd. They lived and worked at St Faith's Mission at Rusape, one of the earliest Anglican Missions in Southern Rhodesia. She was a trained nurse. She entered very fully into the life of the Mission, writing regular reports for the *Mashonaland Journal* and frequently joining her husband on his itinerations throughout the district.

died in 1962 the Diocese took over the school. Nowadays, as in Britain, the idea of training girls specifically for marriage is outdated and the Langham school has become a conventional academic school for girls, occupying the original site, with the early wattle and daub dwellings replaced by modern brick dormitories and classrooms.

Mabel Shaw was a qualified teacher sent out by the LMS to M'bereshi in Northern Rhodesia in 1915, where she founded a school for girls in which she initiated experiments which were to be of utmost value for Christian education in Africa. Her special gift lay in a sensitive imagination which enabled her to make conceptual connections between the widely different cultures of Europe and Africa. She wrote in the Preface to her book *God's Candlelights* (1932):

> All around is the forest, green and shadow-filled . . . . The only sounds are those of familiar intimate things; the shrill clear voices of children, the men's loud talking, the calls of birds, the hum of many insects, the sighing of winds and movement of the trees . . . and yet just behind me, so near that if I turn round I almost see them, are London streets . . . . The wonder of it all is that the difference between life here and in London counts for so little. It is perhaps because these differences lie mostly in the visible and audible and tangible. Life is the same here and there, there is a deep underlying unity . . . . It is a passionate pilgrimage towards God.

She brought a sympathetic curiosity and some of the analytical skills of an anthropologist to her work of teaching and managing a girls' school. The school was part of a larger mission complex, which included a maternity hospital and clinic. A general education was provided and domestic skills were acquired as the older girls learned to share responsibility for cleaning, laundry, cooking and care of the younger pupils. As in the case of the Langham experiment there was keen competition for places and many had to be turned away. Girls entered from the age of five and most remained until adulthood and usually marriage. As a consequence of her empathy with her pupils and with their parents she was trusted to counsel the older girls at a more intimate level when they confided in her about their anxieties and difficulties, often in their marital relationships. 'Tuesday evenings were set aside' for the married old girls to come back with their problems. If they had left the neighbourhood they would sometimes write letters to be read out and discussed.

Langham and Shaw were contemporaries; they both arrived in Africa during the early years of the twentieth century. They both focused their energies on the education of girls and women, but there was a significant difference in their aims and methods. Langham addressed herself to bringing about behavioural change and presented her pupils with a model of English domestic virtue; Shaw was more concerned with the achievement of harmonious relationships within a changing society through a synthesis of Christian values with traditional beliefs and practices. The distinction is important and has relevance in the current debate on multicultural education.

Marriage

The matter of wives of or for missionaries arose in a different context following the increasing recruitment of single women. The debate moved to arguments for and against marriage for both men and women working in the field. In the Societies the question was under continuing review from the early years of this century. The arguments against marriage were different for men and women. For men it was said that salaries were too low to support a family and that the Society could not afford to pay any more; there was no question of paying salaries to both husband and wife, even if the latter served as a teacher or in any other capacity. Furthermore, men were required to travel widely within their districts and would necessarily be away from home a great deal. For women the requirement of an undertaking not to marry within three or five years was based on the probability that if she married a young trained worker would be lost to the Society. One member of the SPG CWW wrote,

> Those who have deliberately offered themselves for missionary work know that this work involves sacrifice and that not only on their own behalf, for they go heavily 'freighted' with the prayers and self denial of those who send them. (SPG CWW Papers, 1902)

One Committee member went so far as to suggest that it should be impressed on men missionaries that they should not 'propose to the girls', that is to young women missionaries[10]. But Sister Clementine of Truro declared that a promise to remain celibate could hardly be justified; where there was a sense of vocation it was not necessary, where there was not it would be useless. The problem was still under discussion in the 1930s when the general ruling was that, 'Marriage severs the connection of a missionary unless she is appointed as an Associated Worker by the Bishop of the Diocese' (SPG CWW Papers – Marriage, 1910–15).

10. So-called 'mixed marriages' between men or women missionaries to partners from the receiving communities were scarcely envisaged and do not appear to have been openly discussed. Church disquiet over 'mixed marriages' in general was evident in the case of the marriage of Seretse Khama and Ruth Williams in 1948 as described in a recent book by Michael Dutfield.

The current position with regard to the engagement of married missionaries is both fairer and more complicated. In the USPG usually only one salary is paid unless the wife (or husband) has a separate appointment to a specific post. For example, at a mission in Zimbabwe recently the husband, a medical doctor, received a salary, while his wife, a veterinary surgeon, was unpaid, though her services were frequently in demand. There is no obligation on a wife to be seen as a missionary, but she would be expected to take part in the training for all out-going missionaries. In the CMS, in the case of married couples both need to be willing and appointed to serve as 'mission partners' of the Society and a married woman is regarded as a mission partner in her own right. If a single person marries and his/her spouse does not wish to become a 'mission partner' the couple normally resign. Married couples are paid a joint allowance and a woman's pension rights are protected. Appointments are now generally made in response to specific needs expressed by the local church.

The pattern of mission work itself has altered. Local priests carry the main responsibility for evangelism and expatriates are recruited for their special skills and services in education, health and medicine and 'development' work. Missionaries and their families no longer spend an entire lifetime in the field; they are recruited for perhaps one or two 2–4 year tours. Much of the work overlaps with that of the agents of overseas charities such as Oxfam and Christian Aid. The CMS reported recently that it had approximately 350 personnel in the field of whom 60 per cent were women.

A Personal View of Missionary Life

An informant, now in her seventies, who served in the LMS in the 1930s as a single woman and who later married a colleague, explained the practical implications of her change in status. Although she continued to work she received no salary. This caused considerable hardship, especially after the birth of their children. She also told how marriage altered her relationship with the indigenous women. Married women missionaries were regarded as 'mothers' and friends, while spinsters, as virgins, were accorded great respect, but from a social distance. (Mabel Shaw's experience was perhaps different from that outlined here.)

My elderly informant confirmed the 'marginality' of mission life, especially in those countries where there was a significant white settler, administrative or military presence. Mission stations were often located on the geographical margin marking the divide between the designated black and white living space, or alternatively they formed small 'islands' in the midst of large, sometimes extended, sometimes dense, indigenous populations. So far as other whites (administrators, settlers, traders) were concerned missionaries were assumed to be 'on the side of the natives', potential troublemakers, at best foolishly sentimental, at worst dangerous. On the other hand, no matter how great the sympathy and liking the missionaries had for the host community they could never identify wholly or completely with them; cultural differences were a reality though not incompatible with mutual regard and respect. Thus marginality to both the black and white communities could lead to a loss of identity, homesickness and loneliness. Whether men or women suffered more from these emotions remains to be researched, and the assumption of the SPG CWW about the excessive sensitivity of women must be questioned. There are many examples of nervous breakdown and discord among men, and there is little doubt that some who volunteered were temperamentally unsuited to the life.

While it would be unwise to generalise, there is evidence to suggest that some mission children developed an unusually sympathetic understanding for the people among whom their parents worked. The late Dr Louis Leakey, son of missionaries in Kenya wrote:

'I am in so many ways a Kikuyu myself – I am a member of the *Mukanda* age group . . . and I am also an initiated first grade elder of the tribe' (Leakey 1952: vii). Dr Jacqueline Eberhardt-Roumeguère from a family of Swiss Protestant missionaries in the Northern Transvaal was welcomed by the Venda people, among whom her parents worked, as a full member of the tribe; she later became a distinguished anthropologist at the Sorbonne, well-known for her work among the Masai people.

Conclusion

This paper has been written largely from the missionary side. It would be difficult within the compass of such a short essay to do more than suggest the possible impact of missionary women on women in the receiving societies. Others (e.g. Tabitha Kanogo, this volume) have given accounts from other standpoints. As has been outlined above it was hoped that married women would serve as models of domestic virtue within the context of Christian monogamous marriage. They were 'incorporated' in their husbands' work to a far greater degree than any of those described in *The Incorporated Wife* (Callan and Ardener, 1984); the 'premiss' of their dedication was more emphatically stated than in the case of the wives of diplomats analysed by Hilary Callan in *Perceiving Women* (Callan, 'The Premiss of Dedication: Notes Towards an Ethnography of Diplomatic Wives', in Ardener ed. 1975: 87).

Single women introduced a new model – that of the professional woman achieving economic independence outside marriage and the family. The late Lavinia Scott,[11] who worked with the American Board Mission in South Africa epitomises this different model. She was Headmistress of Inanda Girls' Seminary, a High School for girls near Durban and gave an important lead in academic education for African girls. Alumni from Inanda can be found throughout Southern Africa holding positions of responsibility in a variety of professions; one is currently a Cabinet Minister in Zimbabwe. Thus the possibility that girls could choose between marriage or a career, or choose both, has gradually become a reality, at least partly as a consequence of the advent of missionaries (see Kanogo, this volume).

What is beyond dispute is that the missionaries themselves were sustained throughout many vicissitudes by the confident belief that, through their response to the instruction to go forth and preach the gospel to all mankind, they were helping to further God's purpose for womankind as well.

11. Lavinia Scott was Principal of Inanda Seminary from 1936 to 1969. The School was founded by Mrs M. K. Edwards of the American Boards Mission in 1869. My husband and I visited Inanda in 1987 and were pleased to find the school flourishing and expanding. Pupils come from all over South Africa. The present Principal is Mrs I. Zulu, who was happy to show us round and bring us up-to-date with recent developments. A *History of Inanda Seminary* was written by Agnes A. Wood and published in 1969 to celebrate the school's centenary.

Bibliography

Ardener, S. (ed.) (1980) *Perceiving Women*, London

Bible, Good News Version

Callan, H. and Ardener, S. (eds) (1984) *The Incorporated Wife*, London

Charles, Pierre (1951) *Rôle de la femme dans Les missions*, Desclée de Bronwer, Paris Edit universelle BKC

Clinton, Iris (1989) *Those Vessels: The Story of Inyati* – 1859–1959, Bulawago

Church Missionary Society. Miscellaneous Papers relating to Women's Work, Bodleian Library, Oxford

Coillard, F.(1902) *On the Threshold of Central Africa* (translated by C. W. Mackintosh from the French original *Sur le Haut Zambeze* ,1899)

Douglass, B.(1888) *The Rise and Progress of Women's Work for Women in Heathen Lands*, London, CMS Papers

Dutfield, Michael (1990) *A Marriage of Inconvenience: the Persecution of Ruth and Seretse Khama*. London

Footman, David (1974) *Dead Yesterday: An Edwardian Childhood*, London,

Fripp, C.E. and Hiller, V.W. (eds) (1949) *Gold and the Gospel in Mashonaland*, Oppenheimer Series for Central African Archives, London

Gibbon, G. (1973) *Paget of Rhodesia*, Bulawayo

Goodall, Norman (1954) *A History of the London Missionary Society 1895–1945*, London

Groves, C. P., (1945) *The Planting of Christianity in Africa*

Holden and Littlewood (1991) *Anthropology and Nursing*, London

Leakey, L. S. B. (1952) *Mau Mau and the Kikuyu*, London

Lee, A. W. (1949) *Once Dark Country*, London

Livingstone, David (1956) *The Zambezi Expedition*, ed. J. P. R. Wallis for the Central African Archives, London

Mackintosh, C. W. (1907) *Coillard of the Zambezi*, London

Oliver, R. (1952) *The Missionary Factor in East Africa*, London

Oxford Dictionary of Saints (1978) Oxford

Pascoe, C. E. (1901) *200 Years of the SPG*, London

Shaw, Mabel (1932) *God's Candlelights*, London

Stock, E. (1916) *A History of the Church Missionary Society*, Vol. 1V

Sunday at Home, monthly periodical (available in the Bodleian Library, Oxford) 1856–1940

United Society for the Propagation of the Gospel, Formerly SPG. All archives now in Rhodes House Library, Oxford. These include:
 • *The Mashonaland Quarterly Journal*
 • Papers relating to the *Committee for Women's Work*
 • *The Mission Field* (monthly journal) 1856–1941

Wallis, J. P. R. (ed.) (1945) *Matabele Mission: A Selection of the Correspondence of J.S. and E. Moffat, David Livingstone & Others 1858–78*, London

Wood, Agnes A. (1969) *A History of Inanda Seminary 1869–1969*, Lovedale Press, South Africa

3

'The Missing Link': The Recruitment of Women Missionaries in some English Evangelical Missionary Societies in the Nineteenth Century

Peter Williams

Introduction

Though Ann Judson and Mary Moffat demonstrated that there was 'nothing unwomanly in bearing the utmost travails and labours of the Missionary life', they were, concluded Miss Rainy speaking at the 1888 London Missionary Conference, 'regarded as rather exceptional instances' in the first half of the century. Many would recall, she continued, a time 'when the sphere of women, and especially of unmarried women', in connection with missionary work, 'was generally supposed to consist in collecting and contributing money, reading Missionary records, and remembering the work in prayer'.[1] (To the well-read, Mrs Jellyby's concern for the mission of Borrioboola Gha, and Thackeray's observation that foreign missions, astronomy and the labouring classes provided a solace for the strong-minded women of the middle classes,[2] would have facilitated such a recall.) Yet by 1900 women were beginning to outnumber men in some missionary societies,[3] and were clearly a very significant force, as was demonstrated at the Ecumenical Missionary Conference of that year in New York. The editor of the conference report remarked that they were evident as never before, reading papers, taking part in discussions and holding ten sectional meetings on

1. Johnston, *Report*, 1888 Vol. 2 143; Prochaska, *Women and Philanthropy* 1980: 23–9 and ch 2.
2. Mrs Jellyby was a character in Charles Dickens' *Bleak House*; for the Thackeray reference, see Neff, *Victorian Working Women* 1966: 207.
3. Williams, 'Recrutiment and Training', 1976: 303; Hunter, *The Gospel of Gentility,* 1984: 13–14.

'various aspects of woman's work'. At these meetings the crowds were so great that at some 'it was found necessary to lock the doors, while an immense number were turned away'. He recalled the 'contagious' enthusiasm and one woman's remark: 'If any man has had lurking in his heart any objections to woman's work, they must melt away before the impressive demonstration of these woman's meetings!' (New York, 1900, i: 46). Only forty years previously at the missionary conference in Liverpool there had been no women's representatives or speakers. It well reflected the climate of 1860 in its underlining of the importance of ladies' missionary working parties in 'enlisting sympathy in the cause' and in its advice that such parties should begin with prayer and a portion of Scripture 'and the passages read should be well selected and interesting' (Liverpool, 1860: 63). The purpose of this paper is to explore the nature of and the reasons for this burgeoning recruitment of women, and to investigate how the societies adapted to this new (and sometimes unwelcome) phenomenon in the structures they provided for assessing, training and over-seeing women missionaries.

That there were few roles for single women missionaries in the first half of the century reflects the reality that there were few roles, in any accredited professional sense, for them at home. The leaders of the evangelical missionary societies we will be examining – the Wesleyan Methodist Missionary Society, the Church Missionary Society, the London Missionary Society and the China Inland Mission[4] – were (with the exception of Hudson Taylor of the CIM) conservative figures. They accepted that a woman's place was in the home, subject to male control and protection, and that consequently it would be wrong in most circumstances to expose them to the unpredictable indignities of missionary life.[5]

Missionary wives were, however, accepted, indeed welcomed (Beaver, 1967: 210–11), and inevitably they undertook some missionary work, particularly among secluded women and in female education. Domestic and family responsibilities often limited their capacity to achieve their missionary objectives. Consequently, the case for single women missionaries began to be made. Societies such as the Society for Promoting Female Education in the East (1834) and the Indian Female

4. Wesleyan Methodist Missionary Society (MS, London, School of Oriental and African Studies, Archives of the Methodist Missionary Society); Church Missionary Society (MS, London, CMS and Birmingham, University of Birmingham); London Missionary Society (MS, London, SOAS, Archives of the Council for World Mission); China Inland Mission (MS, Sevenoaks, Overseas Missionary Fellowship).

5. See Beaver, *All Loves Excelling,* 1968: 59; White, 'Counting the Cost', 1988: 21.

Normal School and Instruction Society (1854) were established and single women were recruited.[6] The mainline societies showed no inclination to follow their lead,[7] though they did occasionally use women missionaries for educational work among girls (Stock, 1899, iii: 367). Even then they quite often employed widows or daughters of missionaries who continued a work which they had begun with their husbands or fathers.[8] The case for women missionaries was only infrequently heard. Significantly, some of its most ardent advocates were in China – a notoriously difficult 'field'. From that base missionaries such as Robert Morrison (1782–1834) and the somewhat maverick Charles Gutzlaff (1803–51), urged the necessity of women if families were to be reached (Broomhall, 1981–9, i: 164–5, 331–2). By the 1850s functions which, by contemporary estimates, seemed to call for women missionaries were acknowledged but little thought had been given to their role and they were no more than on the very outer fringes of missionary endeavour – still a largely male and clerical activity. They were not quite in the category of real missionaries and no doubt somewhat below that other inferior species – lay male missionaries. Typically, the 1860 Liverpool conference accepted the need for girls' schools (Liverpool, 1860: 112–3, 127, 150–1), but managed in its minute on education to say nothing about women missionaries (ibid.: 150–1). One demanded the other but the timescale remained very uncertain, particularly as teaching was not yet held in very high regard by the missionary societies (Williams, 1976: 274–5).

Hudson Taylor, the China Inland Mission and the Holiness Milieu

The Most Powerful Agency

The case for women missionaries was much more quickly heard and accepted by those outside the mainline societies. What is significant

6. By 1859 the older society had recruited 85 women teachers (Donaldson, 'The Cultivation of the Heart', 1990: 437); see also Donaldson, passim; Stock, History 1899–1916: 398; Beaver, All Loves, 1868: 88; Potts, British Missionaries, 1967: 122–6; Pollock, Shadows Fall Apart, 1958.

7. MS, CMS, C/AC 2/2: 238, 29 July 1873, the Revd C. C. Fenn to a prospective candidate assuring her that the CMS does not normally 'entertain offers from ladies'. The CMS in 1864 turned down a request 'from several ladies' for zenana work, and in 1867 rejected a proposal that it should become more involved in zenana work (Stock, ibid).

8. See Murray, 'Anglican and Protestant Missionary Societies': 111. She shows that by 1840 the CMS had sent out only twenty–four women, half of them related to male missionaries or former missionaries.

here is not merely the argument but its provenance. It came not in the main from the heart of the establishment but from the revivalist and holiness periphery which was fighting a successful battle for greater recognition and influence. There was a long history of revivalist sympathy for the ministry of women seen for example in John Wesley, in Hugh Bourne of the Primitive Methodists and William O'Bryan of the Methodist New Connexion and in much local cottage religion.[9] The 1859 revival and the holiness movement which flowed from it, with women such as Mrs Hannah Pearsall Smith and Mrs Phoebe Palmer playing prominent parts, was in the same tradition. The rights of women were not, in themselves, central issues but what was central was the right of all, including women, to enter into an experience of holiness and the resulting power and, as a consequence, to be able to minister (in a way which could include preaching) more effectively.[10]

Hudson Taylor (1832–1905), the famous founder of the China Inland Mission, was part of this circle. He was quintessentially a romantic much influenced by Gutzlaff's vision of China being won by the simple proclamation of the Gospel (Hood, 1986: 11–22, 41–52). For him nothing was more true than that God empowered men and women by his Holy Spirit to do his work whether or not they had formal status and qualifications (Williams, 'Recruitment and Training': 112–13). Such thinking was common in mid-nineteenth-century holiness revivalism. Revivalism was, argues David Bebbington, an expression of the 'counterrevolution of values' against the gradualism of the social consensus of the high Victorian years (1989: 166–7). It was Romanticism doing battle with the values of the Enlightenment. In missionary terms the contrast is most vividly seen in the different perspectives of Henry Venn, the much revered CMS honourary secretary, and Hudson Taylor. Venn's objective was to send out as missionaries carefully chosen and trained, obviously gifted clergy who had established that they were fully acceptable to the authorities of the parent church to build up a church in a relatively confined geographical area before moving on to 'the regions beyond'. There was then little or no room for laymen, let alone lay women. Hudson Taylor, by contrast, sought to send out large numbers

9. Townsend, Workman and Eayrs (eds), *A New History of Methodism*, 1909, Vol. 1: 228 and 332; Davies, George and Rupp (eds), *A History of the Methodist Church,* 1965–88, Vol. 2: 295, 298, 303, 312 and 325; Valenze, *Prophetic Sons and Daughters,* 1985.

10. Bebbington, *Evangelicalism in Modern Britain*, 1989, ch. 5.; on women preachers in the revival context, see Anderson, 'Women Preachers' 1989: 468–74. Lewis points out that the number of women home missionaries rose from perhaps about 50 in 1858 to 270 in 1866 ('"Lights in Dark Places"', 1990: 415).

'from the class that missionaries societies think beneath their notice' (Pollock, 1962: 113), believing that 'private soldiers are not less important than officers'.[11] He was convinced that if the Lord should call 'the most illiterate man and send that illiterate man forth', then he could do a mighty work through him 'perhaps because he is illiterate, and God Himself will have the glory' (Johnston, 1888, ii: 17). God had his own universities,[12] and formal training was not greatly emphasised (Williams, 1976: 112–16). Missionaries, identified as much as possible with the local culture (and particularly by wearing Chinese dress), would move quickly from one part to another preaching the Gospel while there was yet time. Evangelism was central. The structures of the traditional societies (so much concerned with education and the Church and dominated by clergy) were unnecessarily complicated, encouraged missionaries to become comfortable and diverted their energies into subsidiary tasks. It was a vision self-consciously different and in it the use of women missionaries was but one part of a generally subversive, anti-establishment, anti-clerical radicalism.

There were a number of British models, particularly in revivalist circles, of how women could be used in the cause of the Gospel (Taylor, 1918: 48–9). The one that seemed to make the greatest impact on Hudson Taylor was Mrs Ellen Ranyard's Bible-women. He was attracted by her conviction that working-class women should be used in working-class evangelism,[13] as well as by her vigorous anti-clericalism – the people, she declared, 'are tired of what they call "parsons" and "humbug"'.[14] She, in turn, had been influenced by the missionary emphasis on 'native agency'[15] and sought, through her Bible-women, to provide

11. MS, CIM, Howard Taylor's notes on a conversation with Hudson Taylor in 1894; Broomhall also draws attention to the Venn/Taylor contrast (*Hudson Taylor*, 1981–9, Vol. 4: 149).

12. *CM*, July 1888: 94.

13. Her conviction was that to reach working-class women it was necessary to have 'a woman of their own class who could speak as they spoke, understand their difficulties and be as it were like themselves, only transformed by her faith and her Christianity' (Platt, *The Story of the Ranyard Mission*, 1937: 12). To this end she had started using Bible-women in the late 1850s and by 1867 there were 234 working in London. The use of working-class women was highly controversial (Lewis, '"Lights in Dark Places"': 21–2). See also Ranyard, *Missing Link*, 1859: 40, 269, 272, 285. For more on Mrs Ranyard, see Prochaska, *Women and Philanthropy*, 1980: 126–30 and entry in *Dictionary of National Biography*.

14. Ranyard, *op. cit.*: 275, see also pp. 274, 277, 281, 285 and 286.

15. Lewis, *op. cit.*: 221; also Ranyard, *op. cit.* 272 and 279.

the 'missing link' with the very poor which would bring about the rebuilding of spiritual and family life. If this worked in England, why not in China?

Taylor started to recruit for his new society in 1864 and, from the beginning, he looked for 'brothers *and sisters*',[16] and for those who had been engaged in working-class evangelism in England. At home 'our sisters have free access to the women in their own homes....In its actual influence on the people at large, I am strongly inclined to consider it the most powerful agency at our disposal....There is every reason to believe that female labour – the "missing link", as it has been well called at home – will prove to be no less indispensable and no less successful here.'[17] Such a work could not be done by wives of missionaries because their time is 'so fully taken up with family duties, so as to leave but little leisure for going among the native women'.[18] In these objectives Mrs Ranyard provided more than theoretical support. She was committed too to the cause of missions in China and appears to have financed at least some of the unprecedentedly high proportion of women recruits – ten out of sixteen (eight single and in their twenties) – who sailed with him to China in 1866.[19]

Powerful Opposition

Taylor's radical missionary methods were not popular in the European community in China. It was, however, the presence of single unattached young women which focused the opposition by providing it with easy to use ammunition. His aspirations reckoned without the prurience (and jealousy) of the other missionaries. They disliked his policies and particularly his decisions not to live in their neighbourhood and to adopt Chinese dress. Their imaginations dwelt on the 'unmarried females' domiciled with him (and remote from other Europeans) in 'very confined premises', 'the restraints of social etiquette relaxed' by the fact that he was their physician and 'their only easily accessible friend and

16. Broomhall, *Hudson Taylor*, 1981–9, Vol. 3: 399 (my emphasis).

17. *Occasional Papers of the China Inland Mission* (hereafter OP), October 1867: 13.

18. *OP*, June 1868: 21. Wives were, however, given a greater missionary role than in other societies (see note 81 below).

19. 'Mrs Ranyard agreed to support two more Bible-women' (MS, OMF, Hudson Taylor's Journal, Vol. 12, 15 November 1865). She also was editor of a revision of a Chinese New Testament Taylor was working on in conjunction with the Bible Society (Broomhall, *Hudson Taylor*, 1981–9, vol. 3: 483, note 53). For details of the first party of missionaries see Broomhall, *op. cit.*, 1981–9, vol. 4: 154–5; Pollock, *Hudson Taylor,* 1962: 151.

adviser of experience in China' ' . . . *you would*', one of them wrote, '*be more than human if you were not capable of being tempted to lay aside* in some measure the reserve with which for their sakes and your own they ought to be treated.'[20] The vision of woman as temptress brought such an essentially negative reaction that Taylor's bold experiment foundered. Not only did he have to face the consequences of the criticism from the missionary community but his own married missionaries were unprepared to have single women living in their homes.[21] This partly reflects the extreme difficulty Taylor had with his first party of missionaries,[22] but it also surely indicates that the reluctance to use women missionaries was much more than a concern for their physical safety. It was a fear of a role for women outside of well-ordered and known relationships within the family. Consequently, as early as May 1867, his Home Director, William Berger, was making it public that Taylor had written saying that he 'could not encourage us to send any more single sisters at present'.[23] The policy was not formally abandoned, but (apart from an occasional declaration) Taylor kept such a low profile about it that his English-based secretary wrote in 1873 complaining that nobody knew what his mind was on the matter.[24]

Significant Advances

His mind had not, however, altered. Times would change. 'Ere long', he believed, the work 'of our sisters among the women' would be as generally accepted 'as it is in our city missions at home'[25] He was therefore waiting an opportune moment. In 1874 he was encouraging one of his married women missionaries (while she was on furlough in England) to look for 'one or two suitable sisters, to come with you, live with you and work under your supervision'.[26] Women began to be recruited again in 1876 (Broomhall, 1981–9, vi: 57 and 234), and this may have been because the missionary families recently recruited were more sympathetic. A couple of years later a famine in Shansi Province and, in particular, the sufferings of women and children provided Taylor with what

20. George Moule to Taylor, 15 February 1867, quoted in Broomhall, *Hudson Taylor*, 1981–9, vol. 4: 288, see also Vol. 5: 143–7 and 264. He was castigated in the local press as a 'knave' (ibid., Vol. 4: 226–7).

21. Broomhall, *op. cit.,* 1981–9, Vol. 4: 275, 333, 349; Vol. 5: 393.

22. See, for example, Pollock, *Hudson Taylor*, 1962, ch. 16.

23. *OP*, 7, 3 May 1867: 1.

24. MS, CIM, 8 October 1873, R. H. Hill to Taylor.

25. 'Brief Account', *OP*, June 1868: 20

26. MS, CIM, 28 January 1874, Taylor to Mrs Duncan.

he had been waiting for – a compelling argument for women missionaries. This he used, allowing his own wife and two single women missionaries to enter the afflicted and remote inland province to aid courageously the relief operation.[27]

The argument was the more compelling to Victorian philanthropic mores as the women and children had been in moral, as well as physical, danger. The success of this venture established much more than that women could be useful missionaries, it proved to Taylor's satisfaction that they could survive alone in the interior of China. To get women into the interior had long been 'the consuming desire' of his heart,[28] and it is entirely explicable that, once he had found a way of achieving this which cut out total dependency on unwilling men, he seized it. In the next decade a remarkably high proportion of his missionaries were single women[29] – by 1888, 120 out of a total of 329.[30] Taylor moreover employed them in much more pioneering roles than he thought it wise to admit – 'Keep it quiet until success or otherwise appears,' he urged (Broomhall, 1981–9, vi: 387). Indeed by the mid 1880s he was sanctioning their use not only in the interior but in provinces where there were no other missionaries.[31] He was the leading British exponent of what was nothing less than a revolution in the understanding of the role of women in missionary work.

Mildmay, Taylor and Women's Ministry to Men

He could scarcely have been as successful as he was had he not continued to enjoy the support of the revivalist/holiness constituency for his policies. One significant organ of this was the annual Mildmay Conference. It was one expression of the so-called 'Mildmay Circle' of William Pennefather who had been holding holiness, adventist conferences since 1856 and who gave particular attention to the spiritual needs and ministerial potential of women.[32] These conferences, John Kent

27. Ibid.: 165–87; Taylor, *Hudson Taylor and the China Inland Mission,* 1918: 310–14.

28. MS, CIM, 26 October 1880, Taylor to Mr Sowerby.

29. Williams, 'Recruitment and Training', 1976: 354; Broomhall, *Hudson Taylor*, 1981–9, Vol. 6: 232–6 and 449.

30. *CM*, 1889: 103. It means that 55 per cent of his missionaries were, by this stage, women. Sixty-one of the missionaries were wives and, if these are not counted as missionaries (as they were not in other societies), 45 per cent of his missionaries were single women (36 per cent if they are counted).

31. Ibid.: 394–9; Guinness, *The Story*, 1893–49 Vol. 2: 374–8.

32. Braithwaite, *Life and Letters of Rev. William Pennefather,* 1878: 336, 362, 408–9, 471–2.

points out, were 'a crossing-point' for all manner of new thinking within evangelicalism,[33] and were sometimes explicitly concerned with missionary issues. One such was in 1878 and there the support for women missionaries was strong, particularly for those 'female disciples, who have wealth, cultivation and leisure to lay at His feet'.[34] The role of women in relation to the family was prominent in the apologia for women missionaries. Thus Mrs Urmston argued that Western education had undermined the old faith but, because women had not been reached, there was no alternative way presented at home:

> We have left them without hope. The mothers are weeping for the decay of faith. They are breaking their hearts over children who are throwing off the old customs and the good ways; and the mothers, what can they teach them? The mothers know nothing better to teach them. The young men are laughing at the old gods and turning them to derision.[35]

Convert these women and the whole picture would be transformed for 'though the women's sphere may be very limited, they have great influence in the house'.[36] Hudson Taylor was encouraged by this and also by a call which mentioned the need for women in China. Taking up some of the themes of the conference, he stressed the place of women's work because half the population of China were women but, more so, because they form 'the early religious and moral education of the whole rising generation and the strongest and most constantly operating influence that is brought to bear upon the whole male part of the population through life, is in the hands of women' who could 'only be effectively reached and instructed by their own sex'.[37]

Whether through this or by other routes, Taylor increasingly emphasised the importance of women in converting men. As we have seen, he moved in the 1880s to a justification of single women missionaries in provinces where there were no male missionaries and where therefore their work neither could nor should, he urged, be confined to women and children. Chinese men were not, he explained, afraid of women and, while ostensibly an approach was made to women and children, they would listen: 'I imagine that, perhaps it is in this way, through

33. Kent, *Holding the Fort,* 1978: 105; Pennefather had, for example, given Taylor support at Mildmay in 1865 (Guinness, *The Story,* 1983–4, Vol. 1: 248–9) when his ideas were still comparatively unknown.

34. Mildmay, *Proceedings,* 1878: 187, see also pp. 264 and 295.

35. Ibid.: 306.

36. Ibid.: 311.

37. *China's Millions* (hereafter *CM*), February 1879: 15. For the call to China, see Mildmay, *Proceedings, 1878*: 264.

lady-workers, that the men of some of the higher classes are to be won for CHRIST.'[38] Indeed he declared that it was 'a very serious question . . . whether those cities in China which are utterly closed to male evangelists may not prove open to our sisters.'[39]

There were revealing objections to such a use of women. It appeared to many to be unbiblical but this interpretation Taylor brushed aside asserting that Paul, when he spoke of the ministry of women, was doing no more than bringing order to the Church and reiterating the headship of husbands.[40] He felt strongly, furthermore, the radical egalitarian implications of all being in Christ. 'In Him', he told the twenty-five year old Emily Blatchley, 'the weak is strong, the ignorant wise, the mute eloquent, the incompetent all-sufficient'; in Him 'there is no male or female'. Consequently, she was 'no longer a girl whose place it is to keep back, retired and silent, but His instrument, called to adorn Him who is your adornment'.[41] She was in Britain at the time. His particular commission was that she be his *unofficial representative* as he felt that she had a far better grasp of his mind than his formal officers. It was a ploy he often used. Thus he encouraged CIM women to work behind the front of an indigenous male pastor, who could therefore take responsibility for the more public ministry. So, concluded Geraldine Guinness (later to become Taylor's daughter-in-law), the pastors were 'made to think, and work, and pray, and take the lead, *at any rate outwardly*'.[42] It was a device used also in Britain as the opposition to women preaching to men increased,[43] at least in part because the immediate impact of the revival had receded. Taylor was not a man, in any event, to be over-concerned with formal position and, no doubt very conscious from his early experiences of the inhibiting consequences of opposition, he judged that it was more appropriate to further the cause of women by being quietly subversive than by being controversially confrontational.

There was, too, the charge that women, without European male protection and in the heart of hostile China, were exposed to excessive dan-

38. *CM*, July 1889: 107–8.

39. Shanghai, 1890: 263.

40. MS, CIM, 26 December 1895, Taylor to his son Ernest.

41. 24 May 1870 and quoted in Broomhall, *Hudson Taylor*, 1981–9, Vol. 6: 233.

42. *The Story*, 1893–4, Vol. 2: 384 (my emphasis); Taylor, *Hudson Taylor*, 1918, Vol. 2: 397–8, note 2; Broomhall, *op. cit.*: 232.

43. Anderson sees the 1860s as a particularly 'militant period in the history of the extension of female activity', while in the next decade female preaching had to assume 'more discreet forms', such as giving Bible classes 'ostensibly (though often no more) confined to female audiences' (1969: 481–2).

ger. Taylor's response was characteristic and well indicates the implications of his spirituality in relation to the greater independence of women. God would guard them. They walk with him 'and the beauty of holiness gives a dignity before which lewdness cannot live'. The Lord is their escort. 'And He is faithful to the trust, and does keep those who are committed to Him.'[44] There was finally the fear that women dressed in Chinese clothes were offensive to Chinese culture. Taylor agreed but saw this as part of the offence of the Gospel which was integral to the whole missionary enterprise (Guinness, 1893–94, ii: 374–8).

Though the belief that women could minister to men was common enough in revivalist circles particularly in the 1860s (Anderson, 1969: 477–82), it does not seem (Taylor excepted) to have had much impact in Protestant missionary circles. Once more Mildmay supplied the support which he needed. In 1886 it was again on missions. It provided a platform, in an essentially sympathetic environment, for one of his missionaries, C. H. Judd, to give a powerful theological case for a much wider ministry for women than was the normal expectation. The starting principle was that God used 'those which He prefers' (Mildmay, 1886: 31). The gift of the Spirit in prophecy, he said, taking up an oft-used text in revivalist justification for women preaching, had been promised in Joel 2 to both sons *and daughters* and, consequently, 'there was no separation at Pentecost'. The Spirit did not arrange a special 'women's meeting'.[45] As for the apparent prohibitions of women's ministry in Paul, he was merely regulating a practice (1 Cor 10: 11 and 14), or addressing wives rather than women generally (1 Tim 2: 8–12).[46] In fact, he continued, there were supportive New Testament examples of women prophesying,[47] but 'the devil' has 'too long blinded our eyes, so that we have for centuries bound up one of the most powerful arms of the church of God'. The logic, which he fully accepted, was the ministry of women to men.[48] And that was Taylor's position too – surely strengthened by such a bold exposition in the heart of the evangelical holiness movement.

44. MS, CIM, 14 July 1890, Taylor to Dr Hopper.

45. Mildmay, *Proceedings, 1886*: 32. For the use of Joel in revivalist circles see Anderson, 'Women Preachers', 1969: 480–1.

46. Mildmay, *Proceedings, 1886*: 33–4.

47. In Corinthians, he argued, the prohibition had been on women prophesying with their heads uncovered *not* against women prophesying in principle (I Cor 11: 5–6). The prohibition of women speaking (I Cor 14: 34, 35) was against them chattering (the literal meaning of λαλειν). There were 30–40 biblical passages in favour of prophesying together with notable examples – Hannah, Huldah, Priscilla, Junia and Paul's female fellow labourers (Phil 4: 3) (ibid., 33–5).

48. Ibid.: 34–5.

The Established Missionary Societies

Keswick, the Church Missionary Society and Women Missionaries

The holiness conference, which had begun in Keswick in 1875, was an altogether more middle-class and Anglican affair. It was thereby much more influential on the cautious, establishment-inclined and Anglican CMS. Keswick was just beginning in the second half of the 1880s to accept a role in encouraging missionary commitment (Stock, 1909: 203–4). It was also the arena where those on the periphery and those in the centre of establishment evangelicalism were most likely to meet. Hudson Taylor-like ideas mingled with those whose heritage was the logical gradualism of Henry Venn. The cautious Venn tradition in fact remained dominant long after his death in 1873. One mark of it was the CMS's attitude to the ministry of women. When its then honourary sec- retary, Henry Wright, attended the 1878 Mildmay conference he refused to sit on the platform because women were to speak (Gollock, 1929: 114–15). When it was pressed, as it was, to take a significant number of women missionaries, it refused, arguing that the needs of women were adequately met by the smaller societies devoted to female education (Stock, 1899, ii: 398).

The real breakthrough for women in the CMS came however in 1887. First a number were accepted for particular, atypical assignments in China; then an episcopal appeal for three women missionaries in East Africa brought a ready response and the commitment of money from the congregation of a leading Keswick figure, H. W. Webb-Peploe (ibid., iii: 368); finally at Keswick a CMS missionary, Longley Hall from Palestine, requested (without consulting the Society which would very probably have refused permission) that an appeal be read for 'Christian ladies with private means . . . who would come out here and work among the Moslem women'. He asked for ten, and soon the Soci- ety had seventeen prepared to go to different parts of the world (ibid.: 289, 369). The CMS was effectively trapped. Ten of the seventeen were prepared to support themselves and that was an immensely attractive financial inducement (ibid.: 369). The *ad hominen* argument for women missionaries had for some time been that there were a great number of ladies of private means who, unlike their male counterparts burdened down with wives and children, could support themselves.[49] This seemed

---

49. Mildmay, *Proceedings, 1878*: 187–8, 264 and 295; even the CIM, despite its commitment to missionaries from a different background, seemed happy that George Williams had used its platform to appeal for such women (*CM*, January 1881: 14).

now to be established and not only did those volunteering at this time have means, they had influence – one a daughter of a deceased bishop of Sierra Leone, another the niece of the Earl of Dalhousie and yet another the daughter of Henry Wright, the former honorary secretary who had refused to sit on the platform at the 1878 Mildmay Conference (Stock, 1899, iii: 368–9). The Society tried to accept these missionaries without committing itself to a firm policy about women,[50] but that was impossible. The climate was towards a much wider definition of those who could become missionaries and that included women.

Three years later it was being pressed, again at Keswick, to appeal for 1000 additional 'mechanics and working-men and women whose hearts God has touched' and it agreed to invite 'lay and female evangelists . . . *from all classes*'.[51] What was being accepted here was the validity of recruiting those without the education (and status) previously regarded as necessary for missionaries (if for no other reason than they had to be ordained and ordination required a background or training at least comparable to that of a 'gentleman'). It was the partial concession within CMS to a Taylor-like analysis. Similar concessions were being made on a number of fronts as the CMS realised the attractiveness in the later 1880s and early 1890s of Taylor's anti-clerical radicalism and simplicity within the evangelical Anglican constituency, particularly as (ironically) his principles had the greatest impact on the middle and upper-middle classes which the CMS had always been anxious to recruit (Williams, 1990: 149–52).

As far as women were concerned it was, none the less, an immensely significant step. One remarkable criterion of its importance is the fact that between 1891 and 1900 the CMS recruited 388 women, or over 51 per cent of its total intake (Williams, 1976: 303).

Other Pressures for Change

The pressure to change did not only come from holiness, revivalist sources. The WMMS and the LMS accepted women missionaries as part of their normal recruitment from 1858 and 1875 respectively. They were not so close to Mildmay/Keswick circles, though the fact that Methodism's holiness roots were reactivated in this period (Bebbington,

---

50. MS, CMS, G/C 1, Vol. 52: 199–200, 4 October 1887, Committee of Correspondence Minutes.

51. *Church Missionary Intelligencer*, September 1890: 579–80 (my emphasis); MS, CMS, G/AK 1, 27 February 1891, Report of Sub-Committee A on the Keswick Letter was accepted by the General Committee (G/C 1, vol. 55: 356, 15 April 1891).

1989: 153–5), and that it had never quite abandoned the use of women,[52] must have been influential. Equally influential were the pressures in society and the churches to give women a more prominent role. Higher education was beginning to be accessible, as were a growing number of professions, and some of the most onerous legal disabilities were being removed. To those disinclined to listen to such arguments the emphasis on the problem of 'surplus women' (the excess of women over men of marriageable age) provided a justification for women to go abroad (Deacon and Hill, 1972: 87–102) and, if to the colonies to find husbands, why not to the mission-field to save souls?[53] The Protestant Churches too were using women in a host of new ways – as fund-raisers, as philanthropists, as bible-women, as deaconesses and as Sisters in Orders. Strong-minded, forceful women and their male supporters had models of the liberating roles open to women in other areas and were prepared to seize any opportunities and advantage of position to press their case. Thus when in 1858 the wife of a missionary suggested the use of women missionaries by the WMMS, it was taken up by Miss Farmer who was already predisposed towards the greater use of women and who, as daughter of the treasurer of the WMMS, was in a position to influence (Findlay and Holdsworth, 1921–4, iv: 20). Thus in the CMS the influential R. N. Cust, who 'could not *abide* "Keswick"' (Stock, 1909: 137), argued the case for women. There is, he said, 'a new power . . . a very sweet and healthy one'. Their numerical preponderance was a further factor in the missionary call:

> In every town there is a sweet superfluity of women, to whom a vocation is not marked out, or sought for in vain, or at least not found. Endowed with talents, education, and spirituality, they stand, as it were, in the market-place of this great world, seeking employment . . . many even in early life have outlived the natural ties which held them to the spot where they were born, and they stand wistfully, and with weary spirit, looking into the dim remote future, with the inaudible cry of the heart: 'My life, what shall I do with it? Lord, what will thou have me to do?' (Cust, 1888: 65–6).

There was, in brief, social and ecclesiastical justification for change and, even when this was not allied to the revolutionary, anti-clericalist spirituality of the holiness movement, it could effect new policies. Thus in 1875 the LMS decided to set up an organisational structure to accept

52. They were admitted to Leaders' Meetings and Quarterly Meetings (Townsend et al., *A New History*, 1909, vol. 1: 72).

53. Note the explicit use of the one million surplus women as part of an appeal for women missionaries – 'truly the missing link' – by the Bishop of Exeter at the London Missionary Conference of 1888 (Johnston, *Report*, 1888, vol. 1: 421).

women because it saw the need, perhaps because it thought that those who were already recruiting them were gaining an unacceptable advantage, because it judged 'the number of suitable ladies prepared to offer their services as female missionaries' was increasing,[54] and because it had an example from another society, the American Board, which, they observed, had 'enlarged' its 'own efforts in this direction with much success'.[55]

The presumed availability of suitable women was a powerful incentive. The societies particularly hoped to recruit numbers of self-supporting women missionaries. They soon found, as we shall see, that they were not as numerous as the propagandists had led them to believe.

Background, Training and Motivation

Background

Initially, the three traditional societies would no doubt have agreed with the LMS that they sought 'women of education and refinement'[56] and would not have been surprised that a candidate of some education, force and energy was turned down because 'her parentage and associations' were deemed to be deficient.[57] In the 1890s Stock was still able to argue that 'the average social status' of women was higher than that of men, taking as evidence the fact that there were more self-supporting women.[58] None the less, the reality of supply and demand and changing social mores dictated brought rapid change. We have already noticed a social broadening in the CMS in the 1890s as it was persuaded of the case for recruiting from a more working-class background. It had consequently to send about 15 per cent of its women to a college it established in 1892 at Highbury for those who lacked the means 'or adequate

54. MS, LMS, Box 1 Book 1, 13 July 1875, letter from the Directors in the Ladies' Committee Minutes; Lovett, *History*, 1899, vol. 2: 714–16.

55. MS, LMS, Box 1, Book 1, 'Memorandum'.

56. *Report of the LMS* (hereafter *RLMS*), 1882: 14.

57. MS, LMS, Box 1 Book 1: 82, 12 November 1882, Ladies' Committee Minutes. The WMMS, with its stronger working-class links, would not have put it in those terms but it was clear that it preferred 'sending out ladies who, as children, were well taught...' (Ladies' Auxiliary, *Occasional Paper*, 8, 1861: 149– 50). It specified that for India candidates of 'lady-like habits and associations' were 'very desirable' (ibid., 1, 1859: 5).

58. *Report of Church Congress*, 1896: 338.

educational advantages' to enter other (more middle-class) institutions.[59] Stock in 1896 pointed out that only a few years before it had been very difficult for 'a factory girl' to be accepted, but now, he implied, there were no social barriers.[60] It may be assumed that those candidates who were not self-supporting and who did not go to Highbury were middle class; indeed the Principal of the Willows, where some of them trained, commented in 1897: 'The class of students is somewhat mixed but they are mainly ladies.'[61] If that reveals a fine class awareness, it also demonstrates that the CMS had come to take seriously recruitment from a wide social range. It was, likewise, in order 'to enlist the co-operation of all classes of society without distinction' that in 1894 the WMMS changed the name from the 'Ladies Auxiliary' to the 'broader and simpler title', the 'Women's Auxiliary'.[62]

The societies moved in this direction partly because of external pressures to broaden their understanding of who could be recruited for missionary work, but partly too because of the reality that highly educated, self-supporting women were not applying in sufficient numbers. The WMMS constantly appealed to the young women of Methodism, 'educated cultured and without urgent home duties' who would be prepared to become missionaries 'without cost to the society',[63] but in vain.[64] Such appeals were somewhat more successful in the CMS with its strong middle- and upper-middle-class base and it was better able to tap into the resources of single women supported by family settlements. During the 1890s 20 per cent of its women missionaries were, at least in part, self-supporting (Williams, 1976: 304–5). It was, however, a smaller percentage than some had predicted and there is some evidence that it did not recruit the most able women. There were few graduates and

59. Stock, *History*, 1896 Vol. 3: 672; see also p. 704 and Williams, 'Recruitment and Training': 305; *Proceedings of the CMS*, 1892: 9; MS, CMS, G/C 1, Vol. 55: 471, 8 June 1891, Report of Sub-Committee on the Training of Women to General Committee.

60. *Report of Church Congress*, 1896: 338–9.

61. MS, CMS, G/CC b 8/1, 15 July 1897, Miss Goodwyn to the CMS. Highbury students could graduate to the Willows or the Olives – private institutions used by the CMS.

62. *RWMMS*, 1894: 132.

63. *Report of the Wesleyan Methodist Missionary Society* (hereafter RWMMS), 1889: 20 and for the same theme 1894: 135; 1895: 148; 1898: 127; 1900: 154.

64. Ibid., 1894: 135.

even fewer students who had been to Oxbridge (Williams, 1976: 305) and that is not explained wholly in the low numbers of women in either category. The small number of Oxbridge women was regarded as worthy of note by Stock (1899, iii: 371). It will be suggested below that one reason for this was that the mainline societies remained too male-dominated to be attractive to the most able women.

Ironically, for the CIM the movement was, in some measure, in the opposite direction, Taylor's desire had been to recruit from 'a more humble class' than he had met among missionaries in China,[65] and he had had some success.[66] CIM's asceticism, however, became immensely attractive to the middle and upper classes and, while continuing to recruit broadly, the numbers from a higher social bracket were certainly higher than he had originally contemplated.[67] As a consequence, by the end of the century the societies, taken overall, probably provided their women missionaries with a greater social mix than was possible in most occupations.

Training

One of the early WMMS candidates was judged to be 'simple-minded and earnest and fitted for teaching'.[68] Such an assessment seems to indicate that expectations were not so high for roles which were regarded as less important or, at any rate, more practical. Nevertheless its candidates needed 'to have some attainment in elementary knowledge' and 'rather more than the average power of learning a foreign language'.[69] To this end training was given but was not always required for individuals and was often measured in months rather than years. Apart from the CIM, where training in England did not have a high priority in any event, it was much less extensive than for male missionaries. It was more practical (particularly in relation to educational method, domestic knowledge and some basic medical skills)

---

65. *The Revival*, 1 September 1864: 135.

66. Of the ten women recruits in the first party, two were Bible-women supplied by Mrs Ranyard (and almost certainly working-class), and Pollock judges only three as being socially and educationally 'of better class' (*Hudson Taylor*: 151).

67. See Cable and French, *A Woman Who Laughed,* 1934(b): 145 and 147; Williams, 1976: 312–13).

68. MS, WMMS, M/WW, Box 1, Book 1: 101, 17 June 1862, Ladies' Committee Minutes.

69. Ladies' Auxiliary, *Occasional Paper*, 1, March 1859: 5.

than theoretical. The most ambitious project was the CMS Highbury course which could take up to two years prior to graduating for topping-up to the Willows.[70] This was exceptional and training was most often, the relevant Edinburgh World Conference report pointed out critically, in small, privately-run institutions, remote from academic centres and without adequate staffing or libraries (Edinburgh, 1910, v: 84). The case for establishing institutions which the societies controlled seemed strong[71] but was only very partially implemented in this period.

The reasons for the different sort of training for men and women, it was argued, related to their different intellectual background. The 1910 Edinburgh Missionary Conference judged that women candidates often had 'inadequate intellectual equipment'. This, it hastily continued, was no worse than for the 'average woman', and reflected the general weakness in the educational provision for women. However, it proceeded to provide a rationale for courses for women being widely based and different to those for men. 'To give special training to a comparatively ignorant and untrained person would inevitably produce a want of a sense of proportion, intellectual narrowness, and a tendency to conceit and self-satisfaction on the part of those who do not know enough to know how much there is to know' (Edinburgh, 1910, v: 83). A woman, it was implied, could do useful missionary work but as both her background and her future were very different from a man's, it followed that her preparation would be distinct and less intellectually demanding. None the less, the societies occasionally showed some heightened concern about standards. Their worries related to the perceived theological naivety of women rather than to their lack of more general missionary skills. Thus Stock complained that many were 'imperfectly taught' on doctrinal matters and consequently were 'an easy prey' to various heretical ideas.[72] A CMS committee which looked into the matter wor-

70. The course at Highbury was to include 1. Bible; 2. doctrine; 3. laws of health and ambulance; 4. vocal music; 5. domestic training and, where possible, nursing; 6. home mission work; 7. general instruction as necessary; 8. instruction in school management (MS, CMS, G/C 1, vol. 55: 480–1, Report of Sub-Committee on the Training of Women to the General Committee). The Willows was similar but with a little more specifically related to mission work (Spottiswoode, *The Official Report 1894*: 592–5. For more on training see Williams, 'Recruitment and Training', 1976 : 112, 304–5, 307, 309).

71. MS, CMS, G/CC b 8/3, February 1899, Report of Section IX of Centenary Review Committee B.

72. MS, CMS, G/CC b 8/1: 71, 16 September 1897, Stock to the Centenary Review Committee (Section IX).

ried that there was little assimilation: 'While note-books may be full, minds may be ill-stored.'[73] There was, however, little in the way of sustained effort to alter the situation, possibly because of the widespread assumption that women did not have the capacity for abstract theological reasoning.[74]

The institutions used might be even more formidably disciplined than those for men and be governed by the shibboleths of a narrow and rather defensive evangelicalism. Evangeline French, an upper-class CIM candidate, recollected the trauma of the CIM Candidates' Home where well-cut clothes were frowned upon and where dowdiness seemed the hallmark of respectability. She had to learn 'to walk circumspectly' and to keep 'her strong personality in check', thus her biography suggests, inhibiting her personal development (Cable and French, 1934a: 33 and 38). Certainly, as Edinburgh judged, if the test of such institutions was the training of character, discipline, devotional life and a 'capacity to work with and for each other' they would pass, but, it concluded devastatingly, the other manifest weaknesses to which it had drawn attention made 'adequate preparation for future work abroad' 'almost impossible' (Edinburgh, 1910, v: 84).

Motives of Women Missionaries

The exploration of missionary motives is a vast subject and all this section can attempt is to ask how far the motives of women missionaries may be distinctive from those of men. The societies set out consciously to appeal to those 'whose energies find little scope in their own land'.[75] They were obviously well aware of the great reservoir of female compassion that the philanthropic organisations of the century had tapped. Prochaska has demonstrated how 'the profession of charity' became central for many nineteenth-century women. For some at any rate it required a total commitment (1980: 161–3 and passim). The biographer of one missionary, Irene Petrie, urged revealingly that the 'duty' 'of that large class of women who have health, leisure, good education and sufficient means' was not fulfilled by 'occasional guineas to charities' or by bazaars but 'only . . . by living out altruism, not as a nineteenth-century phrase, but as a first-century principle' (Carus-Wilson, 1901: 27).

73. Ibid., G/CC b 8/3: 7, Report of Section IX of the Centenary Committee B.

74. Thus Mother Emily Ayckbowm, who worked tirelessly for the extension of women's role in the Church and who founded the Sisters of the Church in 1872, judged that women generally being 'neither logical nor deep-thinkers' were 'far more liable than men to be led astray by inaccurate and sophistical arguments...' (Vicinus, *Independent Women*, 1985: 72).

75. *RLMS*, 1882: 32.

Manifestly, as in the case of Miss Petrie, missionary work provided one such outlet – the more attractive because it was linked with the opportunity for independent adventure.[76] She was from an upper-middle-class background, but the sense of feminine duty spilled over class boundaries.

If the societies encouraged self-fulfilment, they were constantly afraid that their women missionaries would use the new opportunities to forge marriage relationships which they had not been able to make at home. So Mrs Wiseman, the effective female leader of the women's section of the WMMS, actively discouraged marriage and advised her missionaries as to their conduct on the voyage to their destinations, 'Speak to no man on board' (Webb, 1958: 86–7), and Taylor warned his women of the 'worldly' atmosphere of the ship where 'ungenerous use' might be made of their efforts to do good.[77] Warnings apart, the chief weapon to deal with the problem was an agreement that the costs of training, outfit and travel would be repaid on a sliding scale according to length of service by those who left the societies within an agreed period – typically five years (Williams, 1976: 307 and 310). A sufficiently large number married for the 1910 World Missionary Conference to regard it as a 'grave problem' which was sometimes 'the direct result of a mistaken vocation' (Edinburgh, 1910, v: 150–1).

Romance was one motive it was thought necessary to guard against; the prospect of financial gain was another. Wardlaw Thompson of the LMS was concerned that the typical salary of about £100 per annum – more than could be expected in many other spheres – together with accommodation, would become 'a temptation to many women to enter upon mission work who ought never to go into it'.[78] Such self-interest may have been part of the calculation for a few. It was, of course, never articulated and, for most, was furthest from their thoughts. Rather, they sought to give up everything for their Lord. Many came, as we have seen, from a holiness background. Bebbington speculates that for women the holiness call 'to total surrender undoubtedly had attractions in an age when female submission was axiomatic'.[79] What missionary work added to this ingredient was the prospect of suffering for Christ's

76. Carus-Wilson, *Irene Petrie,* 1901: 198–201, 219–20. For the attraction of adventure and duty see also Vicinus, *Independent Women,* 1985: 48.

77. MS, CIM, 'Proof of Tentative Revision of the Principles and Practice and the Arrangements of the CIM': 15–16.

78. Quoted in Goodall, *A History,* 1954: 12. The salary was less than for a single man who could expect about £140 per annum (MS, LMS, Box 2, Book 3: 338, 4/3/1886, Funds and Agency Committee and cf White, 'Early Female Missionaries', 1988: 26).

79. *Evangelicalism,* 1989: 175; Williams, 'Recruitment and Training', 1976: 312.

sake. Geraldine Guinness recalled how Philippians 3: 10 ('that I may know Him and the power of His resurrection and the fellowship of His sufferings') affected her as a twenty-one year old: 'From that moment it became the ardent desire of my soul to know Him. To know the power came first, but also the longing to know Him in the fellowship of His suffering. The sacred ambition never lessened, it grew. It became like a guiding star to me and controlled everything' (Guinness, 1950: 49–50). It was, it must be said, a theme much in evidence in holiness circles generally (Williams, 1976: 176–82) and to suggest that it had a greater appeal for women is to impose a psychological theory on evidence which will yield no more than the reality of its influence on both men and women.

The great success of the CIM in attracting women[80] casts further light on motives. It had, it is reasonable to surmise, much to do with a responsiveness to Taylor's firm commitment to the place of women missionaries and his willingness to grant them responsible and independent roles far beyond the normal expectations and also to disregard formal academic standards. He clearly regarded them as being the equal, and not infrequently better than male missionaries. 'The women at Shansi are incomparably superior to the men as evangelists,' he informed a senior missionary and, he asked playfully, 'Cannot you . . . get possession of that useful [Buddhist] machine that grinds men into women and vice versa?' (Broomhall, 1981–9, vii: 41). To be so valued encouraged response and loyalty. It may be, too, that the call for absolute dependence which he made had a particular attraction to the feminine psyche. It is clear that he had a deep need for the companionship of women (Williams, 1976: 331, n. 196). He was also unusually open about his vulnerabilities. He combined great moral and spiritual certainty with apparent physical weakness; and considerable authority with unusual sensitivity. Such characteristics may have been the more compelling to the maternal affective instincts of women, though any such assessment needs to be qualified by the undeniable fact that he

80. Taking the last decade of the century (1891–1900), the CMS recruited 51.46 per cent women, the LMS 36.60 per cent, the WMMS 27.71 per cent and the CIM probably over 60 per cent (its records are incomplete and it included wives as missionaries which the other societies did not. This obviously reduces the value of the comparison) (Williams, 'Recruitment and Training', 1976: 339, 345, 351 and 354). A better comparison is between the total number of women in the two societies which recruited them most successfully. In 1899 the CMS had 281 (34.64 per cent) out of 811 missionaries (Stock, *History*, 1916, iv: 16). In 1901 the CIM had 261 (46.28 per cent) out of 564 missionaries – omitting, for the purposes of a more exact comparison, the 181 wives (*CM*, 1901, 100).

attracted too because he pushed them beyond the expected role models. 'Unless you intend your wife to be a true missionary, *not merely a wife, home-maker and friend*, do not join us,' he wrote to missionary candidates.[81] It was a bold challenge to Victorian notions of womanhood and it goes far to explaining the mainspring for his actions and its drawing power.

The appeal which Taylor articulated extended well beyond the CIM. Though other societies were more conservative and offered far less than Taylor, they benefited in recruitment because of his contribution in enlarging the understanding of what was possible[82] and because they at least held out the prospect of a greater challenge and more freedom than was available for most women in Britain. In brief, though revolutionary thinking about the role of women missionaries may have been confined to the CIM, its impact was by no means so confined.

The Relationship between Women Missionaries and the Societies

What the societies sanctioned in agreeing to women missionaries was an apparently revolutionary change in policy, strategy and personnel. This should not, however, be exaggerated. They took good care (with the exception of the CIM under Taylor) to ensure that it was conservative and limited in its scope. Many battles had to be fought concerning the relationship of the committees of women set up to oversee women's work (recruitment, training and service) to the existing power structure. Though they achieved a measure of self-control and were important arenas for the development of female leadership (Williams, 1976: 305, 307–10), they remained ultimately subordinate to often exclusively male central power structures.

The WMMS is a good example. Despite the fact that their early committee was dominated by members of the family of the secretariat (Findlay and Holdsworth, 1921–4, iv: 21 and 33), they were soon telling the General Committee that they were 'hardly prepared to submit to them their movements in detail'.[83] A few years later we find them

81. Broomhall, *Hudson Taylor*, 1981–9, Vol. 6: 234 (my emphasis). Another indicator of this is that from the very beginning he saw to it that the CIM registered wives as full missionaries, rather than as the wives of missionaries as in most other societies (see Williams, 'Recruitment and Training', 1976: 310–11).

82. Thus Irene Petrie was clearly influenced to consider the missionary call by being in a CIM circle (Carus-Wilson, *Irene Petrie*, 1901: 47), though she joined CMS.

83. MS, M/WW, Box 1, Book 1: 118, 31 March 1863, Ladies' Committee Minutes.

defending themselves against the General Committee, which asserted that 'it never was contemplated and never will be possible for the Ladies' Auxiliary to embrace the whole of Female work abroad'.[84] By a clever use of its foundation documents the Ladies' Committee forced a concession on this point but only at the cost of recognising their overall subjection to the General Committee.[85]

The LMS established a Ladies' Committee in 1875 but did not permit women to sit on its main Board until 1891.[86] The CMS did not allow them to serve on its General Committee until 1917 (Stock, 1899–1916, iv: 456), even though the case was pressed strongly by Cust in 1892. When his proposal to that effect was rejected, he resigned. 'Concede in time what is inevitable', he warned in his parting shot, 'they cannot be excluded . . . ; they will have equal rights because they are fit for them: what fools some men, old and young, are' (Penner, 1987: 299). Equality was not conceded because it had, as yet, no theological justification that would have been recognised in these more cautious and conservative circles. Women's role in most societies was still seen as primarily to women and children and always under ultimate male control. There was no dissent from J. N. Murdock's conclusion at the 1888 London Missionary Conference: 'Woman's work in the foreign field must be careful to recognise the headship of man in ordering the affairs of the kingdom of God . . . .Woman may not assume, nor may man shirk, the duty of leadership in the great enterprise of bringing the world to the feet of our Immanuel' (Johnston, 1888, ii: 167).

If such opinions were acceptable in the late 1880s, they were in need of modification by the early twentieth century. Miss Gollock, who was closely connected with the CMS (Stock, 1899–1916, iii: 694), vented her frustration in 1912. The ablest women, she argued, were not entering the Church but going rather to secular spheres where they could use 'all the mind as well as all the heart' and where their opinion was valued 'apart from all questions of sex'.[87] She quoted a recent report of a special committee of the Conference of Missionary Societies of Great Britain and Ireland:

83. MS, M/WW, Box 1, Book 1: 118, 31 March 1863, Ladies' Committee Minutes.

84. M/WW, iii: 20, 9 July 1878, Ladies' Committee Minutes.

85. Ibid.: 52, 19 February 1879 and 71, 5 June 1879, Ladies' Committee Minutes; M/G 6: 511, 11 June 1879, General Committee Minutes. For the general struggle see M/WW, iii: 48, 28 January 1879, Ladies' Committee Minutes.

86. *RLMS*, 1891: 3.

87. 'The Share of Women', 1912: 677.

It seems only good that the natives should see the Christian women missionaries not segregated, not treated as if they must by reason of sex be kept out of authority and responsibility, always subordinate, even the wisest and ablest, to the most callow and tactless young man; but treated by fellow-missionaries as honoured and trusted fellow-workers, fellow-thinkers – able to serve with self-control and with a sacred sense of responsibility which comes not from the commands of man, but the consecration of the Christian to the service of the Master. The women cannot give their best, either in example or precept, till this opportunity is afforded them.[88]

Here the pain of less than equal treatment is plain. It undoubtedly helps to account for the fact, noted above, that the numbers recruited from 'advantaged' backgrounds were smaller than might be expected. It is surely significant that the graduates recruited by both the CMS and the LMS were mainly medical doctors (Williams, 1976: 305) – a profession which gave an immediate role and status. For those, in contrast, from less privileged backgrounds missions held out a cause and the possibility of self-fulfilment. This, together with the development of subsidiary organisations to oversee their recruitment, training and work, undoubtedly advanced the cause of feminism.[89] Missionary work in the traditional Protestant societies remained, however, a male-dominated activity unlikely to be attractive to the most privileged, able, ambitious and liberated women of the period. Indeed, this may help to explain why women often appear to have shared the imperialist assumptions of the times and to have accentuated rather than challenged the sense of missionary/'native' division in the areas where they worked.[90]

However that may be, women came, in forty years, from being a negligible percentage of the missionary force to being 50 per cent of the recruits in some British and American societies. Hudson Taylor and his holiness milieu were important, though by no means the only, catalysts in achieving this. Outside of the CIM, women had not gained an influence remotely commensurate with their numbers, nor even with the secular roles which were being prised open for some in Britain. The traditional societies had made adjustments for women. What they offered was undoubtedly, for many, more challenging, exciting and fulfilling (both

88. Ibid.: 684. Ruth Rouse echoed Gollock's analysis and was quite clear that the risk was to repeat the historic failure to recognize women's gifts and thus lose, once again, 'their gifts and powers' ('The Ideal of Womanhood': 163).

89. See also Potter, 'The Social Origins', 1974: 226.

90. See Pirouet, 'Women Missionaries', 1982: 236–7 and 240. Women missionaries, of course, by their very existence often challenged the heart of the cultures in which they ministered (see Garrett, 'Sisters All', 1982: 224 and 228–9), but that is another subject.

spiritually and personally) than most (probably any) other available options but, in the main, the societies had taken much and given little.

Bibliography

Please note that conference proceedings where an editor's name is not given are to be found under the location of the conference.

Anderson, O. (1969) 'Women Preachers in Mid-Victorian Britain: Some Reflexions on Feminism, Popular Religion and Social Change', *The Historical Journal* 12: 467–84

Beaver, R. Pierce (1968) *All Loves Excelling: American Protestant Women in World Mission*, Eerdmans, Grand Rapids, Michigan

——— (ed.) (1967) *To Advance the Gospel: Selections from the Writings of Rufus Anderson*, Eerdmans, Grand Rapids

Bebbington, D. W. (1989) *Evangelicalism in Modern Britain: A History from the 1730s to the 1980s*, Unwin Hyman, London

Braithwaite, R (ed.) (1878) *The Life and Letters of Revd William Pennefather, BA*, John F. Shaw & Co., London

Broomhall, A. J. (1981–9) *Hudson Taylor and China's Open Century*, Books 1–7, Hodder & Stoughton, Sevenoaks

Cable M. and French, F. (1934a) *Something Happened*, Hodder & Stoughton, London

——— (1934b) *A Woman Who Laughed*, CIM, London

Carus-Wilson, A. (1901) *Irene Petrie: Missionary to Kashmir*, Hodder & Stoughton, London

Cust, R. N. (1888) *Notes on Missionary Subjects*, Elliot Stock, London

Davies, R., George, A. Raymond and Rupp, Gordon (eds.), (1965–88) *A History of the Methodist Church in Great Britain*, 4 vols, Epworth, London

Deacon, A. and Hill, M., (1972) 'The Problem of "Surplus Women" in the Nineteenth Century: Secular and Religious Alternatives', in Hill, M. (ed.), *The Sociological Year Book of Religion in Britain*, Vol. 5, SCM, London: 87–102

Donaldson, M. (1990) '"The Cultivation of the Heart and the Moulding of the Will . . . ": The Missionary Contribution of the Society for Promoting Female Education in China, India, and the East', in W. J. Sheils and Diana Woods (eds), *Studies in Church History: Women in the Church*, Vol. 27, Blackwell, Oxford: 429–42

Edinburgh (1910): World Missionary Conference, 1910 (n.d.) *Report of Commissions*, 10 vols, Oliphant, Anderson & Ferrier, Edinburgh

Findlay, G. G. and Holdsworth, W. W. (1921–4) *The History of the Wesleyan Methodist Missionary Society*, 5 vols, London

Garrett, S. S. (1982) 'Sisters All: Feminism and the American Women's Missionary Movement', in Torben Christensen and William R. Hutchison (eds), *Missionary Ideologies in the Imperialist Era: 1880–1920, Papers from the Durham Consultation, 1981*, Aros Publishers, Arhus: 221–30

Goodall, N. (1954) *A History of the London Missionary Society, 1895–1945*, OUP, London

Gollock, G. A. (1929) *Eugene Stock: A Biographical Study, 1836–1928*, Church Missionary Society, London

Gollock, M. C. (1912) 'The Share of Women in the Administration of Missions', *International Review of Missions* 1: 674–87

Guinness, M. G. (1893–4) *The Story of the China Inland Mission*, 2 vols, Morgan and Scott, London

Guinness, J. (1950 [1949]) *Mrs Howard Taylor: Her Web of Time*, 2nd ed, CIM/Lutterowrth, London

Hood, G. A. (1986) *Mission Accomplished? The English Presbyterian Mission in Lingtung, South China: A Study of the Interplay between Mission Methods and Their Historical Context*, Peter Lang, Frankfurt

Hunter, J. (1984) *The Gospel of Gentility: American Women Missionaries in Turn-of-the-Century China*, Yale University Press, New Haven

Johnston, J. (1888) *Report of the Centenary Conference on the Protestant Missions of the World*, 2 vols, James Nisbet, London

Kent, J. (1978) *Holding the Fort: Studies in Victorian Revivalism*, Epworth, London

Lewis, D. M. (1990) '"Lights in Dark Places": Women Evangelists in Early Victorian England', in W. J. Sheils and Diana Woods (eds), *Studies in Church History: Women in the Church*, Vol. 27, Blackwell, Oxford: 415–27

————— (1986) *Lighten Their Darkness: The Evangelical Mission to Working-Class London, 1828–1860*, Greenwood Press, New York Liverpool (1860): Secretaries to the Conference, *(1860) Conference on Missions Held in 1860 at Liverpool*, James Nisbet, London

Lovett, R. (1899) *The History of the London Missionary Society, 1795–1895*, 2 vols, Henry Frowde, London

Mildmay (1879): Secretaries to the Conference, eds., (1879) *Proceedings of the General Conference on Foreign Missions Held at the Conference Hall, in Mildmay Park, London, in October 1878*, John F. Shaw & Co., London

Mildmay (1886): Secretaries to the Conference (eds.) (1886) *Proceedings of the General Conference on Foreign Missions Held at the Conference Hall,{ILE} in Mildmay Park, London, October 5th to 7th, 1886*, John F. Shaw & Co., London

Murray, J. (1990) 'Anglican and Protestant Missionary Societies in Great Britain: Their Use of Women as Missionaries from the Late Eighteenth to the Late Nineteenth Century' in Marie-Therese de Maleissye, (comp.), *Femmes en Mission*, Lyons: 105–27

Neff, W. F. (1966) *Victorian Working Women: An Historical and Literary Study of Women in British Industries and Professions, 1832–1850*, Frank Cass, London

New York (1900): Ecumenical Missionary Conference, New York (1900) *Report of the Ecumenical Conference on Foreign Missions, Held in Carnegie Hall and Neighbouring Churches, April 21 to May 1*, 2 vols, Religious Tract Society, London

Penner, P. (1987) *Robert Needham Cust, 1821–1909: A Personal Biography*, Edwin Mellen Press, New York

Pirouet, M. L. (1982) 'Women Missionaries of the Church Missionary Society in Uganda, 1896–1920', in Torben Christensen and William R. Hutchison (eds), *Missionary Ideologies in the Imperialist Era: 1880–1920, Papers from the Durham Consultation, 1981*, Aros Publishers, Arhus: 231–43

Platt, E. (1937) *The Story of the Ranyard Mission, 1857–1937*, Hodder & Stoughton, London

Pollock, J. C. (1962) *Hudson Taylor and Maria: Pioneers in China*, Hodder & Stoughton, Sevenoaks

———, (1958) *Shadows Fall Apart: The Story of the Zenana Bible and Medical Mission*, Hodder & Stoughton, London

Potter, S. (1974) 'The Social Origins and Recruitment of English Protestant Missionaries in the Nineteenth Century', University of London PhD

Potts, E. D. (1967) *British Baptist Missionaries in India 1793–1837: The History of Serampore and Its Missions*, CUP, Cambridge

Prochaska, F. K. (1980) *Women and Philanthropy in Nineteenth Century England*, Clarendon Press, Oxford

Ranyard, E. H. (1859) *The Missing Link or Bible Women in the Homes of the London Poor*, James Nisbet & Co., London

Rouse, R. (1913) 'The Ideal of Womanhood as a Factor in Missionary Work', *International Review of Missions* 2: 148–64

Shanghai (1890): Records of the General Conference of the Protestant Missionaries of China, Held at Shanghai, 7–20 May, 1890, Shanghai

Spottiswoode, G. A. (ed.) (1894) *The Official Report of the Missionary Conference of the Anglican Communion*, SPCK, London

Stock, E. (1899–1916) *A History of the Church Missionary Society*, 4 vols, CMS, London

——— (1909) *My Recollections, James Nisbet*, London

Taylor, H. (1911) *Hudson Taylor in Early Years: The Growth of a Soul*, Morgan and Scott, London

——— (1918) *Hudson Taylor and the China Inland Mission: The Growth of a Work of God*, Morgan and Scott, London

Townsend, W. J., Workman, H. B., and Eayrs, G. (eds) (1909) *A New History of Methodism*, 2 vols, Hodder & Stoughton, London

Valenze, D. M. (1985) *Prophetic Sons and Daughters: Female Preachers and Popular Religion in Industrial England*, Princeton University Press, Princeton, NJ

Vicinus, M. (1985) *Independent Women: Work and Community for Single Women*, 1850–1920, University of Chicago Press, Chicago

Webb, P. M. (1958) *Women of Our Company*, London

White, A. (1988) 'Counting the Cost of Faith: America's Early Female Missionaries', *Church History* 57: 19–30

Williams, C. P. (1976) 'The Recruitment and Training of Overseas Missionaries in England between 1850 and 1900, with Special Reference to the Records of the Church Missionary Society, the Wesleyan Methodist Missionary Society, the London Missionary Society and the China Inland Mission', University of Bristol MLitt

——— (1990) *The Ideal of the Self-Governing Church: A Study in Victorian Missionary Strategy*, Brill, Leiden

4

Wanted – Earnest, Self-Sacrificing Women for Service in South Africa:

Nineteenth-Century Recruitment of Single Women to Protestant Missions

Cecillie Swaisland

Introduction

The nineteenth-century demand for single women to work in the mission field coincided with problems for British women, especially of the middle classes, of restricted roles and the fear of demographic redundancy. In an age of imperial and evangelistic fervour, the rapid expansion of missionary activity allowed some single women to consider service overseas as an outlet for their energies and frustrations. In view of the demand, however, it is necessary to explain why, when so many middle-class women were in need of employment and so many, both single and married, were involved in church work, it proved so difficult to recruit single women for the mission field.

Some explanation may be found in contemporary misinterpretations of demographic data on the number of single women denied the chance of marriage and therefore available for service overseas. Further explanation may lie in attitudes towards women's roles and work, which resulted in a lack of employment opportunities and to a system of education which left them unqualified for many mission needs.

As with many issues in the field of women's history, direct evidence of female motivation is limited, but my research over several years into the emigration of single women to southern Africa has shown ample proof of a relationship between the social situation in Britain of the single middle-class woman and the likelihood of her offering herself for service overseas, whether lay or religious.

The Ideology of the Lady

Nineteenth-century thinking on the position of women in society was dominated by the idea of the *lady*. It was adopted as a useful strategy by the rising middle classes of an industrialising society who saw their women both as symbols of economic success and as valuable counters in the marriage market on which the precarious wealth and status of many in the entrepreneurial classes depended. As a result, middle-class women were stripped of many of the useful functions of their predecessors and, in the accepted ethos of the age, were regarded as emotionally, socially and intellectually inferior to men.

Education was geared to the ideal of womanhood, so that most middle- and upper-class girls were taught only the *accomplishments* that would ensure early marriage to a suitable husband. As early as 1844, protests about this were made:

> This last century seems to have wrought an ill change on the intellectual status of women. That plan for enforcing 'accomplishments' has at last so diluted and over-sweetened their minds that they gradually become more similar the one to the other than thinking creatures should be . . . . But the most evil sign is an increasing langour and want of spirit . . . (*Quarterly Review*, 1844: 111)

The pursuit of the ideal soon produced its crop of problems as it became apparent that it could not easily be sustained. Wives and daughters trained for a life of idleness and ostentation were expensive for both fathers and husbands and, as the century progressed, there was evidence of a flight from the responsibilities of matrimony by many young men. Should a woman fail to marry, or should an improvident father, by death or business failure, not make adequate provision for his dependent daughters, the prospect was bleak as there were few employment opportunities for them.[1]

There were strong penalties for those who, by choice or necessity, broke the social norms. Loss of caste, and with it the chance of a suitable marriage, was the most feared. At the same time it was admitted by some that active, energetic, unmarried women too often felt

> cramped and depressed in their narrow circle of duties to which they are confined. They are conscious of power and may not exert it; of ambition and must stifle it. The disenchantment of life has fallen upon them, and they cannot take refuge in active occupation to forget it. (*Frazer's Magazine*, 1860: 364)

---

1. For a perceptive account of the problems of unsupported women see George Gissing's novel, *The Odd Women*, 1893.

The Myth of Redundancy

As marriage was virtually the only acceptable career for middle-class women, the claim, often repeated, that there was a surplus of over one million women in Britain, struck fear into female breasts. Analyses of census date, however, from 1851 until the myth finally faded in the early years of the twentieth century, have shown that, real as was the excess of women, it was not among women of marriageable age but among older women, mainly widows. However, the belief that over one million young women were denied marriage and employment was sustained and quoted for over seventy years.

The main source of the belief was an article by W. R. Greg, published in 1862. He claimed that an analysis of the 1851 census showed that there were 1,248,00 unmarried women in the population, of whom 1,100,000 were 'unnaturally so' in that they would like to marry but were denied the opportunity (Greg in *National Review*, 1862: 436.) Even before Greg published his article, however, other analysts of the same census had come to different demographic conclusions. George Sala, writing in 1854 on the same figures, had concluded that there were only 350,000 'excess' women in the whole population. Among unmarried women, 84,000 were over the age of 40, and in the cohorts of 20 – 40 years, there was actually an excess of bachelors of nearly 7,000 (Sala, in *Household Words*, 1854: 221–8).

The belief retained its power for the rest of the century despite statements such as that of 1889, which claimed that 'the enormous preponderance of spinsters has been curiously exaggerated' as, in reality, the number unable to marry was small. The 1881 census, it claimed, had shown that in the age-group 15–45 years there were 79,000 more bachelors than spinsters. The excess of 65,000 women over the whole population was mainly among older widows and must be due to the 'greater longevity of women and in the many risks of life to which men of all ages were exposed'. The author expressed surprise that 'to many estimable persons, the "surplus" female population has been a veritable nightmare, and at its doors have been laid some of the greatest evils of modern society' (*Westminster Review*, 1889: 271).

Belief in the *nightmare* continued and inspired much philanthropic activity, including the energetic espousal of emigration for women. The three main factors that account for the apparent surplus of young middle-class women were the flight from matrimony of young men as they contemplated the cost of maintaining an expensive and possibly frivolous wife with the large family customary at the time; the emigration of large numbers of young men and the difficulty for young women in finding employment.

Women's Education and Employment

Visible distress among unsupported middle-class women was caused by the failure of employment opportunities to keep pace with changes in society. Public opinion was strongly against paid work for *ladies* even when family support failed. Girls' education improved slowly and gave to many who received it the wish to escape from the confines of the home but it could not bear fruit until it became acceptable for women to work and there were adequate opportunities for it.

The only respectable openings for women before the 1879s were in governessing and in charitable works, often through the Church. Even when prospects began to improve with the recruitment of female clerks by the Post Office and a few private offices, the positions were poorly paid and bore no relation to the demand. Training for teachers and nurses began in the 1860s and 1870s but the market for their services was rapidly saturated, leaving many unemployed or obliged to accept low wages, limited security and few opportunities for promotion.

Frances Low, writing in 1897, called for an investigation into the conditions of women's work, especially into those of educated women. Many girls, she said, were sent to newly opened colleges such as Girton College, Cambridge, in order to become high school teachers but there were not enough posts in the new schools to absorb them. Other fields such as *typewriters* were equally overcrowded and underpaid:

> The congested condition of the labour market for educated middle-class women with the competition that prevails therein and the increasing difficulty for middle-aged ladies to obtain any occupation by which they can maintain themselves, are serious problems which will have ere long to be faced, if the present distress is to be prevented from becoming chronic and incurable and of greater intensity. (Low, in *Ninetenth Century*, 1897: 405)

The solutions sought by women of little education or training who failed to marry, were varied. Some remained at home to become *old maids* or valued maiden aunts; some sought such work as they could find as governesses, housekeepers or even shopworkers, and suffered the pangs of downward mobility. Some with means occupied themselves in charitable works, while others retreated into invalidism or even insanity. Some of the more robust emigrated with the help of women's emigration societies and a few went out to overseas missions. The tragedy was, however, that nine out of ten who applied to the emigration societies were rejected as unsuitable. This was also true of applicants for mission work, most of whom proved to be unsuited in temperament, education or training.

Missions in Southern Africa

Before the opening up of East and West Africa, southern Africa, the gateway to the great land mass south of the Sahara, attracted the interest and attention of missionary societies. Many Christian people believed that Britain had a duty to support the maintenance and expansion of the Empire as

> a destiny has been thereby conferred on us by Providence, of universal beneficence – namely to diffuse among millions of the human race the blessings of Christianity and civilisation and it is no less obligatory on nations than on individuals to use the power entrusted them by Providence. (*Frazer's Magazine*, 1853: 487)

The teeming peoples of sub-Saharan Africa offered the greatest opportunity for the fulfilment of that destiny.

Recruitment of women to the Protestant missions in southern Africa reflected both attitudes towards female employment and opportunities for it. In the early years of the century mission women fulfilled a nurturing role as an extension of family duties. Towards the middle of the century, philanthropic and evangelical roles developed but the women were still largely untrained. In the last years of the century, roles became increasingly professionalised with opportunities for women to offer trained skills.

Single Women in the Mission Field

Mission activity had begun at the Cape in 1797 during the first short-lived occupation by the British, when the interdenominational London Missionary Society arrived to work in co-operation with the Dutch Church. After the final occupation of 1806, the LMS spread rapidly to the frontier and even beyond the Orange River to the Griqua people, where Robert and Mary Moffat, the parents-in-law of David Livingstone, spent their lives. Other nonconformist missions arrived with and after the 1820 Settlement and moved up the *Missionaries' Road* into the interior. The Anglican Church played a lesser role in mission work at this time.[2]

In these early years the number of women in the field was small and almost all were the wives or daughters of missionaries. Despite the dangers and discomforts of isolated mission stations, wives were vital to success. As H. H. Johnson wrote in 1887, 'A celibate, young and in the prime of manhood, is prone to be restless and discontented or to find consolation which arouses scandal', but if married to a woman of his own nation and rank, 'he is happy, contented, pure-minded and disposed

2. See Davies and Shepherd (1954).

to devote himself with greater heartiness to his work in Africa' (Johnson, in *Ninetenth Century*, 1887: 717).

There was little place for unmarried women in the early work of the missions. Life in the interior was hard enough for families, and the societies could not see how single women could be used or protected. The Rev. Henry Calderwood, writing in 1857, made it clear, however, that the task of Christianising 'a barbarous people' could not be achieved without the 'affectionate influence of pious, enlightened European females'. In work among native women there were 'a hundred ways and opportunities of reaching the female heart and mind which do not come within the range of male missionaries'. No station, he believed, could be complete without an unmarried woman worker, as the mission wives had too little time to spare from their domestic and child-rearing duties. Their presence might, he admitted, introduce some tension with wives but all must learn to 'bear and forbear for the work's sake'. There was also the danger of 'their position being so much misunderstood by the natives' (Calderwood, 1858: 199–209). Despite these fears, however, single women were gradually introduced to the field, although in no great numbers before the middle of the century.

The first Protestant women workers of whom there are any details were those who went out to the Lovedale Institution of the Glasgow Mission in the 1840s. There is little evidence of the origins of these women other than that most seem to have been the daughters of clergymen and as such would have been both highly motivated and less economically secure.

The Mission had had a chequered career in its early days, being forced to move several times as a result of frontier wars, but by the late 1830s it was established firmly enough to open the Lovedale Institution for the training of native catechists and the education of mission children. Several devout, but largely untrained, churchwomen were recruited to run the school, and these were followed for the rest of the century by a succession of single women with increasing levels of education and training.[3] One of the most notable was Jane Waterston, the daughter of a Scottish banker who, although well educated, was without training. She remedied this by returning to Europe to train as a doctor. As there was no medical training for women in England at the time, she gained her qualifications in Ireland. After a brief period back in the mission field, she spent the rest of her life as the first woman doctor in Cape Town.[4]

3. See Shepherd (1955).
4. For the letters of Jane Waterston and an account of her life, see Bean and Heyningen (1983).

The Expansion of the Anglican Church at the Cape

A dramatic extension of the recruitment of single women to the mission field in South Africa took place after the revitalisation of the Anglican Church at the Cape in the late 1840s as the result of a donation of £35,000 by the London heiress, Angela Burdett-Coutts, for the endowment of two new colonial sees. The Cape which, up to that time, had been part of a huge see that included both St Helena and Natal, was chosen and the see was further broken up in 1853 when bishoprics were conferred on Natal, with oversight of the Zulus, and on Grahamstown for work among the Xhosa. The Rev. Robert Gray was made Bishop of Cape Town in 1847, Dr John Armstrong was given Grahamstown in 1854 and Dr John Colenso arrived as Bishop of Natal in 1856.

Harrowing tales of loss and privation among mission wives and children were much in the minds of the new bishops and all were determined to reduce their burden by introducing single mission women. There were several problems in the way of achieving this, of which the two most pressing were how to recruit sufficient suitable women and how to prevent them marrying soon after arrival in a country starved of suitable marriage partners.

Accompanying the bishops and the clergy who followed in their wake were families and servants and a number of single women who wished to devote their lives to the Church. Some, who had the means to pay their own way, had recruited themselves but were often more devout than useful.

Colenso's Sisterhood in Natal

Bishop Colenso was the first to attempt to solve the problem of marriage soon after arrival. There were six single women in his party and he decided to set up an informal Sisterhood, the Sisters of Mercy sometimes known as the Grey Sisters, and so place them under a form of discipline. A habit was devised, consisting of 'a peculiar costume of blue-grey tweed dresses with large capes of the same, and black and white straw bonnets in the coal scuttle style, simply trimmed with white muslin' (Child, 1979: 64).

Colenso's hopes of retaining their services were slight, as the very presence of unmarried women attracted immediate attention from local men. Eliza Feilden, an acute observer of the local scene, reported that the Bishop was soon having trouble: 'The nurse who was to be such a "treasure" has married and, on being expostulated with, said she did not know there would be white men here!' (Feilden, 1973: 112).

The Sisters did useful work in the mission schools, orphanage and in general mission work but within a few years the scheme was caught up in the theological controversy surrounding the bishop. The original group was soon scattered, either by marriage or by the return of the unsuitable to Britain. The institutions established in the early years were disbanded when, in 1862, Colenso left for England to argue his case.

The Sisterhood of St George, Cape Town

Colenso returned to Natal in 1865 but the Natal Sisterhood was not revived. The idea was, however, taken up by Bishop Gray of Cape Town. The small party of women who had accompanied him in 1847 had married, died or otherwise dispersed, but in 1868 he returned from a visit to England with a party of eleven single women, eight of whom had been chosen to form the nucleus of the Sisterhood of St George. This followed a resolution of 1865 by the Cape Synod to ask an Anglican Sisterhood to go out to establish a penitentiary for *fallen women*. Gray had visited many Communities in Britain but there had been no response to the call, so he interviewed a large number of women 'who felt the desire to work in this way for God'. Eventually, when many had been rejected for a variety of reasons – 'health, objections of friends, reasonable and unreasonable; and an absence of real fitness for the work in the candidates themselves on closer investigation' – the eight were chosen (Brooke, 1947: 125). Most came from parishes influenced by the High Church Oxford Movement and none had been a member of a Community but the bishop hoped to mould and train them himself into a Sisterhood. Their story was published in 1905 by the youngest of the Sisters, Mary Anderson-Morshead.

Two sets of rules were drawn up as guidance. The first, written by the bishop himself, was intended as spiritual guidance for women, no doubt all strong-minded, who would be living together in a close-knit household. 'Your work', he advised them in his inaugural sermon, 'requires the very highest spiritual gifts and graces – humility, faith, zeal, love, devotion, heavenly-mindedness, tenderness, gentleness, self-sacrifice, forbearance towards others, watchfulness over self.' The second set of rules related to membership matters and domestic arrangements, important in an informal Sisterhood in which vows could not be wholly binding (Gray, 1876, Vol. 2: 448).

The Sisters were soon absorbed into pastoral work and in the care of the Cathedral. An orphanage for the children of settlers, a home for destitute children of all races and a refuge, the House of Mercy, for *fallen women* were set up and survived well into the twentieth century. However, despite the hard work of the Sisters and the recruitment of additional workers in 1871, insufficient laywomen could be found in Britain to continue the work. With the exception of the orphanage, all the charitable work was taken over in 1876 by the All Saints Sisters of the Poor from St Albans.

Bishop Webb and the Community of St Michael and All Angels, Bloemfontein

In 1863 an additional diocese was created at Bloemfontein in the Orange Free State and, in 1871, Allan Becher Webb was appointed bishop. Until overwhelmed by the needs of the settlements at the diamond fields of Kimberley when he was obliged to turn his attention to pastoral and medical work, Webb believed that his mission to Africa was to improve and elevate the native population, especially the women. For this he would need the help of a band of dedicated and disciplined women to instil respect for the Christian home:[5] and 'peace and progress in the country must largely depend upon the readiness of England's daughters to take Africa's dark maidens by the hand, bravely, gently and patiently and so lead them out of the shadow of death' (Webb, 1883: 42).

Webb was puzzled as to how to accomplish this as, although women already in the mission field were useful, 'everyone around us is either married or going to be married', and so was lost to the bishop. His first thought was that 'some thoroughly experienced middle-aged ladies should come out from England and open schools', but none could be found. He then looked for an established Anglican Community in Britain to join him but was no more successful than Bishop Gray. He decided, therefore, to follow the Bishop's example and found a Sisterhood 'that could stand upon its own foundations'. He secured the services of Sister Emma of the Oxford Sisterhood of St Thomas the Martyr as Mother Superior to the new Community of St Michael and All Angels. She arrived in 1874 with five associates who had not yet taken vows. Mother Emma agreed to stay for five years but never returned to England.

Bishop Webb on the Role of Women

Webb's views on the role of women in the work of the Church were uncompromising. The central power must rest with the bishop, as father of the family and not in 'arbitrary government by a woman':

5. The effect of such beliefs on the lives of African women is discussed elsewhere in this volume by Modupe Labode.

> All Sisterhood work, to be perfect, ought . . . to be carried on with the real
> central power vested in the Bishop . . . . The work must be under his person-
> al control (as representing the Great Head of the Church) and rule; not under
> the irresponsible rule of any woman. (Webb, 1883: 57)

No doubt the word *irresponsible* has changed its meaning over a
hundred years, for Webb admitted that women were needed in the field
to do 'a work which the clergy can no more do, than women can do the
work of the clergy'. Not for women, however, was

> the originating faculty, which chalks out the lines of action, broad and bold
> and unhesitating. That is man's especial function. But he does not stand
> alone. Here as everywhere else in the world, Woman is Man's helpmeet. For
> the Wisdom for which Woman is the representative, what is it but the organ-
> ising faculty, the executive power.
>   Woman, then, is to exhibit the attribute of Wisdom; good sense and tact
> in practical matters; working ably on the lines laid down for her, as the true
> handmaid of the Church; not reasoning out an idea but working it out, by her
> own womanly intuition. (Webb, 1883: 2)

Ironically for a man of such views, Webb was instrumental in introducing into South Africa two women whose influence and work out-
stripped his own – Henrietta Stockdale and Annie Cecilia Isherwood.

Sister Henrietta Stockdale

The daughter of a clergyman, Henrietta Stockdale was one of the five
who went out with Sister Emma. At the age of sixteen she had met a
group of missionaries on leave from the Orange Free State and had
resolved to become a mission nurse. After training at the Clewer Hospital and Great Ormond Street, she responded to Bishop Webb's appeal
for workers. She took her vows as Sister Henrietta in 1875 and, until her
sudden death at Kimberley in 1911, worked indefatigably to establish
nurses' training and the state registration of nurses in South Africa.[6]

Sister Henrietta was a prime example of a woman who by her dedication broke out of the restrictions surrounding middle-class Victorian
women. The nursing training she set up enabled many women from
Britain to serve as mission nurses in South Africa. In her later years Sister Henrietta worked closely with the women's emigration societies
whose concern was to enable British women to earn their living overseas.

6. See Searle (1965) for an account of Sister Henrietta's life and work.

Mother Cecile of the Community of the Resurrection, Grahamstown

In 1883 Bishop Webb was transferred to Grahamstown in the Eastern Cape and established there the Community of the Resurrection of Our Lord on the same lines as the Bloemfontein Sisterhood. On a visit to England he undertook a preaching tour during which he appealed to churchwomen to join him at Grahamstown. One who answered the call was Annie Cecilia Isherwood. Orphaned early, she had gone to live with family friends in London and there, while worshipping at St Peter's, Eaton Square, had heard the bishop preach of the need for women workers in South Africa. She decided at once to devote her life to mission work and, at the age of 21 years, was one of the first to arrive for service in the new Community. She took her vows in 1887 as Sister Cecile, was soon elected Mother Superior of the Order and was known as Mother Cecile for the rest of her life (Davies, 1951: Chapter 18).

Bishop Webb believed that the Community should be self-supporting and life was hard in the early years. The Sisters lived in extreme poverty but this did not prevent them setting up a variety of institutions in Grahamstown from which, over the years, the work spread throughout South Africa and Southern Rhodesia.

Mother Cecile's greatest achievement was the founding of teacher training at Grahamstown in the 1890s. Like Sister Henrietta she worked with the women's emigration societies and many women teachers were enabled through her good offices, to become teachers in the territory. Appeals were made particularly to 'earnest and devoted Churchwomen' to assist with training and elementary school work in the diocese. The British Women's Emigration Association, through which appeals were made and many of whose members were devout Anglicans including the wives and widows of clergymen, considered it a good opportunity for 'earnest, self-sacrificing women of education who would be willing for a nominal salary of £20 per annum to offer themselves for a most interesting and important branch of work'.[7]

The Expansion of Women's Work

The initiative of the founding bishops firmly established women in the work of the Anglican Church in South Africa. In other Protestant missions, too, single women found their place. As life became more settled

---

7. British Women's Emigration Association – South African Correspondence. File, March 1900. These papers are lodged in the Fawcett Library of Women's History, London.

in the interior of the country, mission schools and hospitals were founded, some by women from Britain recruited directly for mission work. Other British women were recruited to staff them.

Some women who went to South Africa were laywomen reponding to the strong need for Christian service felt by many in the nineteenth century. Some went out by their own means and initiative while others were obliged by their circumstances to seek help from the women's emigration societies, themselves strongly imbued with the aims of evangelisation and the furtherance of empire.

An outstanding example of the women who used their own means to go to South Africa in the hope of spreading the Gospel was Kate Barter. The daughter of the Rector of Sarsden, Oxfordshire, she went to Natal in 1857 to keep house for her brother, Charles Barter, but with 'a latent hope which I had long entertained of being at some time or other engaged in the work of missions to the heathen' (Barter c. 1865: 9). Eliza Feilden described her as 'that singular lady who has been living among the Caffres with a view to Christianize them, sleeping on a mat in a hut, and undergoing various voluntary privations' (Feilden, 1973: 265). Kate's health, Eliza reported, had been undermined by these activities and she was returning to England. She had, in any case, lost her role as housekeeper when her brother carried off into matrimony one of Bishop Colenso's Grey Sisters.

Others, lacking means, made use of the opportunities offered by the emigration societies to work in a land where, they believed, they might both solve their economic problems and have the chance of working out their faith in a 'corner of the Vineyard of the Great Husbandman'. Miss S. E. Hall was one such. She went to South Africa in 1868 with the help of the Female Middle Class Emigration Society. Like so many Victorian women she was reticent about her past but served with distinction over many years first as a governess, then in her own school in the Eastern Cape and finally as the Lady Principal of the Ladies' Collegiate School, Port Elizabeth. From the first she expressed a wish to further the evangelisation of Africa, which she described as 'the most benighted continent of the world'. She hoped that she might help the day to dawn 'when the Gospel light, with its knowledge of peace and love, would shine from Morocco to the Cape'. She wrote to the Society in 1877:

> I have the interest of Africa at heart and I see that by increasing the number of hard-working people, I can do much good and perhaps hasten the coming of the 'Kingdom' for which all Christendom is praying.[8]

8. S. E. Hall in Letter Book 2 of the Female Middle Class Emigration Society, 10 June 1877 (Fawcett Library).

Conclusion – The Problem of Recruitment

Despite the apparent pool of women available for emigration and the evangelising zeal of the period it did not prove easy, for most of the nineteenth century, to recruit single women to the Protestant missions. The reasons for this lie in the circumstances and position of middle-class women in Britain and also in the conditions and needs of the missions in South Africa.

Similar problems of recruitment were experienced by the women's emigration societies. Although there was considerable distress among unsupported gentlewomen there was no vast pool eligible for work overseas. Most of the women in need of employment were unsuited, by the nature of their socialisation and education, to the needs and deprivations of mission life. In addition, the strength of the expectation of marriage as the only acceptable career for *ladies* meant that many lingered on in hope until the time was past when they could make a suitable contribution.

There was little encouragement to mission service in the known hardships of mission life for those without the strongest faith and commitment. Nor, in the early years of the century, were the missions themselves sure of the role that single women could play or of their ability to absorb them. All they could offer in return for devoted service was a hard life of deprivation, ill health and even premature death. It needed a very stout heart to give up home and family, despite the frustrations and difficulties, for this.

Most nineteenth-century women were inexperienced in ordering their own affairs and in travelling alone. It was in this sphere that the women's emigration societies proved so useful. Many of the women emigrationists were clergy wives or widows and were strongly linked to Christian organisations such as the Girls' Friendly Society and the Young Women's Christian Association. They helped with recruitment and through their policy of protected emigration supplied both the means and protection on the voyage. Both Sister Henrietta and Mother Cecile gave their services to enable women to reach the missions in South Africa.

Who Went to the Mission Field?

Of those women whose origins are recorded, many who went out to serve in the mission field were daughters of the clergy. They were particularly suitable because they had grown up in the knowledge of the sacrifices needed for mission work. They were also, in general, better trained in household duties than most women of their class and were more likely to have to earn their own livings as their fathers were less able to provide for them.

Other women who were attracted to the mission field were those who had already had experience of church work in Britain. Some of these were older women who possessed the means to make their own way but, perhaps because they were less willing to submit to discipline, often proved unsatisfactory. Some made their way to the mission field to look after bachelor brothers or to help with their brothers' families. If the brother were a clergyman the sister's role was clear-cut, but others like Kate Barter, joined brothers who were not clergy and made their own arrangements for Christian service.

As the century progressed and the education and training of women improved in Britain, the missions became more demanding in the qualifications required for their servants abroad. Although the role of the general mission worker survived the century, increasing stress was laid on the need for teachers, nurses and other trained women for work in the more specialised institutions that were emerging.

Bibliography

Anderson-Morshead, A. E. M. (1905) *Reminiscences of Robert Gray*, Skeffington, London

Barter, Kate (c. 1865) *Alone Among the Zulus*, SPCK, London

Bean, L. and van Heyningen, E. (eds) (1983) *The Letters of Jane Elizabeth Waterston, 1866–1905*, Van Riebeeck Society, Cape Town

Brooke, Audrey (1957) *Robert Gray*, Oxford University Press, Oxford

Calderwood, Rev. Henry (1858) *Caffres and Caffre Missions*, James Nisbet, London

Child, Daphne (ed.) (1979) *The Diaries and Letters of Joseph and Marianne Churchill*, Balkema, Cape Town

Davies, H. M. (1951) *Great South African Christians*, Oxford University Press

Davies, H. M. and Shepherd, R. H. W. (1954) *South African Missions, 1800–1950* Thomas, Nelson & Sons, London

Feilden, Eliza W. (1973) *My African Home*, Interprint (T.W. Briggs) Durban (first published 1887)

Frazer's Magazine 'Female Labour', Vol. 61, March 1860: 364
   'Lord Grey's Colonial Administration', Vol. 47, May 1853: 487

Gissing, George (1980) *The Odd Women*, Virago, London (first published 1893)

Gray, Rev. Charles (1876) *The Life of Bishop Gray*, 2 vols. Rivington, London

Grey, W.R. 'Why Are Women Redundant?', in *National Review*, Vol. 15, No. 28, April 1862

Johnson, H.H. (1887) 'British Missions in Africa', in *Nineteenth Century*, Vol. 22, November 1887: 717

Low, Frances (1897) 'How Poor Ladies Live', in *Nineteenth Century*, Vol. 41, March: 405

Quarterly Review (1844) Article 5, Vol. 75, No. 144, December

Sala, George (1854) 'The 1851 Census', in *Household Words*, Vol. 10, No. 239, October

Searle, Charlotte (1965) *The History of the Development of Nursing in South Africa*, Struik, Cape Town

Shepherd, R.H.W. (1955) *Lovedale, South Africa, 1824–1955* Lovedale Press, Cape Town

Swaisland, Cecillie (1993) *Servants and Gentlewomen to the Golden Land* Berg, Oxford and Providence, (USA)

Webb, A.B. (1883) *Sisterhood Life and Women's Work*, Skeffington, London

Westminster Review (1889) 'Women and Work', Vol. 131: 271

5

'God and Nature Intended You for a Missionary's Wife': Mary Hill, Jane Eyre and Other Missionary Women in the 1840s

Valentine Cunningham

Victorian India Texts

In an arresting accident of chronology the year 1847 witnesses an illuminating convergence between the lives of two missionary-minded Protestant Englishwomen. On 7 September 1847 Mary Hill, wife of the Rev. Micaiah Hill, a Congregationalist missionary to Bengal and acting pastor of the Congregationalist Union Chapel in Calcutta, died in that city, aged 57. Just a month or so later there appeared in London a novel called *Jane Eyre*, apparently from the pen of one Currer Bell, actually written by the daughter of the Anglican minister of the parish of Haworth in Yorkshire. Charlotte Brontë's sensationally successful plot featured a young woman who would eventually find marital happiness only after refusing to go out to Calcutta as the wife of a missionary.

The tombstone to Mary Hill is now in the British graveyard in South Park Street, Calcutta. It was moved there, along with other missionary memorial stones, in April 1987 from the Scottish Cemetery just around the corner in Karaya Road. Cheek by jowl with the scores of graves of East India administrators, river pilots, clerics, clerks, scholars, soldiers, younger sons, young men all seemingly in their twenties and early thirties, young wives and mothers, many of them scarcely out of their teens, babes in arms, toddlers, small children, Mary Hill's stone takes its place among the mouldering remains and collapsing mementoes of all those once deeply grieved-over ones who gave up their lives in the service of King or Queen, Empire, Duty, Mammon, European education, the religion of Christ. South Park Street Cemetery is a moving place, full of compelling public texts of pious testimony and tribute. The text of Mary Hill's tombstone runs thus:

In Memory of
Mary Hill,
Wife of the Revd Micaiah Hill,
of the London Miss.ʸ Society
And Acting Pastor of Union Chapel, Dhurrumtollah.
Obit 7th Sept 1847, Aetat 57.
This monument is erected by the church and congregation
From respect and esteem for her Christian virtues;
and missionary zeal,
In establishing and superintending religious schools,
Both for heathen children and poor Christian females,
during a period of 24 years at Berhampore;
and also to record their grateful remembrance,
of the deep interest she untiringly took,
in the spiritual and temporal welfare,
of the people among whom in the providence of God,
she came for a time to reside,
and among whom she closed her earthly career
of usefulness and Christian benevolence.

She was born Mary Beardmore in 1790 in Newcastle-under-Lyme. She married Micaiah Hill, a man of her own age, from Walsall. She was an Anglican; he was a Congregationalist, a member of Birmingham's famous Carr's Lane Chapel, then pastored by John Angell James. Dutifully, Mrs Hill joined the Congregationalists. Micaiah Hill was ordained into the Congregationalist ministry in July 1821, and on 10 October 1821 Mr and Mrs Hill sailed for India under the auspices of the still young London Missionary Society. It took them until 5 March 1822 to get to Calcutta. There they laboured in the station already established around the Union Chapel. Mr Hill did some journalism. After two years and various abortive ventures in the region they were posted to Berhampur, 120 miles or thereabouts from Calcutta, a large military centre, to set up a new Dissenting missionary outpost. It was hard going, 'a wilderness of Idolatry and sinful abomination', as a letter of Micaiah Hill puts it (11 December 1824), 'far from European friends and severed from Christian Society'. (Hill's letters that survived the journey home are now kept in the London Missionary Society archive at the London School of Oriental and African Studies.) Mrs Hill was often ill. After prolonged physical suffering she returned to England with three of her children, sailing from Calcutta on Christmas Day 1836 and arriving in London on 24 April 1837. In 1838 Micaiah Hill's health was sufficiently broken down to compel him to make the return journey home, and he arrived in London on 22 May 1839. After three years of his recuperation the family returned once more to India, setting sail on 14 July 1842, arriving in Calcutta on 29 October, and then going on to Berhampur. In January 1847 they left Berhampur for good: Hill was appointed replacement pastor for Dr Boaz of the Union Chapel who had returned to England. After only eight months in Calcutta Mrs Hill died, her death 'occasioned by severe injury received from a fall about six weeks before'.[1] Her husband survived her by only sixteen months: he died on a boat on the Ganges, sailing to Benares in order to recover his health.

The bare narratives of the tombstone text and the simple published chronological record[2] reveal something of what such missionary labours involved – for instance, the huge number of months spent aboard ship, merely in transit, just travelling between England and India. But the heroic physical and spiritual endurance test that India imposed is something that these public glimpses scarcely touch on. Nor are the published Annual Reports of the London Missionary Society and the *Quarterly Chronicle of Transactions of the LMS* (which turned into the *Missionary Magazine and Chronicle*) much better at registering either the distresses of the Hills, or their few successes. The British Christian public was clearly felt by the LMS's London administrators to need stories of spiritual triumph – distinct conversions of the heathen, pagan temples cast down, idol worship vanquished, positive missionary action and positive missionary thinking. They got a little of that from Micaiah Hill. But not much. He was in fact nagged at by the LMS Secretaries in London for his dilatoriness in sending publishable news, journals of itineraries, diaries of life on station, and so on. On one occasion in 1831, accused of not communicating since 1828, he replied that 'remissness in correspondence' was caused by heavy work-loads, a dislike of diary keeping (too 'egotistical'), and of repetition (reporting a 'sameness of occurrences and events') and, in any case, there was yet no triumphalist outpouring of the Spirit, no 'shaking' in 'this valley of vision'. If he produced a daily record the result would be, every month, 'an octavo volume of disappointments' (letter of 18 August 1831). The very paper for extensive correspondence was hard to come by. In 1836, when Hill was embroiled in a quarrel with fellow-missionaries about how the Bengal mission should be managed, a debate that provoked very lengthy epistles, he expostulated at the end of one enormous and

1. Mary Hill's death is noticed in *The Missionary Magazine and Chronicle*, CXXXVIII, November 1847: 174. Extracts from the funeral sermon appeared in this LMS journal, CXLI, February 1848: 28–9.
2. James Sibree (ed.), 1923: 22–3. Micaiah Hill was missionary No. 222.

closely-written missive (29 September 1836) that he was 'unable to comply' with London's 'request to write my letters on Fool's cap with a broad margin': paper was short; the Directors' last consignment of paper had sunk on its way up-river; and that was ten years previously.

Medicinal Living and Soldierly Dying

What such correspondence as survives does reveal (and Hill claimed that numbers of letters were going astray) is the awful physical truth behind the bare public records of illness and death. 'We are constrained in this climate to live medicinally' (18 August 1831); 'My eldest boy has been several times on the verge of the grave and last year was ten months under the influence of Mercury' (16 June 1828); 'perpetual mortality around us' (18 August 1831); 'death is making havock of many around' (30 December 1832). The Hills' eldest boy, William, had to be sent home to England for his health ('has every year more or less been so ill that we have despaired of his life', 21 August 1827). Their fifth child, a boy, died aged eleven months in February 1832. They were luckier than some. One of their colleagues the Rev. Gogerly wrote home in January 1831 of the sudden death through cholera of his thirteen-year-old son, which meant he had lost three children and a wife in India; his nine-year-old boy was 'almost reduced to a skeleton' and must return to England lest he become 'the *fifth victim* of the insalubrity of the climate in Bengal'. Mary Hill was repeatedly ill: 'continual illness in the first years (*sic*) residence in Bengal' (11 December 1824); 'has twice been dangerously ill with no medical person at hand' (June 1824); travelling about with her husband in the cold season in order to stay healthy she has been, two years running, 'unable to walk across the room' (5 October 1836). On one occasion in 1830 the Hills were evicted at short notice from their military-owned bungalow in the rainy season and had to move themselves and their belongings three miles in pouring rain: 'I was just able to walk about. Mrs Hill could not rise from her bed & . . . our second son lay to appearance at the point of death' (23 September 1830). The published records tend to skim over such plights. They note them, of course, bluntly in obituaries. But the letters of the LMS archive are, by contrast, a long litany of illness and deaths through epidemics, dysentery, fever, cholera. They tell of ailing children, dying wives, dead missionaries, missionary widows and orphans, as well as the occasional mad woman who has to be shipped home (at great expense, accompanied by costly female attendants, against the will of reluctant ships' captains who increase the fare in consequence of their worries). They offer urgent pleas and present accumulated medical evidence for returning to England, costly to the Society and heartbreaking to the missionaries though these journeys are.

At the end of 1837 Hill reports his alarm 'at the large numbers of missionaries whom Mrs Hill met in London' – the Devil has evidently been busy making mission-fields too pestilential for God's servants to stay in them – and he regrets that illness is compelling him to add himself to their number: 'a return to England is opposed to the plan I have always cherished, viz as the Venerable Waugh charged me on leaving England "To die with my face towards the foe" never shall I forget those words'. And, of course, Hill would in fact die in just that way upon his subsequent return to India. So would Mary Hill. So would the Hills' eventual colleague at Berhampur, James Paterson; and Paterson's first wife, Isabelle, who died there in April 1847 only months before Mary Hill's death; and the second Mrs Paterson, who was brought out from Britain to die at Berhampur in 1853.

Just how soldierly a death Mary Hill's (and Isabelle Paterson's and the other Mrs Paterson's) would be accounted by the LMS's London organisers and the Christian public in Britain is something of a moot point. For missionary work at this stage of the LMS's history was clearly perceived as a task performed by men which women merely supplemented. *Missionary* was a male noun; it denoted a male actor, male action, male spheres of service. Mary Hill was not a missionary by the definition of her day, she was a missionary's wife. In the standard printed LMS 'Schedule of Returns' form the slot headed 'Missionaries' would be for a long time filled with the names of men only. Wives and children occupied the form's space for dependants. The Society was solicitous of wives' welfare, conscious of their value, but it is possible to detect an official suspicion that they might not always pull their weight unless kept up to the mark. 'In answer to your question Is Mrs Hill endeavouring to learn the language? I answer, from continual illness in the first four years residence in Bengal she was not able to attend to the language, but since that period she has daily studied with the Pundit and now reads in the Bengallee Testament' (11 December 1824). When Micaiah Hill pleads with London for 'a fellow-labourer to strengthen my hands' (5 February 1825), he is asking for a male coadjutor: his fellow-labouring wife is not accounted a fellow-labourer in the fullest sense (and, in fact, she only itinerated the villages with him of health necessity: had she been well enough, paradoxically, she'd have stayed behind in Berhampur).

The LMS was a male affair. Hill's letters to the 'missionary rooms' in London commonly begin 'Dear Fathers and Brethren'. A man speaks to men about this mission-field. The official history of the Society by

John Morison is entitled *The Founders and Fathers of the LMS*. John Angell James's commemorative sermon of 1849 was entitled a 'Tribute to the Fathers and Founders of the LMS'. The Society's *Quarterly News of Women's Work* seems not to have been founded until 1887. There are signs that some womanly details got edited out of the letters that the (male) missionaries sent home, when they were prepared for publication. For example, the one from Micaiah Hill (1 March 1828), corrected for publication in the *Monthly Chronicle* of January 1829, has the details of the difficulties encountered in their girls' school by Mary Hill and her colleague Mrs Warden ('Mrs Hill regrets to state are not so encouraging as she could desire') deleted by an editor's pen. Letters from wives rarely appear in the archives. There is an occasional communication from a returning widow conveying an update of the work. But only one missive from Mary Hill appears. It is a complaint (12 April 1825) that she and her husband receive letters too infrequently. Some they have just received 'lay' more than eleven months at the London 'Rooms' before being sent on. 'In consequence of this delay I did not hear from my beloved Mother for nearly two years after my arrival in Bengal.' But this little outburst of womanly querulousness, so rare in the correspondence, instantly collapses into the expected notes of wifely duty: she attaches to her missive a copied-out extract from the journal of her 'dear partner' about a fair he recently attended for purposes of evangelism – the sort of report Hill would later declare himself too busy to send.

The Prom. of Fem. Educ.

There is some discussion in the 1820s correspondence from northern India about whether 'unmarried females' should be sent out. A letter from Calcutta signed by Messrs Trawin, Warden and J. Hill (no relation) opposes the idea: single women would be a nuisance in that they could only accompany married couples; they might get married to Europeans not belonging to the mission and so quit the work; they cost as much to send out and support as unmarried (male) missionaries, so why bother; and (male) missionaries can just as easily found girls' schools as females can (31 August 1824). Women widowed in the field were also felt to be a problem.

Warden and Trawin both died in India. J. Hill (16 January 1826) had to obtain London's support for Mrs Warden's staying on to help with 'female schools' (she was the Mrs Warden of the edited letter from Micaiah Hill). For her part the widowed Mrs Trawin earned a generous tribute from Micaiah Hill when weakness from perpetual dysentery compelled her return to England. She was, he wrote, not only 'the most useful female in our Mission in Bengal, as she has obtained a knowledge of the Bengalee and a partial knowledge of the Hindustanee language' (21 August 1827), she was also 'a most excellent Missionary' (16 June 1828). As good as a man in fact. But such a male concession was rare at the time, and women were not to be allowed officially to show whether they were equal to male missionaries for some time after this. There were only three officially appointed female LMS 'missionaries' before 1875. The first of these in the LMS register is Maria Newell – 'appointed to carry on Women's Education among Chinese at Malacca'. She left England in 1827, but is clearly the object of some oversight or afterthought, so anomalous was she, since she is tucked late into the list at No. 270a. There is not another registered woman missionary until No. 605 – E. M. H. Sturrock, and hers is no straightforward appointment either. She is said, carefully, to have been 'Connected with the Society for the Promotion of Female Education in the East, by which she was appointed to Peelton, Kafirland, South Africa, and which bore the expenses of her voyage and journey to *Peelton*; while the LMS paid her salary at her station.' She spent twenty years in Peelton, then 'In 1884 it was arranged that her connection with the LMS as one of its missionaries should cease, and that she should be regarded solely as an Agent of the Soc. for the Prom. of Fem. Educ. in the East'. The third independently listed LMS woman is Lilly White, 'appointed to superintend *Caste Girls' Schools*' in Madras – the first widow of an LMS missionary to be granted separate official status (her husband died in Madras in 1866). It is only after 1875, when policy clearly changed, that the flood of acknowledged LMS women missionaries begins – Mary Anne Heward, Edith Annie Tubbs, Mary Teresa Bliss, Emmeline Mary Geller, Lucy Margaret Bounsall, Christina Brown, E. Bear, and so on and on.

For all the early hesitancies and grudging tributes, though, the work of the wives and widows was obviously indispensable, especially among women and girls, both Indian and European, and among orphan boys. The 'Prom. of Fem. Educ.' relied on them. The allegation that (male) missionaries might found girls' schools just as readily as women did, seems not have been much put to the test. Women's education in India was firmly in women's hands; so was ministering to women in general. Very soon after she arrived in Berhampur Mary Hill had one Girls' School in operation, was 'erecting' another, and had 'two others in contemplation' (11 December 1824). In 1826 Mrs Warden was running a Sunday School for children of the European regiments stationed in Berhampur, and she and Mrs Hill were devoting 'a portion of each day' to the European women attached to these regiments (14 March 1826). The Bengali girls of the Orphan Asylum that was being planned in 1831 were to be 'instructed in Mrs Hill's school in reading, sewing, plaiting straw for Bonnets, spinning, &c' (18 August 1831). In 1834 Hill's new colleague James Paterson reports that the dozen boys in Mrs Hill's Orphan Asylum are being taught by her several 'arts' for their future self-support. Mrs Paterson and Mrs Hill ('when she is able') run the Bengali Girls' School, where the girls every day sing hymns, repeat the Catechism and the Lord's Prayer and 'write on the ground', as is the Bengali custom (7 October 1834).

There was local support for the education of women. In 1828 the Moha Raja Oodwent Singh donated 500 rupees towards Mrs Hill's Schools, in which, according to the *Quarterly Chronicle of Transactions of the LMS*, 'Some of the girls . . . could read more fluently than many Sircars. Those in attendance read *Mala Konya*, learn the Catechisms and Mr Jetter's spelling-book.'[3] Despite some opposition from (male) missionaries in the LMS (correspondence in the archive suggests the effort to educate Indian women to be an unrewarded waste of time) the first printed *Report of the Native Female School Society, Connected with the London Missionary Society* appeared in Calcutta in 1828. And on the second of January 1832 one Agnes Gogerly of the Native Female School Society of Calcutta addressed a fund-raising pamphlet *To the Members (more particularly the Female) of the Churches of Christ in England and Scotland*. She declared that there were fifty million females in India and fewer than 2000 of them perhaps could write their names. Christian women must support the 'movement in favour of Female Education' lately manifest in India. The Native Female School Society is the last to be formed of the twenty-two voluntary aided institutions of Calcutta and so the least supported. The former neglect by British Christians of the 'female part of the population' of India must be remedied. Sympathy and help are therefore requested 'for the daughters of India, who, through the degrading influence of a most abominable system of idolatry, are suffered by their natural protectors to remain in the grossest ignorance and vice, and in consequence are thrown upon the charities of strangers'.

Women's education, conducted by missionary wives and widows

---

3. *Quarterly Chronicle of Transactions of the LMS, 1825–8*, III: 418. Sircars were local political or domestic or financial officials. *Mala Konya:* enigmatic, but sounds like a school primer for girls, or a slightly misrecorded title of a fairy story about a girl with flowing black hair; at any rate, a text for young girls (my thanks to Richard Gombrich for this clarification).

('the female department of the Mission' as Hill called it, 14 March 1826), would be supported above all by women's contributions. In 1824 Hill reports that the European regimental 'ladies' of Berhampur have 'nobly patronised and generously contributed towards' Mrs Hill's schools to the tune of 456 rupees, which will pay for three schools for a year. Mrs Hill has written to her friends back home in Newcastle-under-Lyme for 'their assistance in female education'. She called one of her earliest schools the Newcastle. And support came from England in the form that ordinary chapel-going and generally propertyless (because married) British women could contribute it – in womanly stuff. The 1832 Schedule of Returns from Berhampur reports that 'a box of articles' has come 'from Sandbach Ladys Sewing Society which sold for 75 rupees' and was 'applied to Female School'. 'From Miss Bayley London' came 'some pincushions which sold for 5 rupees 10 annas', which was applied to the same purpose. In 1834 James Paterson writes that 'Mrs Paterson will feel obliged if the Directors will take the earliest opportunity of inserting in the Monthly Chronicle her thanks to Mrs Romanis . . . and other friends for a box of fancy articles which she has just received, in aid of the Girls' School. As soon as the articles are disposed of, she will inform her friends of the amount they have realised' (7 October). Presumably these female offerings were sold to the European women attached to the local garrison. Occasionally, as well, English women with private wealth at their disposal are envisaged as supporters. In 1824 Hill regrets the absence of medicines which would grant an entrée for 'Mrs Hill and myself' into people's abodes: perhaps 'some pious Druggist or Lady' would supply medicines if the need were publicised. The 1832 Schedule of Returns reports 'A very acceptable supply of medicine received in Aug. last'.

Marginal People

For all the evident caginess within the male-dominated LMS, in India and at home, about missionary women, their status and their labours, it is nonetheless clear that a sort of radical emancipatory motive, rooted in particular interpretations of Scripture, inspired the likes of Mary Hill in her work among women, and shaped the rhetoric that was employed to describe it:

> As female education in raising morals of a nation is so important, we earnestly entreat Honoured Fathers and Brethren your prayers and those of the Churches, will assist our efforts and help to draw upon us the influence of the Holy Spirit, that we may soon see a reformation here of Males and Females, congregated together in the name of Him who has said 'There is no Male or Female but all are one in Christ Jesus'. (4–24 June 1824)

What exactly the Honoured Fathers and Brothers thought of this particular quotation and application of that Scriptural text is only guessable. What is clear is that already – and this would still be the case later on when the ranks of all Protestant missionary societies filled up dramatically with women missionaries – the rhetoric and the cause of women and women's ministry were running ahead more speedily in mission-field circumstances than at home. It is no accident that the ordination of women in the Anglican Church would be in the twentieth century accepted first in what were Anglicanism's missionary branches. More pertinently, it seems even less accidental that in the earlier part of the nineteenth century this radical-sounding tone should have been adopted by a Congregationalist pastor and his wife (even if she had been brought up in the Church of England). It is at least arguable that the Hills' interest in the marginal people of India was incited by their own status as marginals within English religious society and within the versions of British society exported to India.

As a woman, of course, Mary Hill was by definition a marginal person. When she married her Congregationalist husband she left the religiously and socially centrist Church of England, and so added a religiously inflected marginality to the already given marginality attaching to her gender. The Hills were made to feel the sharp end of that Dissenting marginality in all of their Indian dealings with what Micaiah Hill continually refers to in his letters as 'the Establishment'. The Bishop of Calcutta – from 1823 to 1826 he was Reginald ('From Greenland's Icy Mountains') Heber – and his clergy were at the centre of this colonial outpost. They wielded and represented its authority and privileges in ways utterly denied the LMS's nonconfirmist preachers and educators. The Berhampur Anglicans seem, for a start, to have had greater wealth for their mission, at any rate early on in the Hills' work. In 1824 the Anglicans were luring children from the Hills' schools with a 'system of presents' (4–24 June 1824). Since Berhampur was a garrison town the smile and frown of the European military jurisdiction mattered in all aspects of day-to-day functioning. The only decent houses the Hills could rent were owned by the military, which generated native suspicions as well as giving them particularly bad moments like the eviction in the monsoons of 1830. And 'the Establishment' sometimes presented a united hostile front of military authority in collaboration with its official Christian expression, the Anglican Church.

The Hills had gradually won the respect of the pious churchgoing soldiery of Berhampur, to the extent that the men of regiments like the 38th, the Buffs, came to regard Micaiah as their pastor and the Berhampur Mission as their church, to be supported by gifts of money even when they were posted elsewhere. Even Anglican soldiers were receiving the 'dissenting sacrament' and were happy to worship 'on Congregational principles'. But in 1835 there arrived as Anglican and 'government' chaplain the Rev. Richard Chambers. He regarded himself, so James Paterson sneered (21 August 1835), as 'the government (and therefore divinely appointed) guardian of the spiritual interest of the European soldiers'. Clearly peeved to discover Hill's pastoral success with English soldiers and other English speakers whom he thought should be his flock, Chambers provoked a division between the Anglicans and Dissenters attending the Hills' ministries. Going further, he published a sharp attack on missionaries such as Hill who preached in English. His article 'On the Proper Sphere of Missionary Labour' appeared in the Calcutta *Christian Intelligencer* in June 1835, and at a time when, as Paterson pointed out, the Hills had just buried their youngest child, their next youngest was severely ill with dysentery, and Mrs Hill had had to remove up country for her health. The kind of hostility and disabilities imposed upon Dissenters at home were thus being transposed with a vengeance to the foreign field. No wonder a large packet of letters accumulated as Hill defended his right to minister to whomever he felt led, and above all to preach in English. (The truth was that his English-speaking congregation essentially paid for the much smaller Indian one.)

It is not difficult to imagine that the Hills' care for local outcasts was infected by their own position as outcasts in relation to the Establishment. The man from Walsall and from Carr's Lane Birmingham, and the wife who had gone down-market, religiously and socially speaking, were not gentlefolk. Their dealings with 'the upper classes' were, Hill reported, 'always visits of necessity', tempered by religious not social ambition, and thus were conducted in the evenings after dinner. They were not much on calling terms with the Empire's more accredited agents. If they were invited to tea, they would, Hill wrote, always produce a Bible immediately afterwards and conduct family worship (23 September 1830). In any case their more natural social inclinations were towards the 'women of colour' who get mentioned in the same letter. Certainly from the start in Berhampur they had directed their attentions to the illegitimate children of Spanish, Portuguese and British men by native women, and to the females who lost caste by being sold by their parents (11 December 1824). The girls in Mrs Hill's and Mrs Paterson's Bengali School were all (7 October 1834) of the 'lowest caste'. The behaviour of the Rev. Richard Chambers can only have rubbed their Dissenting noses into the fact that the Establishment thought them fittest, socially and religiously speaking, for ministry to these cast-outs, the lowest castes, and the half-caste. And as a woman, of course, Mrs

Hill was, by a consensus that Dissenting and Anglican males more or less agreed on, closer still to the condition of these marginalised ones, not least the females, among whom she toiled.

Fellow-Missionary?

The kinds of social, religious and genderised marginalities that Mrs Hill lived with were well known back home. Charlotte Brontë was by no means unfamiliar with them. She was not one of those who enjoyed what Matthew Arnold designated 'the tone of the centre'. She was a woman of the provinces, acquainted with spartan conditions and deprivations of all kinds, living at a great distance from the geographical and cultural centre and centres, brought up in Church-Methodism as a kind of surrogate Dissenter under the hand of a loving, but also rough, eccentric, evangelical Ulsterman of a father. And she knew about India and missionaries, not least through the magnetic influence upon her father's life of Henry Martyn, the Cornishman who, before the likes of David Livingstone stole his thunder, was the most famous English missionary of the nineteenth century. The translator of the New Testament and the Prayer Book into Hindustani, and of the New Testament, the Psalms and the Gospels into Persian, Martyn had been a chaplain to the Bengal establishment of the East India Company in Calcutta. He laboured at his translations in various locations across northern British India, travelled widely in Persia, translating his Christian texts and disputing with Muslims, and finally died of the plague, aged thirty-one, 16 October 1812, in Turkish Tokat on his way back from St Petersburg (where his Persian New Testament was printed) to England in order to marry Lydia Grenfell and take her back with him to the East.

Martyn had gone up to St John's College, Cambridge, in 1797, and had served as curate to the great evangelical Charles Simeon at Holy Trinity Church in Cambridge before leaving for Calcutta. In 1804 he had arranged for a poor evangelical Irish student of St John's, at that time called Patrick Brunty, to receive £10 a year from each of Henry Thornton and William Wilberforce. This piece of patronage was a key stepping stone in a career of evangelical patronage that was gradually leading Charlotte Brontë's father from Ulster, via Cambridge, through a chain of plum Simeonite Yorkshire parishes, to Haworth. It has been assumed, and with good reason, that Charlotte Brontë read Sargent's Memoir of Henry Martyn in the Keighley Public Library copy.[4] When

4. *DNB* (for Henry Martyn); T. J. Wise and J. A. Symington, 1933: 1, footnote p. 172; and I: 2–3 (for Martyn's letter to Wilberforce about Brunty/Brontë).

her father read *Jane Eyre* he believed he was being presented with old family stories and that Charlotte had had Henry Martyn in mind when she conceived St John Rivers. For one thing, he bore the name of Martyn's and Patrick Brontë's old College.

But for all the family enthusiasm for Henry Martyn (the national enthusiasm too: Samuel Wilberforce's two-volume edition of Martyn's *Journals and Letters* appeared in 1837), Charlotte Brontë calculatedly resists having Jane Eyre accept St John Rivers's plea to go to India with him as a missionary wife. Jane would not join the ranks of the Mary Hills. To be sure, she submits to learn Hindustani, 'poring', under Rivers's tutelage, 'over the crabbed characters and flourishing tropes of an Indian scribe'. But she is resistant to going out as 'a conductress of Indian schools, and a helper among Indian women' (Ch. 34), though not because of fear of dying prematurely. She is, of course, mindful of India's terrible climate, mindful that she would probably succumb to illness like so many missionaries – 'I feel mine is not the existence to be long protracted under an Indian sun'. But it is Rivers's sister Diana, not Jane herself, who thinks the very suggestion of going to be 'frantic folly', on the grounds that Jane is 'much too pretty, as well as too good, to be grilled alive in Calcutta'. Nor does Jane allow her manifest snobbery to stand in the way. St John Rivers is an evangelical Anglican, so that his labours would not have been so socially *démodé* as Micaiah Hill's. But if Jane finds her northern peasant pupils so degrading to teach – 'I felt degraded. I doubted I had taken a step which sank instead of raising me in the scale of social existence. I was weakly dismayed at the ignorance, the poverty, the coarseness of all I heard and saw around me' – there is little doubt that India would have seemed even more so. But this is not allowed to intrude. Jane's resistance focuses rather on the issue of the only role that St John will allow her: the missionary wife. 'God and nature intended you for a missionary's wife.'

For St John Rivers, as for Micaiah Hill and the fathers of the LMS, a missionary is a man. Charlotte Brontë recognised this contemporary fact: her poem entitled 'The Missionary' celebrates a travelling male hero of the faith. And in Rivers' view the place for a woman in the mission field is as a wifely supplement or subordinate to the male missionary. 'I want a wife: the sole helpmeet I can influence sufficiently in life, and retain absolutely till death.' Jane is prepared to go out as an unmarried assistant, a free, 'unenslaved' helper. But for St John Rivers, as for the LMS at the time, there's little or no role for independent women missionaries. By then current definition, a female 'fellow-missionary' does not really exist. When Jane consents to 'go with you as your fellow missionary' (Ch. 35) she is projecting an impossibility. As the LMS males readily assumed, there's no room in all decency for unmarried women on mission-stations with only a single white male colleague. 'How can I', Rivers demands, 'a man, not yet thirty, take out with me to India a girl of nineteen, unless she be married to me? How can we be for ever together – sometimes in solitude, sometimes amidst savage tribes – and unwed?' Jane's reply is a refusal to accept this piece of conventional wisdom. Even though she were single she would be able to accompany Rivers 'very well': 'under the circumstances, quite as well as if I were either your real sister, or a man and a clergyman like yourself'. No wonder Rivers labels her words as 'violent, unfeminine'. Jane would be 'a man', would invade and break down the preserves and prerogatives conventionally assigned to and possessed by missionary and clergyman.

These conventional agreements as to the social and religious nature of woman and wife, their proper sphere of action and selfhood, are then, being put sharply to the question in *Jane Eyre*, and in direct reference to Indian missions. The novel grants that great good is being achieved among Eastern people, and particularly women, by missionaries like St John Rivers and by missionary wives such as Rivers wished Jane to be and that Mary Hill actually was. But Jane Eyre's refusal to join in this work on Rivers' terms – which were the LMS's terms – focuses a logical flaw and a serious moral contradiction in a Christian endeavour that would seek to elevate, educate, emancipate Eastern women but saw no need to challenge the kinds of subordination required of the very married European women who were invited, to become, as Jane Eyre is invited, to become, the agents of that foreign liberation. There is also much good to be achieved at home, Jane thinks. Were Rivers to marry the fair Rosamond Oliver and 'become the possessor of Mr Oliver's large fortune, he might do as much good with it as if he went and laid his genius out to wither, and his strength to waste, under a tropical sun' (Ch. 32). And for Jane Eyre it is the subordination of wives – subordination particularly pronounced in the case of the missionary's wife, but shared by all British wives – that demands particular reformation. And the plight of the wives of Britain is reflected in the mirror of the missionary wife that St John Rivers holds up to Jane, and to us.

Eastern Allusions

Jane refuses to go East. But all her life she's been in an Eastern condition. As girl, young woman, wife-to-be and ultimately as wife, her condition is presented by the text as pointedly Eastern. The opening chapter of the novel has Jane sitting reading Bewick's *Birds* in her window-seat refuge, 'cross-legged, like a Turk'. She reads 'Arabian tales' and 'usually' finds them 'fascinating' (Ch. 4). But Arabian tales and Turkish reading positions are no consolation for, nor any ultimate refuge from, the brutalities of British males for this young Victorian girl and woman: Master John Reed soon interrupts Jane's solitary enjoyment of Bewick, throws the book at her, makes her head bleed; the Rev. Mr Brocklehurst upsets Jane so much with his terrorising talk and texts about Hell for naughty girls that she cannot concentrate on reading her Arabian tales. What Charlotte Brontë is teaching her heroine and us is that British women are by no means as free of Eastern bondage as we all might have supposed. 'You are like a slave-driver,' Jane tells John Reed. Even males who appear in kindlier guise, as Rochester does in the immediate run-up to the aborted marriage ceremony with Jane, cannot shed their part as Eastern tyrants. Marriage in Britain is demonstrated to be enslaving along Eastern lines. The arresting charades enacted by Rochester and Blanche Ingram (Ch. 18) have the pair 'attired in oriental fashion'. She is got up like 'some Israelitish princess of the patriarchal days'. He, turbanned, swarthy, with 'Paynim features', 'looked the very model of an Eastern emir'. The scarcely cryptic meaning of the pantomime turns out to be 'Bridewell' – the name of London's notorious penitentiary for women. And this notion of English marriage as an Eastern transaction and of the bridegroom as an Eastern-style potentate, pervades the text. When Rivers fantasises himself as a husband of Rosamond Oliver (Ch. 32) he imagines himself 'stretched on an ottoman in the drawing-room'. And Jane's resistance to wifely subservience is cast in what are in these circumstances appropriate Eastern terms.

On the eve of the aborted marriage attempt (Ch. 24) Rochester 'obliges' Jane to go to a 'silk warehouse' with him where he 'orders' her to choose material for half-a-dozen dresses. Hostile to extravagance, she beats the number down to two. She cannot 'bear being dressed like a doll by Mr Rochester'. He is not to be her 'idol' –Christianity forbids idol worship – and she will not allow herself to be his. He smiles possessively: 'and I thought his smile was such as a sultan might, in a blissful and fond moment, bestow on a slave his gold and gems had enriched'. Jane expostulates ('You must not look in that way') and there follows an exchange about harems which is peculiar only if it is read outside of the novel's carefully contrived set of 'Eastern allusions':

> He chuckled; he rubbed his hands, 'Oh, it is rich to see and hear her!' he exclaimed. 'Is she original? Is she piquant? I would not exchange this one little English girl for the Grand Turk's whole seraglio – gazelle-eyes, houri forms, and all!'
>
> The Eastern allusion bit me again. 'I'll not stand you an inch in the stead of a seraglio,' I said; 'so don't consider me an equivalent for one. If you have

a fancy for anything in that line, away with you, sir, to the bazaars of Stamboul, without delay, and lay out in extensive slave-purchases some of that spare cash you seem at a loss to spend satisfactorily here.'

'And what will you do, Janet, while I am bargaining for so many tons of flesh and such an assortment of black eyes?'

'I'll be preparing myself to go out as a missionary to preach liberty to them that are enslaved – your harem inmates amongst the rest. I'll get admitted there, and I'll stir up mutiny; and you, three-tailed bashaw as you are, sir, shall in a trice find yourself fettered amongst our hands: nor will I, for one, consent to cut your bonds till you have signed a charter, the most liberal that despot ever yet conferred.'

'I'll be preparing myself to go out as a missionary to preach liberty to them that are enslaved.' But the idolatrous sultans and pashas, the purchasers of female flesh are at home too. They are called husbands. Jane Eyre does not have literally to go out East to aid the cause of women's emancipation. That particular Eastern missionary work is, metaphorically speaking, required to be done also at home. And Charlotte Brontë and her novel *Jane Eyre* will co-operate in the insistence that this particular missionary enterprise, laudable and necessary though it also be overseas, must start at home.

In Darkest England

As the great nineteenth-century missionary ventures became a more and more prominent feature of British religious and social life, so the sense grew that Britain too was a mission-field in ways that simply mirrored the overseas ones. Africa, India, China, the world's dark continents, were plundered by Christian rhetoric to provide metaphors for the work of home evangelism. 'And this also has been one of the dark places of the earth': Marlow's comment at the end of the century in Conrad's story *Heart of Darkness*, a fiction that shows morally proud Europeans their own face in the corrupted African mirror, that confronts Europe with its Congo Doppelgänger, is only a secularised version of what had become by then a recurrent trope of Christian rhetoric. Dickens' criticisms in *Bleak House* (1853) of African missionary enterprise, are built upon a heavily ironised parallelism. Mrs Jellyby's involvement in charitable missionary works in Africa simply disables her as a mother of a family in London. This woman's missionary goodwill should be concerned in the first place with her own daughter's welfare. Neglect of home duties makes nonsense of her massive care for Borrioboola-Gha. The very word is gibberish. Just so, the Society for the Propagation of the Gospel in Foreign Parts should do more for the needy of London, the waifs pausing to breakfast on dirty bits of bread on its splendid doorstep. (Joe, the crossing-sweeper, 'admires the size of the edifice, and wonders what it's all about. He has no idea, poor wretch, of the spiritual destitution of a coral reef in the Pacific, or what it costs to look up the precious souls among the cocoa-nuts and bread-fruit', Ch. 16.) When John Henry Newman thought of missionary work he saw foreign and home missions as running necessarily in parallel – 'missionaries for China or Africa . . . evangelists for our great towns'.[5] And what was perhaps the most potent written home-evangelistic summons ever uttered in Victorian times was structured on an extended analogy between Darkest Africa and Darkest England, namely *In Darkest England and the Way Out* by William Booth, founder of the Salvation Army (1890). The 'African Parallel' it draws is inspired by what Booth calls the literary sensation of 'this summer', 'the story which Mr Stanley has told of "Darkest Africa".'

Noticeably, women feature recurrently in such parallels. Dickens is actively concerned with the mess Mrs Jellyby is making of her daughter Caddy's life. Among the most impressive of the many impressive analogies Booth makes in his In *Darkest England* is the paragraph comparing the lot of 'the negress in the Equatorial Forest' with the plight of penniless girls in London:

> The lot of a negress in the Equatorial Forest is not, perhaps, a very happy one, but is it so very much worse than that of many a pretty orphan girl in our Christian capital? We talk about the brutalities of the dark ages, and we profess to shudder as we read in books of the shameful exaction of the rights of feudal superior. And yet here, beneath our very eyes, in our theatres, in our restaurants, and in many other places, unspeakable though it be but to name it, the same hideous abuse flourishes unchecked. A young penniless girl, if she be pretty, is often hunted from pillar to post by her employers, confronted always by the alternative – Starve or Sin. And when once the poor girl has consented to buy the right to earn her living by the sacrifice of her virtue, then she is treated as a slave and an outcast by the very men who have ruined her. Her word becomes unbelievable, her life an ignominy, and she is swept downward ever downward, into the bottomless perdition of prostitution. But there, even in the lowest depths, excommunicated by Humanity and outcast from God, she is far nearer the pitying heart of the One true Saviour than all the men who forced her down, aye, and than all the Pharisees and Scribes who stand silently by while these fiendish wrongs are perpetrated before their very eyes.[6]

5. John Henry Newman, 1974: 423.
6. General William Booth, 1970: 13–14.

But *Jane Eyre* is unique in working the overseas/home-mission parallel exclusively in terms of women and wives. Even at their most feminist – and the indignations of *Bleak House* and *In Darkest England* on behalf of women do run at times very high – the other parallel-mongers are at best only partly preoccupied with the female aspects of the case. But *Jane Eyre* is wholly so. And specialisation of the home/overseas issue as a matter of and for women and wives makes one more reason for regarding this fiction as a fully, and not just crypto- or ur-feminist text.

The Last Word?

And yet, for all her resistance to being the enslaved wifely possession of the English version of an Eastern male, Jane finally married Rochester. And for all her refusal to accept the terms offered by the Indian missionary, the novel's last word is granted to St John, and to St John twice over – St John Rivers quoting the last words of the last book of that greatest male text, the Judaeo-Christian Bible, the words of St John the Revelator. Why? Is Jane Eyre succumbing after all, by some terrible failure of nerve, to the Sultanic conventions of English marriage and to the terms offered English women by the missionary societies? Yes; but also not altogether so. Granted financial independence at last by her uncle's will ('What, Janet! Are you an independent woman? A rich woman?' Ch. 37), Jane surrenders her freshly liberated self and what is left of her newly acquired cash (some went to the Riverses), giving it and herself to the charge of her husband (as all contemporary married women had to). Rochester is her master, for all that he has been purged by fire, reduced physically, and has also undergone a spiritual or moral conversion. And even though a certain Biblical rhetoric, suggestive of mutuality in union – and rather shockingly outspoken in an overground novel of the time – clusters about their marriage, it remains a rhetoric of female submission: 'I am my husband's life as fully as he is mine. No woman was ever nearer to her mate than I am: ever more absolutely bone of his bone and flesh of his flesh.' His bone, his flesh. Adam is still Adam, Eve still Eve. The potential missionary liberator of the harems of Istanbul succumbs to English wifehood. Radical critique gives place spectacularly and with apparent completeness – it is like the end of *Emma* or *The Mill on the Floss* – to convention.

But with St John Rivers the case is less cut and dried. The novel's last paragraph does indeed reinstate him as the heroic male missionary in India: 'resolute' and 'indefatigable', a 'pioneer', 'firm, faithful, and devoted, full of energy and zeal, and truth, he labours for his race; he clears their painful way to improvement; he hews down like a giant the prejudices of creed and caste that encumber it'. He is laden down with approving analogies and textual parallels from *The Pilgrim's Progress* (he's Greatheart besting Apollyon) and from the New Testament. And when he has the last word, when those words from 'the last letter' that Jane received from him turn out to be the last words of the last book of the Bible, it would seem that endorsement and ultimate tributes could scarcely come more fulsomely.

But this array of last words is not quite all that it at first seems. Letters are, of course, crucial here, as they have been all along in the novel. This ending endorses not least the power and importance of the foreign mails that have been felt repeatedly through the text. Letters from abroad are the occasion both of the interruption of Jane's first marriage ceremony with Rochester and of her financial emancipation. Overseas correspondence – utterly central to the management of empire – naturally feature prominently in this and other Victorian fictions (the plot of *Great Expectations*, for instance, relies heavily on the Australian mail). *Jane Eyre* is special in bringing home the centrality of letter-writing in the running of the missionary enterprise. It is a recognition in a fiction of what the LMS correspondence brings home – that, chancy, irregular, subject to loss and delay though it was, missions could not exist without the mail. It is also a recognition of what the LMS Bengal correspondence manifests above all else – that that correspondence was in male hands. The public epistolary dealings of the missionary scene in Charlotte Brontë's time have little space for women writers. Their private letters – to and from mothers and children and female well-wishers – have scarcely survived. They rarely have the temerity to correspond, as Mary Hill did on that one occasion, with the male Directors at home. In terms of the record the pen has – to use the words of Jane Austen's *Emma* – 'ever been' in the hands of the male missionary. And so it is in *Jane Eyre*, apparently: the epistle from India that's put on the record is one from St John Rivers.

A Stranger's Hand

But on closer inspection this 'last letter' is not, in fact, the last letter. After all, St John Rivers's last word is not contemplated as the actual last word. At this final moment of our text, in this very moment of apparent total surrender to the words of St John Rivers, this surrender of the Indian correspondence to this man, it turns out that another voice, other words, the words of another, the presence of a subsequent epistle, are anticipated. 'I know that a stranger's hand will write to me next.' Admittedly this stranger is anticipated as endorsing St John once more, and in Biblical terms ('to say that the good and faithful servant has been called at length into the joy of his Lord'). But it is the case that this voice, this pen, this letter from the stranger are to have their say when St John and his last piece of male missionary mail are silenced.

And there is, clearly, much affinity between the pen-holding hand of the stranger and the pen-holding hand of Charlotte Brontë. Throughout the novel, the stranger, the alien, the Other has been a woman – especially Rochester's women, Bertha Mason and Jane Eyre, the one a madwoman in the attic, a Creole from the West Indies, literally the dark stranger who is finally burnt to death in a terrible conflagration which consumes her and her person, the other a woman and wife who is presented as Easternised, a European version of the dark stranger – both of them women who have been as it were struggling to get their voices, their texts, their stories heard above the din of the predominant male discourse. Now, right at the last moment, even as the male discourse looks and sounds so predominant, it is suggested that a stranger from India will have the last word. And it is, of course, the manifest case that some of the English versions of that stranger, our narrator Jane Eyre, and behind her our author Charlotte Brontë, are already having the final word. The pens are, in fact, already in their hands. These are hands, female ones, that have yielded to Rochester in marriage, and that are quoting, repeating, and on the face of it endorsing a dense palimpset, a whole tradition of male writings – St John Rivers's, St John's, Christ's, the Bible's, the mass of male missionary correspondence of the time. But they are also hands that, at this very last moment, are lifting the curtain, turning the page, to reveal a future in which the hand of the stranger will hold the pen, will command the correspondence, will provide discourses that are currently unheard or scarcely heard, filling the page with alternative voices from the likes of Jane Eyre, Bertha Mason, Charlotte Brontë, Mary Hill, Isabelle Paterson, the women who were 'grilled alive', sickened, went mad and died in Calcutta and Berhampur for the cause of Eastern women's betterment, and the women who went mad and burned and bled in England for what *Jane Eyre* suggests was an identical or analogous cause, the betterment of the lives of the women of England. *Jane Eyre* ends: 'Amen; even so, come, Lord Jesus.' In opening the future to the 'stranger's hand' it is also saying 'even so, come, the letter, the text, the discourse, of the stranger, the (present) female Other' – which includes the wife as missionary, to be accepted at last as 'your real sister, or a man and a clergyman like yourself'.

Bibliography

Booth, General William (1890, Salvation Army; 6th reprint edn, 1970) *In Darkest England and the Way Out*, Charles Knight and Co., London

Newman, John Henry (1845, edn 1974) *An Essay on the Development of Christian Doctrine*, Pelican, Harmondsworth

Sibree, James (ed.) (1923, 4th edn) *London Missionary Society: A Register of Missionariesl Deputations, Etc., from 1796 to 1923*, London Missionary Society, London

Wise, T. J. and J. A. Symington (1933) *The Brontës: Their Lives, Friendships and Correspondence*, Shakespeare Head, Oxford

PART II

MISSION IMPACT ON WOMEN

6

Were Women a Special Case?

Adrian Hastings

Introduction

Were women a special case in the impact that the Christian missionary made upon nineteenth- and twentieth-century Africa? I think that a first answer to that could rightly be 'No'. They were an integral part of a society challenged as a whole by the Gospel and a vastly different way of life connected with it. Women and men shared the same beliefs, the same fears, the same sense of right and wrong. Custom, taboo, marriage and kinship obligations, all this and much else was accepted by all in an essentially unreflective way. It was moreover one vast web in which the religious could not be separated from the secular, the personal from the public. Female duties were, evidently, largely different from male duties but they were correlative and integrated within a unitary whole, which provided support, meaning and some degree of happiness for all participants.

Missionary Christianity in its Western garb and never entirely hidden colonial connections challenged that unitary whole from top to bottom. But it challenged some societies a good deal more sharply than others, and it challenged some aspects of that unitary whole more obviously and immediately than others. African societies were anyway mostly anything but static in the late nineteenth century. They were already subject to tension, if not caught within large-scale conflict; they were changing; they had their own internal contradictions. It was natural and inevitable that missionary Christianity found a way into them very largely through fissures already produced by tension, change and internal contradiction. In all societies there was a range of personal roles and in the more complex societies there was a structural classification such that while some people must benefit from the maintenance of the status quo, others could benefit by its dissolution.

Men and women, old and young, chiefs, commoners and slaves, polygamists and non-polygamists, priests, diviners, traders – they were all, in a way, special cases when it came to the impact of the Christian mission. Just as Buganda, for instance, proved as a whole to be very much a special case, to some considerable extent every other society was so too. There was no absolutely standard response, impact or reaction. This becomes particularly obvious when one adds in the variables of Christianity itself (Moravians or Holy Ghost Fathers?) and of the degree of linkage with European conquest and trade.

Yet it strikes me, as I look at the literature, how little consideration there has been of the feminine case. All in all African society was apparently so male-dominated that the impact of Christianity upon it has been treated overwhelmingly in male terms. But this also derives from the nature of nineteenth-century Western Christianity. It allowed almost no public role to women in the main Churches. Outside the Salvation Army and suchlike this was definitely not the century of women's ordination. A largely male-dominated missionary church encountered a largely male-dominated traditional Africa. Two forms of patriarchy appeared to fit together well enough. Where African custom was matrilineal, missionaries could be bewildered and attack this (like so many other aspects of custom) as opposed to the law of God. For the most part in the history of the wider encounter, women have had the briefest of mentions. This remains the case when one turns to thoughtful and critical re-examinations by modern African historians, like Jacob Ajayi and Emmanuel Ayandele, of nineteenth century missionary history – studies with such subtitles as 'The making of a new elite' or 'A political and social analysis' – one still finds no extended consideration at all of what all this meant for women: the social analysis has stopped well short of a gender analysis. Even the routine discussion of the issue of polygamy is conducted overwhelmingly in male-oriented terms. Only John Waliggo's still unpublished thesis on the *Catholic Church in the Buddu Province of Buganda, 1879–1925* begins to do justice to the female side of life.

Women Missionaries as Role Models

Nevertheless, things were not as simple as that. African tradition no more entirely subordinated woman to man than did European tradition, while the missions would appear to have provided scope for female initiative to a degree rarely possible in the sending society. By the later nineteenth-century there were many women, married and unmarried, engaged in missionary work. They would soon be a majority of all mission workers. Doubtless they were mostly in rather subordinate positions in terms of the missionary hierarchy and few indeed stand out clearly with the strength of a Mary Slessor. Nevertheless, the missionary church saw itself as champion of the dignity and education of women, and in terms of a local African environment the impact of a woman missionary must often have been very considerable: the impact on education, midwifery, dress and deportment, the washing of plates, the airing of blankets, but still more upon the psychology of individual expectations. The ministry of all the Churches had to be a great deal more flexible in the missionary and frontier situation than it was at home, and such flexibility could only redound to the advantage of those who at home were deprived of much opportunity to express or assert themselves. Despite obvious rigidities the missionary situation should be seen as one of comparative freedom in which things could be done, sometimes well, sometimes disastrously, which would have been almost unthinkable elsewhere.

That sense of freedom, of a co-operative effort in which men and women were both strenuously engaged, was quite often, I believe, communicated to African converts, women particularly. So that a first reason why women were different was due to the character of some missions themselves – the impression they communicated, in life as well as by formal message, that women were equal, free and capable of independent responsibility. This led on naturally enough to the experiencing of this freedom by African women especially in the early, less structured, phases of the missionary enterprise. It is noticeable that the first converts were often women. This may in part have been due to a feeling that they did not matter: the adherence of some women to the missionaries was seen at first as permissible, simply because it was socially and politically so insignificant. The same could be true of male slaves. But their presence within the young – or indeed hitherto non-existent – Church could not in fact be socially insignificant. And, of course, biblically-conscious missionaries would be glad enough at that point to lay stress on the Christian equality of men and women, following Galatians 3:28, 'there is neither male nor female'. In a fair amount of early African mission history one has the impression of a certain amount of what one may reasonably call female exuberance, and self-assertion, not wholly unlike that communicated in the New Testament itself at the start of the Christian Church. In the early days this was even occasionally linked with the marriage of white missionaries to black women. The black wives of Johannes Vanderkemp and James Read, for instance, must have made a very considerable impact upon the early Christian Church in South Africa. The white missionary was so much the leader and if he was married to a black woman, this could not but affect quite considerably the overall status of African women. Later on, of course, missionary societies opposed the interacial marriage of missionaries very emphatically. Indeed missionaries so doing were almost invariably disconnected.

The Rights of Women

The next reason was that missionary Christian morality tended to impinge particularly upon various specific aspects of female existence, and in such a way as a few at least would regard as liberating. In some cases the liberation may be more a matter of the missionary's perspective, even a missionary misunderstanding, but there can be no doubt that in terms of what the modern feminist position would see as the rights of woman, the missionary was by and large standing clearly enough on the liberationist side against the bondage of tradition. We could instance polygamy, the payment of bridewealth, cliterodectomy, the killing of twins, the pursuit of alleged witches. The missionary onslaught on these areas – even if at some points, as in the matter of bridewealth, it was much mistaken – was certainly, as we shall see, one capable of reverberating in the feminine heart.

A fourth, not unconnected, reason is that converts were often dropouts – people who in one way or another no longer belonged to a society, either because that society was actually disintegrating or because it had driven them out or wished to kill them and they had fled. Such drop-outs were by no means, of course, all women, but quite a number were. They might be escaping cruel husbands, a marriage they did not want, confinement to a chiefly harem, punishment for some offence, being sacrificed at the death of a king, or whatever.

Female Converts to Mission Christianity

If Samual Ajayi Crowther, the Yoruba slave boy liberated by the British navy, educated at Freetown by the CMS and in due course sent back to Nigeria to evangelise it, is the primal figure of nineteenth-century West African Christianity, his most symbolic action was surely his return to Abeokuta to find his mother and there baptise her.

Again and again in a mission history the early significant baptisms were mostly of women. Bethelsdorp was the first black Christian comunity in southern Africa. By the end of 1806 its total baptised consisted of 43 women, 18 men and 62 children.[1] That may provide something of a guideline – with women rather more than twice the number of men –

1. Sales, 1975: 38.

though the Hottentot and coloured people of the western Cape were clearly not typical of Africa. Yet Dr Akama remarks of the very different society of Isokoland, Nigeria, in the early twentieth century, 'It is a noticeable phenomenon that with the growth of Christianity in the area, the number of women converts in all the congregations became decisively larger than those of men.'[2] Again and again one notes how the first Christian in a place is a woman like Fiambarema, the Moravians' 'first fruit' in 1897 in Rungwe, or Kapuleya-Ndondolilwe, in 1909 at Mkoma's.[3]

In the very early period of a mission too, while boys would see no point in coming to school, girls might begin to do so. That was true of Mrs Smith's knitting school of Bethelsdorp from 1805, or the sewing school of Mrs Wrigley and then Elizabeth Waldron at Cape Coast from 1836. Again it was true of early times at Onitsha where the first primary school, opened in November 1858, consisted of fourteen girls. Occasionally there, we read, a group of boys 'would rush into the house, proudly gaze at the alphabet board and with an air of disdain mimic the names of the letters pronounced by the schoolmaster and repeated by the girls, as if it were a thing only fit for females'.[4] Even in Buganda the first boarding school opened by the CMS was one for girls – at Gayaza in 1902. The boys' boarding school at Budo followed two years later. Attending a mission school involved wearing clothes of some more or less European sort. Dress seemed essential to Christianity and in many parts of Africa the missionary invented forms of female dress for the first schools which became in due course extremely popular – the 'Bordingi' in Uganda, the 'Cabasroto' in Ghana – but to begin with such dress must have enhanced the strange liminal character of females-out-of-line: out of line yet at the same time obtaining thereby a sort of motherly power in the still shadowy new dispensation. At Rungwe Fiambarema's position as senior Christian was institutionalised by the convention that subsequent applicants for baptism would approach her to intercede on their behalf.

A little to the south in modern Zambia two early headmen appointed by Bishop Dupont at the great White Father mission of Chilubula were in fact head women, Nandola and Chipasha. Each was subsequently murdered by her husband and each of the murderers committed suicide.[5] To the possible significance of that tragic sequence of events

2. Akama, 1981: II, 231.
3. Wright, 1971: 89–92
4. Sales, 1975: 44–5; Bartels, 1965: 20–1; Ekechi, 1972: 24.
5. Garvey, 1974: 112–3.

we will return. But I have cited enough evidence here to suggest the special position of women in the earliest Christian phase in many though not all places. In Buganda, it has certainly to be admitted, women played a relatively small role even in the earliest phase, but in this as in many other things Buganda may have been the exception rather more than the rule,[6] though even here the exception might be more apparent than real.

Women attached themselves to the missions for a multitude of reasons: they might be escaping brutal husbands or unwelcome marriages, particularly as additional wives to some rich polygamist. They might be objecting to having to let their baby die because it had not cried at birth or because it was a twin. In some African societies twins, if feared, were also much honoured, but in many others – both east and west – their birth was so feared that they were left to die. The brief ministry of Bernard Miseke in Mashonaland[7] and the earlier years of Mary Slessor in Calabar were punctuated by battles to save the lives of twin babies but, quite often, this could mean a battle to save the mother too. At no point did deep maternal feminine instinct cry out so emphatically against custom and in favour of the Christian view, just as at no other point did the Christian missionary feel so required to challenge immediately and absolutely the practice of custom.

Let us consider the story of the conversion of southern Isokoland, an area near the Niger Delta where at the beginning of this century Christianity had still not penetrated. There was an Ijo woman named Berebolo Brigrina who became a Christian in 1905 when near the CMS mission at Patani. She later gave birth to twins and according to Ijo tradition was required to put one of them to death by abandoning it in the bush. As a Christian she refused to do so and was banished from her community. Fellow Christians ferried her and her twin babies across the Patani river and left them alone on an island where a certain Mr Ebiegbe, an Igbide trader returning from a trip to Patani market, met and took pity on her. He took her to Igbide and later married her. At Igbide Brigrina began to evangelise the people and to organise a church so that it became the pioneer Christian centre within Isokoland. However, the growth of the church resulted in persecution until in 1911 Bribrina, her husband and other faithful Christians fled away to found Obhodokpokpo, meaning 'New Town', a Christian community. People were soon coming to it from all parts, so that in 1912 the CMS missionary Aitken vis-

6. The 'Partial Who's Who of the early Christians of Buganda' provided by Taylor, 1958: 261–73, includes 88 names of whom only 5 are women.
   7. Farrant, 1966: 124–6, 184.

ited it to help organise the new church. Such is the myth, perhaps the history too, of the origin of Christianity in Isoko South and its founder, Bribrina – an extraordinarily rich symbolic account of the start of the conversion of the Isoko – the emergence of the 'New Town', the church, out of the decision of one woman not to allow her twin child to die.[8]

African Marriage versus Mission Morality

In the area of marriage itself the issues are more complex. One might start perhaps, a little provocatively, by remembering the very widespread traditional African preoccupation with female fatness as a sign of beauty. The girl being fattened up for marriage, even caned when she fails to keep on drinking from the milk bottle, is a recurring motif in nineteenth-century literature from east, west and south Africa. It was not, for the missionary, a pleasing practice. And so in 1879 Mrs Price, daughter of Robert Moffat, sister-in-law of David Livingstone and wife of the missionary Robert Price, wrote to her Kwena friend Bantsan (daughter of the chief Sechele), in the following way: 'In civilised and especially Christian countries,' she declared, 'a slender figure is admired', unlike the fat African model, because it it thought a dishonour to eat too much. 'The more civilised and more Christ-like' the Bakwena became, continued Mrs Price, the more they would admire slenderness and not fatness.[9]

The African woman had then, on becoming a Christian, to be reshaped as well as reclothed. She had, quite possibly, also to be remarried or at least married in a very different way from that of tradition. The battle with twin-killing was a relatively short one in which missionaries had behind them the weight of colonial authority. The battle with polygamy was to be a long-drawn one, never really won, in which colonial authority resolutely refused to be involved. Consider a fairly early incident in Mary Slessor's life in Calabar. She was visiting a village called Ibaka on the Cross estuary in 1882. One morning there was a row. Two girl-wives of one of the chiefs had been discovered in the hut of a young man. The village council promptly ordered each to receive a hundred lashes, quite likely a sentence of death. Mary had the council reconvened, harangued all and sundry, and finally got the sentence reduced to ten lashes. The girls were then brought to her, bleeding profusely. She bandaged them, dosed them with laudanum and kept them lying on their stomachs on the floor of her hut for the rest of her

---

8. Akama, 1981: 226–8.
9. *The Journals of Elizabeth Lees Price, 1854–1883*, Una Long (ed.) 373.

stay.[10] That sort of thing reinforced the missionary conviction that African women were, through polygamy especially, in a sort of slavery. And, of course, in some cases they were. Missionaries in the early period had most to do with chiefs and chiefs had large numbers of wives. This kind of polygamy could, for junior wives, be very enslaving. It was, moreover, unlikely to have been entered into with much consideration of the women's wishes. But polygamy could be very different from that and it is not fanciful to think that small-scale polygamy was often desired as much by the women as by the men: it provided companionship, economic co-operation, and enhanced status for the senior wife. When this kind of marriage was terminated by Christian conversion, it was the women who suffered most.

There were missionaries, and not only John Colenso, who thought polygamy temporarily tolerable, but by and large they set their faces against it so firmly that an official monogamy became almost the principal mark of the mission church and later on in some, though by no means all, cases, the acceptance of polygamy became in turn the mark of the independent church. There can be little doubt that the large effect for good and ill of the Christian mission upon African women centred on this. If Christian missions had been weaker, as they easily could have been, the movement towards Islam of black Africa, already well under way in both west and east, would, almost inevitably, have been much quickened by the arrival of colonialism. And Islam could only have reinforced the traditional judgement that the marriage of one man to as many women as he could afford was an excellent thing. The advance of Christianity did not banish so well-established a custom, but it did remarkably alter the public sense of the marital ideal, particularly among women. However much the successful African male may still incline to polygamy, the norm of official monogamy is not seriously challenged.[11] The mission impact upon marriage was, however, a more complicated matter than the disfavouring of polygamy. First and foremost it stressed the necessity for the woman of freedom of choice – something formerly present in many African marriages but by no means in all. Probably missionaries underestimated the proportion of marriages in which it had existed; nevertheless the new Christian stress on freedom and its welcoming acceptance by women are undeniable.

In the areas of bridewealth and divorce the value of the missionary input is less easily gauged. Initially missionaries, especially in southern

10. Buchan, 1980: 74–5.
11. See, for instance, Little: 147–8.

Africa, were emphatically opposed to bridewealth which they regarded as tantamount to the buying and selling of women. Yet they were, of course, strong on indissolubility. It took them a while to realise that within African custom the payment of bridewealth was a guarantee of the bride's recognised value and the most notable force for the permanence of marriage. Some at least did see this as time passed – indeed so much so that in some cases they even tried to introduce the payment of bridewealth among matrilineal peoples where it was not customary. Yet they mostly believed that both insistence upon indissolubility and the restraint (if not abolition) of bridewealth must enhance the status of downtrodden women. In point of fact neither of them did so. In tradition the ill-treated wife would run away to her parents. If a husband wanted her back he would have to convince the parents, offer presents, maybe abase himself. If he failed to do so he would lose his wife. The very missionary stress upon absolute indissolubility undermined the wife's main post-marital source of protection, just as the early attack on bridewealth undermined the wider family commitment to ensuring that a marriage worked. If the missionary assault upon traditional marriage (and, of course, both varied immensely across the continent) certainly gave something of a new sense of freedom to women, it hardly produced the controlled and ordered freedom missionaries were hoping for.[12] 'A wife of the ring' might all in all be less protected in her dignity than her pagan mother had been. She was probably more conscious of her rights and of a feeling of freedom than of the positive advantages her ring marriage in fact brought her. By the 1930s the Nyakyusa were blaming Christians for the practice of wooing in secret before a man has been to the father. 'The Christians say "It is good to woo in secret first" but pagan fathers object, saying "We will not eat the cattle properly".'[13] The dislocation of traditional custom in a heavily Christianised country like Buganda had already brought with it a permissiveness on both male and female sides and a dissatisfaction with the new marital order which alarmed missionaries of the second generation. Thus in 1918 the Provincial Commissioner in Buganda wrote to the Chief Secretary that 'local missionaries of both denominations consider that the women should be punishable [in case of adultery, etc.] equally with the men, as in many cases they are the chief offenders. They also suggest whipping as the most suitable penalty. The chiefs whom I consulted concurred, and myself I consider these recommendations sound.' Accordingly, a

12. Note, for instance, the worries of the perceptive Moravian missionary, Traugott Bechmann, in Tanzania: M. Wright 1971: 106.

13. Wilson, 1957: 251 (material gathered 1934–8).

law was passed for the flogging of women and continued until 1927 when it was abolished on account of abuse (Law of 16 November 1927). A popular women's song of the period ran thus:

> I pity very much the man I shall marry
> That man will die of constant quarrelling
> The only advice I offer him
> is to prepare his beating stick beforehand.[14]

'I am fed up with this Christian marriage,' ran another Ganda song of that period, 'Ssammanyirirwa'. A researcher into Igbo women at much the same time observed that for many 'Christian marriage' was seen as a 'prison', polygamous marriage as a more open and socially satisfying institution.[15] 'Our main grievance is that we are not so happy as we were before,' declared women rioters comprehensively, if vaguely, at Owerrinta, Nigeria, in 1929.[16]

By this time – the 1920s and 1930s – African women had been far overtaken by men on the educational front. We noticed how initially women were often ahead of men in elementary schooling. This did not last long, and it was, surely, an expression of the low esteem in which western education was held. Once society saw the point in schooling, it was the boys who got it. The magisterial Phelps-Stokes report on *Education in Africa* (A Study of West, South and Equatorial Africa by the African Education Committee) of 1920 declared:

> It is rather surprising that missions and schools have not made more serious efforts to bring the girls into the schools and to provide suitable training for them. The chief reason for this apparent neglect is probably the indifference and sometimes the opposition of the native people themselves to the education of their girls. Schools here followed the line of least resistance, accepting the boys who have applied . . . (p. 24)

Compare that with our picture of the little Onitsha school in 1858! The education of girls only really started to improve again on a large scale after the Second World War.

I remember how at the All Africa Conference of Churches in Lusaka in 1974 a distinguished African theologian made an attack on the Western imperialist imposition by missionaries of monogamy upon Africa and called on the African Church to reject it in favour of the indigenous

---

14. Waliggo, 1976: 291–2.
15. Leith-Ross, 1938: 125–6. Quoted in Ayandele, 1966: 337.
16. Perham, n. d.: 219.

tradition of polygamy. He was immediately followed by two ladies of striking stature and forcefulness, one from Sierra Leone, the other from South Africa, who insisted that monogamy was the greatest gift the missionary Church had brought to African womanhood and that there could not be the slightest question of going back upon it. No more was heard about that. In the nineteenth century Christian insistence upon monogamy could be more destructive of the lives of women than of men – women prevented like the Xhosan Princess Emma from marrying into their class at all,[17] women lower down the social scale rejected by their husbands and separated from their children. In retrospect, however, women had here been the gainers and it is hard to deny that the repeated calls of African theologians in the sixties and seventies for the church to accept polygamy have been in part at least an expression of male chauvinism. As a matter of fact, in due course men had won most of the more spectacular prizes, educational and otherwise, to be obtained by membership of the Christian Churches from archbishoprics downwards. In Christian Buganda women were expected to kneel before men as much as ever – and they did so. The acquisition by women of the publicly approved model of monogamous marriage and free marital choice (including the freedom not to marry) is, all the same, not – despite any inconveniences – to be derided or reversed.

Conversion and Commitment

But this discussion has taken me on rather far and I would like to return for a little to the earlier phase, of conversion and the first generation, rather than that of establishment and the second generation. In Barotseland when the Paris Mission Society, led by François Coillard, arrived there in the 1879s they found King Lewanika installed in the capital of Lealui but his sister, Mokwae, as a sort of viceroy in the second city of the realm, Nalolo. Both were much attracted by the missionaries, both were frequently expected to convert but for many years neither did so. Lewanika, like many another African king, said at times that it was just a matter of polygamy – 'without that we should soon be Christians,' declared Moshesh of the Basuto. Yet Mokwae was not a polygamist. What really held her and her brother back was principally a much deeper sense of the coherence of their authority, tribal identity and independence with their beliefs and practices. When one considers a great African lady like Mokwae, women cease to be a special case, even if after 35 years of hesitation, Mokwae, unlike her

17. Janet Hodgson, *Princess Emma*, Ad. Donker, Cape Town 1987.

brother, did actually become a Christian in 1921.[18] Her husband had preceded her.

Mokwae approached things, one feels, not so much as a woman but rather as did her brother the king, with the caution appropriate to people of power. One has much the same impression of the young women of nineteenth-century Buganda when we manage to get a glimpse of them: they could be as headily radical as their brothers. There were indeed no women among the martyrs of 1885–6 but that was not because there were no female Christian converts willing to be martyred, but rather that the customs of Buganda were averse to the killing of women. It is true that one woman, Sara Nakima,[19] had been taken to execution with the very first victims, but she was reprieved. When Noe Mawaggali was martyred at Mityana his sister Munaku actually pleaded with his executioners that they should kill her as well but they refused to do so, simply taking her a prisoner. Women were presumably not regarded as being sufficiently responsible to be executed for their behaviour. This may seem the more odd in that it was the Princess Clara Nalumansi who triggered off the persecution in the first place by behaviour which in traditional terms was no less than outrageous. She had cast away her umbilical cord. The martyrs may have died in consequence but Nalumansi remained at the time untouched. The early Ganda female converts appear, then, to have adopted Christianity much as did their brothers and husbands, with the same heady enthusiasm. Missionary insistence upon monogamy did, of course, affect them differently. They were not polygamists: unlike many of the men they did not have to set aside their additional husbands. On the other hand, a number of them *were* additional wives – divorced by their husbands at the moment of baptism. In some cases they remarried, in others they adopted the role of pious widowhood in the neighbourhood of a mission. That was the easier in that among some women the call to celibacy was immediately heard. Munaku was the first of these. The commitment she entered into immediately after conversion in 1886 she kept until her death in 1938, spending her life teaching catechism and, later, running the gardens and kitchens of Bukalasa seminary.

This proved not only an option open to drop-outs. The call of female virginity could be heard in the greatest houses in the land. The leader of the Catholics over many years was Stanislaus Mugwanya, the second Katikiro (or Prime Minister) and in due course a knight of St Gregory.

18. See F. Coillard, 1902, and Martin Jarrett-Kerr, 1972: 77–86.
19. Taylor, 1958: 270.

His sister, Isabella Birabwa, was married to the county chief of Buddu, the formidable Alexis Sebbowa. Through long years Sebbowa adhered to monogamy despite the childlessness of Isabella – a considerable moral achievement in missionary eyes. And she was all that a great chief's wife should be, leading the sixty or so women of her household to morning prayers in their chapel, and on Sunday to mass at the mission.[20] Her brother's household was run on similar lines. Yet when in 1897 Mugwanya's daughter, Angela Nabbogo, confided to him that she intended never to marry but 'to work all my life for the Fathers' he found it hard to agree: he had already arranged for her a suitable marriage. 'Let both of us pray to our Lady and whatever she will inspire we shall do,' Angela piously replied. Her will proved the stronger and in due course she did indeed become a nun and remained so for seventy years. Naturally, if the great Mugwanya had had to leave his daughter free to do this, lesser fathers could hardly refuse, and this may help to explain the scale of growth of the sisterhood of the Bannabikira. Elsewhere it could be much more of a battle, as in Eastern Zimbabwe (then Rhodesia) where, for instance, in 1937 the Native Commissioner sentenced an aspirant nun named Clara to 14 days hard labour for refusing to return home. Around Triashill this had been a running battle for decades between the Mariannhill Fathers and an alliance of parents and colonial authorities. 'Freedom of conscience', wrote Fr Fleischer back in 1911, 'cannot be taken away by parents or guardians. We think a human soul is of greater value than the lobola.'[21]

Centrality and Marginality

As the church grew more central to African society, it came – as we have seen – to reflect, even reinforce, in most of its central concerns the traditions of male primacy. The training of the clergy and the development of the school system were predominantly to the advantage of men. When the church itself was marginal to society, in an initial liminal period, the women had been more central to it, dangerously central indeed at times as the murder of the Chilubula head women might suggest. At such a moment the church might seem to be reversing society in some sort of on-going *communitas* experience. But as the church became more socially central, women's role within it appeared to grow far more marginal: the basic requirements of patriarchy were reasserted. The dominant impression of African Christian life in the great missionary

20. Waliggo, 1976: 113–5.
21. Ranger, n. d.: 10.

age of the first half of the twentieth century remains not one of the liberation of women but, on the contrary, of a lack of freedom. The new rules of marriage and schooling imposed by the missionary could all in all be more not less restrictive than the old. Catholic girls were not free to marry other than Catholics. The immediate experience of Christian conversion was one of freedom from taboo and discrimination; the lasting experience was too often the imposition of a load of burdens enforced as much as ever upon the young by corporal punishment. 'Mother was very strict and did not like to spare the rod,' wrote one woman of her Christian upbringing in the thirties. 'The Reverend Fathers had taught that it was very wrong to spare the rod, no matter how trivial the offence committed by the child.'[22]

Yet the Catholic sisterhoods, the Protestant female societies like the *Manyano* of South Africa and *Rukwadzano* of Zimbabwe[23] and the striking numerical dominance of women within most Zionist and Aladura churches all suggest that this was only part of the truth. At least from the 1950s one senses a great female comeback in African Christianity, alike in the mission churches and in independent churches. The nuns multiply far more than the priests; the organised *Manyano* becomes, despite much male clerical suspicion, the clear centre of religious vitality; the prophetesses multiply – Ma Nku and Ma Mbele, Alice Lenshina and Mai Chaza, Mariam Ragot and Mrs Paul. As communities the churches in Africa returned to being (if in reality they had ever ceased to be) what they were in most places at the start, predominantly feminine entities – perhaps, indeed, feminine alternative societies to the male-dominated secular world. At the start and then again from the fifties the gospel seemed to appeal to women with a special intensity which we may reasonably relate in a broad way to the issue of specifically female freedoms – freedom not to have to abandon your twin children, freedom not to be married to a rich old polygamist, freedom to be valued sufficiently to be taught in school, freedom to choose your husband, freedom to woo in secret before your father knows, freedom to choose not to marry at all and be a nun, freedom to live an independent existence as a woman, made manifest to the male world by the habit of your order or the red blouse of your Rukwadzano membership. It symbolised a female fellowship, at once communal and freely chosen.

To make the point that women are more religious than men seems so generally true that it hardly helps us here. The question for us is precise-

---

22. Asheri, 1969: 11.

23. Brandel-Syrier, 1962; David Muzorewa, T. O. Ranger and John Weller (eds.) 1975: 256–68.

ly how female religiosity has related to the phenomenal growth of Christianity in Africa over the last 150 years: a process of rapid change. It may, after all, equally be remarked that women are more conservative than men and in point of fact it is a widely observable phenomenon in Africa – particularly in areas of Islamic penetration – that the new religion has come with the men while the custodians of traditional beliefs across several generations of transition have been the women. On this model, female religiosity in Africa would not contribute to its christianising but on the contrary provide the strongest bulwark of resistance. And that, undoubtedly, was at times the case. The people we have been considering were, after all, the tiniest minority among women and most of them were socially, politically and even ecclesiastically insignificant. Yet it is equally true that they proved in the long run far from insignificant in religious, social, cultural and even ecclesiastical terms. They were the new women embracing Christian faith because in particular and exciting ways it liberated and elevated. Cross the river with your twins, cast away the umbilical cord, refuse to marry though it deprive your father of lobola and outrage even the District Commissioner. Early Christianity could be socially revolutionary. It was, of course, intended by the missionaries to be so in some ways: not ways entirely different from those perceived by their early female converts and yet very different too. If the experience of liberation was succeeded in many cases only too quickly by that of a new subjugation, this was hardly alien to the missionary plan but it was for the second generation of christian women a profound disappointment. Patriarchal Christianity wrapped up in a highly legalistic and authoritarian form, whether Catholic or Protestant, seemed none too liberating. Take the third generation, however, and the women are breaking through regardless, reshaping the realities of African church life according to their intrinsic expectations. It was perfectly possible that missionary Christianity would spread in Africa almost entirely through men, offering gifts of education and status to the male, while generally resisted by the religiosity of women adhering to the cults of tradition. But it was not so and Christianity would have been infinitely weaker if it had been so. There was just enough in the Christian package to ensure that women would put their weight behind the new as well as the old, and then the new much more than the old, until in due course they would in their own way assume the lead. In the second half of the twentieth century this would ensure the consolidation of Christianity as the religion, not just of the elite or of the institutions of western provenance, but of the countryside and of the *povo*. Their men might take to politics and esure the triumph of nationalism, the women, while not averse to that cause, would combine it with an at least equal attachment to Christianity. Look, for instance, at Robert Mugabe, the very model of the new African man, and his church-worker sisters or at Maurice Nyagumbo, ZANU's General Secretary, and his sister, a nun. The Christianity of African women with its quest for healing and community and the strength to carry on through poverty, riot and famine, is profoundly other-worldly but profoundly this-worldly too. It is anything but Utopian. It is very patient. It draws at every point upon the traditional religiosity of the pagan past but combines it with a sharper sense of female dignity, social purpose and personal piety culled from Bible and ecclesiastical practice. It is undoubtedly Christianity's principal asset in Africa today and it would probably not be there, at least not with anything like the vigour it has acquired, were it not for the element of feminist liberation which the nineteenth-century male missionary did proclaim – often almost *malgré soi* – and which the female missionary incarnated to very practical effect, though almost never in explicitly feminist terms, not only in such exceptionally memorable figures as Mary Slessor, Mother Kevin or Patricia Chater,[24] but in countless others too. Yes, women were and remain a special case.

24. Caroline Oliver, *Western Women in Colonial Africa*, Greenwood Press 1982; Patricia Chater, *Grassroots*, Hodder & Stoughton 1962; Patricia Chater, *Caught in the Crossfire*, Zim Publishing House, Harare 1985.

Bibliography

Akama, S. (1981) *A Religious History of the Isoko People of the Bendel State of Nigeria*, PhD Thesis, Aberdeen

Asheri, Jedida (1969) *Promise*, African Universities Press, London

Ayandele, E.E. (1966) *The Missionary Impact on Modern Nigeria, 1842–1914*, Longmans, London

Bartels, F.L. (1965) *The Roots of Ghana Methodism*, Cambridge University Press

Brandel-Syrier, Mia (1962) *Black Women in Search of God*, Publisher London

Buchan, James (1980) *The Expendable Mary Slessor*, St. Andrews Press

Chater, Patricia (1962) *Grassroots*, Hodden and Stoughton, London

_____ (1985) *Caught in the Crossfire*, Zim

Coillard, F. (1902) *On the Threshold of Central Africa*, publisher, London

Ekechi, F. K. (1972) *Missionary Enterprise and Rivalry in Igboland, 1857–1914*, Cass, London

Farrant, Jean (1966) *Mashonaland Martyr*, Oxford University Press, Cape Town

Fasholé-Luke, E. et al (1978) *Christianity in Independent* Afmen, Rex Collings, London

Garvey, B. (1974) *The Development of the White Fathers' Mission among the Bemba-speaking Peoples 1891–1964*, London PhD thesis

Hodgson, J. (1987) *Princess Emma*, Donker, Cape Town

Jarrett-Kerr, Martin (1972) *Patterns of Christian Acceptance,* Oxford University Press

Leith-Ross, Sylvia (1938) *African Women – A study of the Ibo of Nigeria*

Little, Kenneth (1974) *African Women in Towns,* Cambridge University Press

Long, Una (ed.) (1956) *The Journals of Elizabeth Lees Price, 1854–1883,* Arnold

Muzorewa, David (1975) 'Through Prayer to Action: the Rukwadzano women of Rhodesia', in T. O. Ranger and John Walker op. cit.

Oliver, Caroline (1982) *Western Women in Colonial Africa,* Greenwood Press

Perham, M. (1937) *Native Administration in Nigeria,* Oxford University Press

Ranger, (1981) *Poverty and Prophetism* Unpublished paper

Ranger, T. O. and Weller, John (eds.) (1975) *Themes in the Christian History of Central Africa,* Heineman, London

Sales, Jane (1975) *Mission Stations and the Coloured Communities of the Eastern Cape, 1800–1852,* Balkema, Rotterdam

Taylor, John (1958) *The Growth of the Church in Buganda,* SCM Press, London

Waliggo, J. (1976) *The Catholic Church in the Buddu Province of Buganda, 1879–1925*, PhD thesis, Cambridge

Wilson, Monica (1957), *Rituals of Kinship among the Nyakusa,* Oxford University Press

Wright, M. (1971), *German Missions in Tanganyika 1891–1941,* Oxford University Press, E. Africa

7

From Heathen Kraal to Christian Home: Anglican Mission Education and African Christian Girls, 1850–1900

Modupe Labode

Introduction

A 'lady correspondent', K. H., reported in 1875 on the state of South African women to mission supporters in Britain:

> I have taken coffee in a native kraal and heard the welcome words, in broken English: 'We are Christians'. How hard it must be to live as Christians amid heathen neighbours, and how arduous is the work set before native women in changing that heathen kraal into a Christian home . . . [1]

From the missionaries' point of view, transforming the kraal to home was the essence of work among African women. Simply converting Africans to Christianity was not enough; the missionaries' goal was nothing less than restructuring African society. 'Restructure' suggested physical changes in the household, such as favouring square houses over round huts; these physical changes corresponded to the spiritual changes which took place in the convert. As the quotation implies, 'kraal' and 'home' were mutually exclusive. But transforming a kraal into a home also required ideological shifts, which included 'creating' African women who would preside over homes in which Christianity could flourish.

This is an exploratory essay which offers an overview of the various ways in which African women and girls were made a particular focus of Anglican missionaries' activity. Before exploring these efforts, it is useful to consider the missionaries themselves. The missionary group

1. *Bloemfontein Mission Quarterly Paper*, October 1875: 23.

which is the focus of this work is the Society for the Propagation of the Gospel in Foreign Parts (SPG).[2] The SPG began sending missionaries to South Africa in the middle of the nineteenth century. While the SPG itself did not constitute the Church of the Province of South Africa (CPSA) – the formal name of the Anglican Church – it played an important role in establishing the church in South Africa through supplying missionaries and providing funds.

Most of the work discussed here was done by women among women. Many of the missionaries were single women sent out under the auspices of the Women's Mission Association (WMA). The WMA, originally called the Ladies' Association, was formed in 1866 as a semi-autonomous branch of the SPG to co-ordinate 'women's work'. Women's work in South Africa included nursing, teaching, home visiting and running orphanages and refuges for 'fallen women', as well as organising sewing groups and mothers' meetings. The WMA also had a home section, which arranged for the selection and training of women missionary candidates, among its other activities. There were other women who worked in the mission field who, although they co-operated with the WMA, were not sent to South Africa by the WMA. For example, there were women who worked in the region as members of Anglican sisterhoods. Further, the ranks of women missionaries included relatives of SPG-funded male missionaries. These wives, daughters and sisters of male missionaries worked without pay, and often without acknowledgement of their contribution.

Although little is known about the background of these missionaries, they seem to have come from middle- to upper-class backgrounds, and were sympathetic to the High Church views of the SPG. An important factor in the missionaries' background, and the subsequent direction which their work among African women took, was the Victorian emphasis on the home. Historians have described the ideology of 'separate spheres', in which men had responsibility for the economic and political life of society, while women were responsible for maintaining the moral tone of the family, and rearing the future generation. In the home, the values of society at large were determined; if the home life of the family was faulty, this was a matter of public concern (Dyhouse, 1981: 30, passim).

Most of the mission work described in this essay occurred in the Eastern Cape and Ciskei, which formed part of the Diocese of Graham-

2. The SPG was founded in 1701 for the dual purpose of sending clergy to British subjects abroad, and sending missionaries to the unconverted throughout the world.

stown. There are also references to the Transkei (Diocese of St John's), Natal (the Diocese of Maritzburg), and Orange Free State (Diocese of Bloemfontein). The African peoples in these areas varied greatly. As a generalisation, those in the Eastern Cape, Transkei, Ciskei and Natal fell into the Nguni groups, including the Xhosa, Mfengu and Zulu. The peoples of the area which is now the Orange Free State were Southern Sotho (Davenport, 1987: 60–5). The Anglican Church in South Africa organised its work by territory or parishes, so in theory the same missionary would minister to both Africans and whites in any given area, although in practise 'mission work' and 'European work' were carried on almost independently of each other. The main concern here will be with the 'mission' side of the clergy's work.

Both male and female missionaries identified work among African women as crucial to the success of Christianising African society as a whole. The missionaries were convinced that their efforts would come to nought if they could not produce the African women who would create a family environment in which African Christianity could grow. Their task took on a certain urgency because from the missionaries' perspective, African women were part of the problem of spreading Christianity. The missionaries' construction of femininity and womanhood was narrowly based on their European experience, and was not inclusive of the non-Western constructions of gender which they encountered in Africa. Because they were often unfamiliar with the attributes of 'womanhood' in African societies, these missionaries often characterised African women as ignorant and backward. In identifying women as a particular missiological problem, their criticism of African women took three, sometimes contradictory, forms.

The first was a perception of African women as intrinsically more resistant to civilisation, and perhaps more atavistic, than men. In the areas where men migrated to towns or the mines to find work, women usually remained in the rural areas. Since these women seldom came into as close a contact with whites as men, they were therefore less familiar with the ways of European society – which the missionaries often called 'civilisation'. But women were also thought to be 'more wedded to heathen custom' than men, and committed to perpetuating the traditional way of life. Bishop Webb of Grahamstown, for example, declared that African women in Zululand were in part responsible for the continuing unrest on the frontier because they would not 'marry men who had not "wet their spears in blood"'(Webb, 1883: 43).

A second view portrayed African women as innocent victims of traditional practices such as *lobola* (or bridewealth) and polygyny. In their literature the missionaries cast themselves as the champions of these down-trodden women. They portrayed African men and, by extension, African society as uncivilised because the men did not show African women the respect due to them as women. Indications of such 'disrespect' included men forcing women into polygynous marriages, and idling their days away while women did the heavy agricultural work, which properly should have been done by the men. In promoting mission work, British women often appealed to their common experiences as women, which presumably bridged cultural differences. The literature emphasised the horrors of heathendom: 'the scarcely credible ignorance, the practical slavery . . . their terrible sufferings in sickness and maternity from the ignorant barbarities of native treatment and their intense degradation.'[3] The backward African women who suffered from this treatment deserved pity and help, instead of vilification.

Thirdly, the backwardness of African women was invoked in the criticism of the home environment and education of women and girls. A few missionaries grudgingly acknowledged that there were some benefits in the education which girls received at home. In their traditional society girls learned to be 'patient and self-denying and enduring'. However, the girls needed to be taught the ways of 'purity and integrity, humility and industry'. These virtues could not be acquired in their homes, because in the final analysis, 'the home life [of Africans] is defective'.[4] To raise the standards of African home life, some girls had to be taken into a European, Christian environment and taught how to live. This premise informed the insistence placed on removing African girls from their homes to mission boarding schools.

These views all emphasised the supposed ignorance of African women. They had to be taught how to be women in ways in which African men did not have to be taught how to be men. Although men were criticised for being lazy or 'sensual' (due to the supposedly enervating effects of polygyny), they were still admired for their 'masculine' skills in warfare and hunting. The remedy for their laziness was to destroy polygyny and force them to work for wages, rather than to teach them a whole host of 'masculine' virtues.

By contrast, the remedy for the ignorance of African women and its consequences was education, and by the missionaries' definition, educational agencies included sewing classes, mothers' meetings and guilds, as well as formal schools. These diverse educational institutions all emphasised domesticity, since the crux of the problem was the supposed ignorance of African women of domestic skills. Many other

3. *Mission Field*, May 1902: 173.
4. *The Net*, May 1889: 68–9.

missionary efforts were aimed at women and girls, and African women also initiated their own mission work among their own people. These all deserve consideration in order to assess the true impact of the concept of domesticity in education and African life, but such a survey is beyond the scope of this paper. This essay examines a narrow aspect of education, girls' boarding schools, and the messages which they embodied about African womanhood.

Mission Schools and African Girls

The majority of African girls who had any contact with mission schools attended the day or night schools in their immediate vicinity. It is important to keep in mind how very few Africans attended school for any length of time. By one estimate, in South Africa there were approximately 9,000 Africans receiving an elementary education in the 1850s. By 1900 the number had risen to 100,000 (Walshe, 1970: 7). Of these students, girls were in the majority at the elementary level (Davis, 1974: 4); boys, however, formed the majority of the pupils at the advanced level (Cock, 1980: 268–80). Very few of the pupils ever attained functional literacy. An even smaller number of children went to the boarding schools; the presence of girls in these schools is, however, instructive because it was in these schools that the ideology of female education was made most explicit. The Anglican missionaries in the Cape Colony worked very closely with the government authorities. The Cape Government gave mission schools grants to defray their costs; in return, the schools were required to comply with government regulations, such as hiring certified teachers, following a standard curriculum, and opening the schools to government inspection. One famous example of the co-operation between Church and State is the collaboration between the Governor of the Cape Colony, Sir George Grey, and the Bishop of Cape Town, Robert Gray, in the late 1850s. In addition to establishing Zonnebloem College, the 'higher school' for sons and daughters of African chiefs in Cape Town, Sir George Grey helped the church found missions on the frontier of the Colony (Hodgson, 1979: 107–08).

It would be misleading, however, to assume that the missionaries were merely the agents of the colonial authorities. They had different goals and methods, and the co-operation was often forced out of convenience rather than conviction. The missionaries did not celebrate their dependence upon government grants, and the colonial authorities were often unimpressed with the efficacy of missionaries as agents of colonialism (Goedhals, 1979: 92–5).

Missionaries hoped that in their schools they would cultivate the leaders of a future Christian African society (Hodgson, 1979: passim). Initially, the missionaries hoped to convert, or at least to influence, the sons of chiefs by sending them to special schools, such as Zonnebloem College, or schools in England. When this plan met with only modest success, the missionaries gradually modified their goals, and decided to create and cultivate a Christian elite in South African 'higher schools'. These higher schools were boarding schools which offered a level of 'secondary' education beyond that available at mission day schools (Davis, 1974: 2). The special status of this elite was not so much defined by traditional criteria, as by education and Christian piety. Most of the boarders in the schools were children of converts, or those sympathetic, to Christianity, rather than sons and daughters of chiefs (Davis, 1969: 206).

Both boys and girls were educated in the 3Rs, but 'industrial education' featured in varying degrees in almost all of the mission boarding schools.Industrial education was an elusive concept and could mean all things to all people. African parents, students, teachers, missionaries and colonial authorities all had their own ideas concerning the purpose of industrial education. For some, its purpose was to inculcate virtue; for others it was meant to prepare Africans for wage labour.

The issue of industrial education for African girls revolved about the question of whether girls should be trained primarily to become domestic servants or wives. Although there was no attempt to bar African women from teaching or other professional careers such as nursing, there was a strong, non-academic bias to education for girls during this time. Missionaries often maintained that it was far more important for girls to learn 'how to live', than to advance academically. One matron of a boarding school remarked,'It seems to me that these schools ought not to have at all the atmosphere of an institution, but that of a home – the model it may be hoped, of future homes in the girls' lives.'[5]

In this essay, only two of the many trends in mission boarding schools during the nineteenth century will be discussed. The first was that of 'homes'. Girls' boarding schools were often referred to as 'homes'; the 'home' was designed to be 'a rival *domestic* establishment' to the child's original home (Gaitskell, 1988: 56). This idea of a rival home was probably true for both boys and girls, but the goals were different. Boys were taken into a home to learn how to live in a civilised manner and prepare for their future, public roles in society. This training was not an end in itself; the end of education for boys was to produce leaders. The girls were supposed to learn how to provide suitable homes for such leaders.

---

5. *Bloemfontein Mission Quarterly Paper*, July 1878: 15.

This type of school flourished in the nineteenth century. These homes were often very small, and academic work was minimised. In this all-female environment, the matron was expected to act as a surrogate parent to the girls. The household was meant to be a model African household, or rather, represented a European idea of how Christian Africans should live. The majority of such homes were found in Natal, and were not exclusive to Anglicans. The Anglican missionaries ran two such homes in Pietermaritzburg: St Margaret's was for younger girls, and St Agnes's was a hostel for girls and women working as domestic servants in the town. There were also Anglican homes in Bloemfontein and Cape Town.

The second type was the 'higher schools' as they were called, or academic boarding schools. These schools were the pride of mission educators; many of those established in the nineteenth century continued to operate until the Bantu Education Act of 1953 forced their closure (Davenport, 1987: 374). These schools offered education beyond the elementary level; most were meant to prepare boys and girls for higher stations in life, such as the ministry, teaching, nursing or government work. Perhaps the most famous was Lovedale, which was established by the Free Church of Scotland. The Anglican equivalent to Lovedale in the Eastern Cape was St Matthew's School at Keiskama Hoek.

St Matthew's began as a small mission school, but by the end of the nineteenth century it had become one of the most prominent mission boarding schools in the region. The boys and girls received a similar education; however, unlike the day-schools, the classes and social life of the students was strictly segregated by sex. The boys and girls at St. Matthew's were divided into three categories depending on their educational course: pupil-teachers, apprentices, and those students attending the elementary school. The male apprentices learned skills such as tinsmithing and carpentry, while the female apprentices studied techniques of laundry, housework and cookery. All of the girls boarding at St Matthew's were required to learn how to sew as well as do some manual labour, which included housework for the school. Government regulations made the curricula of such schools conform to a recognised standard. As the emphasis on domesticity became institutionalised, however, the purpose of the domestic education remained ambiguous. The discussion about domestic education in the schools reflected the roles which missionaries imagined for African women in colonial society.

Langham Homecraft School Domestic Science Class

Plate 7.1 Miss E. K. Preston teaching Dressmaking – 2nd year students

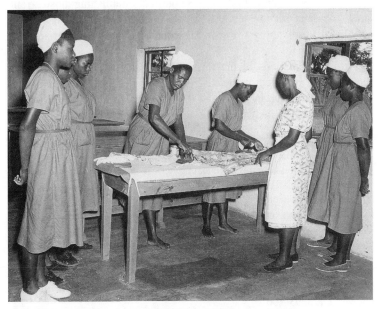

Plate 7.2 Laundry class with Mistress Makuze – Ironing

Domestic Service and Domestic Education

A constant refrain in the education of African girls was the perceived need, on the part of the missionaries, to train girls to become 'domestic'. But it was not clear whether they were being prepared to work in the homes of whites, or to create their own homes; it was one thing to produce Christian wives and mothers, another to create domestic servants.[6] On the one hand, the missionaries and the colonists themselves continually decried the lack of 'good servants' in South Africa. At the same time the colonists were employing, training and, in some instances, expressing a preference for 'raw natives'. There is little evidence to suggest that there was a demand for mission-trained girls to work as domestic servants. Perhaps more importantly, there is little evidence that the girls were requesting such training and education in order to become domestic servants. For example, very few of the girls trained at Lovedale worked as domestic servants at the end of their course (Gaitskell, 1988: 162).

There were manifold practical problems and concerns in training girls to be servants. The towns, and indeed the employer's house, could be dangerous, immoral places for young girls. As a response to these dangers, missionaries consistently made the same, rarely implemented suggestions; they urged the mistresses to take more responsibility for their servants 'after hours', and suggested establishing hostels and labour bureaux for the servants. However, they were not particularly successful in changing the working conditions for domestic servants during this time.

Further indications of the missionaries' ambivalence behind their rhetoric were revealed by the case of male domestic servants. This was particularly an issue in Natal and the Transvaal, where male domestic servants predominated.[7] The missionaries never wholly approved of

6. The role of missionaries in educating African girls to be domestic servants has attracted scholarly debate. See, for example, J. Cock, *Maids and Madams*, 1980, especially Chapters 'Changing Patterns' and 'Education for Domesticity'; D. Gaitskell, 'Race, Gender, and Imperialism – A Century of Black Girls' Education in South Africa', in J. A. Mangan (ed.), *Benefits Bestowed?: Education and British Imperialism*, 1988; 'At Home with Hegemony', paper, Berlin, 1989.

7. In the Cape and Orange Free State, women predominated as domestic servants. See J. Cock, Chapter 8, and D. Gaitskell, 'Class, Race, and Gender: Domestic Workers in South Africa', 1984, *Review of African Political Economy*, Vol. 27/28: 93–100.

male servants, and their literature often reflected the whites' fears of having black men in the homes.[8] Yet the missionaries rarely explicitly advocated replacing African men with women servants, perhaps because in addition to the economic reasons which compelled men to work as domestic servants, women servants brought with them their own set of problems.[9]

Miss Jane Lorimer of the Gordon Memorial Mission in Natal captured some of the ambivalence which was felt by colonists towards African women servants. Writing in the 1880s, she counselled that missionaries should not encourage African women to go into service for two reasons. The first was that the missionaries should concentrate their efforts on cultivating the future generation of African women, not in providing servants for whites. Secondly, she felt that, as much as possible, Africans and whites should remain apart. She explained that Africans and the colonists had very different ideas about household management. But there were also dangers in having African girls about the house: 'Even the excellent mistresses of pure European homes cannot protect their native girls from the immoral people about. Respectable heathen fathers won't allow their girls to be exposed to it.' She darkly alluded to the potential 'Amalgamat[ion] in their domestic life' which would arise if black girls worked in white households.[10]

The persistence of the rhetoric of domestic service might be traced in part to British models; during the nineteenth century 'domestic' training was seen as the appropriate education for working-class girls (Dyhouse, 1981: 79–113). In the schools there was often a tension between the goal articulated by the matron of teaching girls how to cook and clean so that they could be trained to be wives or servants, and the constant potential that the girls' labour could be exploited within the school. In some schools, doing housework was considered part of the girls' 'classwork'.[11] One missionary recognised the risk of exploitation and asserted that he and his wife never 'treated one of these girls as domestic servants' even though the students helped out around the house as part of their education.[12] In Zonnebloem, the missionaries were careful to con-

8. For example, see *The Christian Express*, March 1907: 37–8; N. Etherington, 'Natal's Black Rape Scare of the 1870s', *Journal of Southern African Studies*, Vol. 15, No. 1, October 1988: 36–53.

9. See C. Van Onselen, 'The Witches of Suburbia', *Studies in the Social and Economic History of the Witswatersrand 1886–1914*, Vol. 2, 1982: 16–17.

10. *The Christian Express*, August 1884: 173.

11. *The Net*, August 1882: 127.

12. CWW 192, Rev. J. Gordon, King William's Town, 2 September 1878.

fine the housework that the girls did to the warden's lodgings, so that this practical training would not be misunderstood as servitude (Hodgson, 1975: 467). Other missionaries were not so scrupulous and used the girls as their personal servants in the name of education. Miss Lucas at Keiskama Hoek reported that:

> a few of those [students] who attend to my rooms are quite equal to many English lady's maids, so thoroughly clean and neat, mending & even making my underlinen & keeping everything in the greatest order. They also make good parlour maids, Mrs. Taberer having them in her house when the occasion requires. It is our object to render them good, useful servants, and therefore we insist upon work of every description being done, from hoeing in the mealie fields, to attending upon me personally.[13]

Dissent and Rebellion

Although many Africans supported mission education, there is no reason to assume that they and the missionaries always had the same goals and perspectives. The Anglicans saw themselves as moderates on the issue of educating girls. They compared themselves to the Roman Catholic Trappists in Natal (known from 1909 on as the Congregation of Missionaries at Mariannhill), who in the nineteenth century, did not think that African girls should be taught to read and write in English (Schimelk, 1953: passim). Among those parents and girls who acknowledged the value of mission education, there were various reactions which demonstrated unease or discontent with the type of education which was offered at Anglican schools.

Some dissatisfied parents and students sought education elsewhere. The search for a more 'secular' education on the part of Africans was an issue which was articulated with great force in Natal. This was probably due to the high concentration of missionary activity there and the consequent competition among mission societies for converts. In the 1880s the Anglicans discussed establishing a 'higher school' for girls. However, the Bishop of Maritzburg preferred a non-intellectual approach to education for African girls, and regarded St Margaret's Home as an example for any future educational ventures in his diocese:

> the aim of St Margaret's is, first and foremost, to make the girls good Christians, and then to fit them for that state of life to which it seems most likely that they will be called, the life of a good domestic servant or that of the wife of a Christian native. Good household work, plain cooking, and needlework,

13. CWW 193, Miss Lucas, St Matthew's, 1 May 1880: 59–60.

cleanliness, and tidiness seem to be far more important than the qualifying [of] these girls to be teachers and then leaving them to the great difficulty of finding employment.[14]

For pragmatic reasons, the Reverend Greene found himself on the opposite side of the issue from his bishop. While not enthusiastic about giving African women, or men, access to higher education, he foresaw that the Natal Government would soon be requiring certification for African teachers as a condition of receiving government grants. If the Anglicans did not educate their own teachers, others would, and already were doing so. He asserted that:

> if we wish to spread Church teaching, [we must] be ready to put forward our own teachers, but in order to do this we must not however, be afraid of its civil effects, as long as we endeavour to counteract them with a good sound Church education.[15]

In the end, the Anglicans did not establish a teachers' training school for African women in Natal until the first decade of the twentieth century.

Further evidence of discontent was demonstrated by an 'unsatisfactory' attitude on the part of the girls. This attitude was revealed by what the missionaries termed the 'inappropriate' dress and 'unenthusiastic' behaviour of the girls. They often complained that the girls could be sulky and temperamental, and that it required strong discipline to keep them in good cheer. Some of this discontent can be traced to the girls desiring 'book learning' instead of industrial training. In 1910, the missionary in charge of St Agnes's School, Johannesburg noted that:

> It takes the natives some time to accept and approve of industrial work for their girls – Their one idea of education is book-learning, and many girls have left because they did not like having to do laundry work, house cleaning etc., as well as school work. In time I suppose they will grow to see that there are other branches of education quite as necessary for a woman as book-learning, if not more so![16]

These comments indicate tensions and misunderstandings between the missionaries and the girls. The former harboured many concerns about the effects of academic education upon the latter, as well as doubts whether all the girls were capable of 'book-learning' rather than practical education. Like many colonists, they were concerned that too

14. CWW 196, Bishop of Maritzburg, 25 March 1889: 78.
15. CWW 196, Rev. Greene, Pietermaritzburg, 10 April 1889: 95–8.
16. CWW 119, St Agnes's School, Johannesburg, 4 September 1910, Amy Kent, File 42. See also, Gaitskell, 1988: 163.

much formal education could 'spoil' the African girl if such education was not tempered by manual work. The girls were probably aware of the doubts which the teachers had concerning their capabilities. The reasons informing their desire for 'formal' education were not clearly articulated, but are open to speculation. Perhaps they wished to emulate prominent African women, such as teachers, who were literate and well-respected in society. The opposition to industrial education may also have indicated resentment at being channelled into a type of education which seemed to offer little status, little reward, and which was perceived as being an inferior alternative to 'book-learning'.

A more direct way for the girls to express their dissatisfaction with a school's regime and curriculum was through rebellion. Revolts were not rare in mission institutions, and continued into the twentieth century.[17] Most of these rebellions were small-scale, and it is reasonable to assume that they were not only about the incident which sparked the dissent on the part of the students; rather the incident was the last straw.

The best-documented account of a rebellion in the Anglican schools during this time was that of the girls of the Bloemfontein Training School in 1877, which had been established in 1876. The matron of the school was a Miss Copleston, a WMA-sponsored missionary. Although not a nun herself, Miss Copleston lived and worked with the Sisterhood of the Community of St Michael's and All Angels (CSM&AA) in Bloemfontein, and the school represented a co-operative effort between the WMA and the CSM&AA as well as the diocesan hierarchy. The school was situated near the mother house of the CSM&AA, St Michael's Home. All the girls in the school came from Thaba Nchu, a settlement of the Seleka Rolong in what is now the Orange Free State/Bophutatswana. Most of the girls at the school were related to Moroka, the chief of the Seleka Rolong. There is reason to think that the Anglican missionaries were trying to cultivate Moroka's good will through establishing the school. The Anglicans were relative newcomers in Thaba Nchu, and were 'poaching' on the mission field of the Methodists, who had been working among the Rolong for decades.

The school fitted the pattern of a 'home'. The girls received a very basic education in the 3Rs, and the emphasis was on housewifery, sewing and religious education. Within a year of its opening, the bishop reported favourably on the progress of the school. Perhaps buoyed by her achievement thus far, Miss Copleston made plans to take in the laundry work for St Michael's Home. This laundry served about one

---

17. See *Not Either an Experimental Doll*, ed. S. Marks, 1987: 28; *Sol Plaatje: South African Nationalist 1876–1932*, B. Willan, 1984: 225.

hundred people, including the sisters of the Community of St Michael's and All Angels. This work had hitherto been done by a group of African women who, reportedly, claimed high wages, and food as well. Miss Copleston reasoned that by making the girls do the laundry, she could increase the number of pupils in the school from twelve to eighteen, save money for the CSM&AA and further the girls' industrial training.[18] Somewhat guilelessly she remarked:

> I rather expect a mutiny at first, they will think they are being turned into servants, but of course it will be an immense advantage to them to learn to wash and iron properly, whatever they may do in the future...[19]

Although the accommodation was cramped and the resources overextended, Miss Copleston received the bishop's approval for the plan.[20] The girls were divided into two groups. The first group would take a turn at washing all week long, from 9 to 1, and 2 to 6, while Miss Copleston taught the second group. In the evening, the first group had lessons, while the second group did their homework. During the next week, the second group would work in the laundry while the first group had their lessons. 'I thought [that although] they would have less lessons, the tribe would benefit as much by taking a larger number [of girls].' Unfortunately, Miss Copleston was ill during the first three weeks of the term, and the plan was implemented by a deputy. Upon her return, Miss Copleston found the girls in a fractious mood.

Undaunted, she tried to continue with the plan for another three days, until so many of the girls were ill that she had to call in the doctor, who forbade them from working more than three hours a day:

> [O]n reflection I saw that 8 hours for 5 days must be too much for such young growing girls. They stand to wash the clothes on boxes, they were moreover wet through, partly through throwing the water over each other on purpose.

Despite the respite in the laundry work Miss Copleston found the girls still more rebellious. She thought that this change in their attitude was because they perceived that her authority had been undermined and thought that they could appeal against any decision that did not suit them. In the end,

---

18. CWW 247, Bloemfontein, 2 August 1877: 148–9.

19. *Bloemfontein Mission Quarterly Paper*, October 1877: 25.

20. This quote, and the account of this incident are all from: CWW 247, Bloemfontein, 4 November 1877: 220–6.

the half who were washing one day threatened to run away to Thaba Nchu, as in old times they used to do, and I answered coolly that they had better do so. But they really went early one morning, and in a few days the remaining eight became so unmanageable, always hanging over my head the threat of their being sent for home, that I had no resources but to write to Mr. Mitchell and ask him to send for all.

The rebellion became a *cause célèbre* within the diocese. When the girls went home, they told their relatives that they had not been well treated at the school and the parents demanded an explanation. A delegation consisting of the Archdeacon, the Mother Superior of the Community of St Michael and All Angels and Miss Copleston went to Thaba Nchu to resolve the matter.

On the first day in Thaba Nchu the delegation paid a courtesy call on Moroka and the heir-apparent. At the Sunday service, the missionary in charge, Mr Mitchell, announced that there would be a meeting the following day with Miss Copleston, the Archdeacon and Mr Mitchell to discuss the incident.

Most of the girls and several of the parents attended the meeting. The parents spoke first, and the complaints were aired. These boiled down to 'not enough to eat, not enough lessons, and not enough church, and the washing'. The meeting focused on the last of these complaints. According to Miss Copleston, the parents

Plate 7.3 Chatting in their cottage after school

consider it a breach of engagement; that the girls were to do nothing except for the ladies who taught them as *in loco parentis* and I suppose it was. This must be strictly kept in future, and by washing our clothes, which they have never done yet, they will learn to wash.

The missionaries acknowledged their fault in the matter, and the meeting closed with the girls having the opportunity to speak to Miss Copleston; they apologised and shook hands. Presumably they were readmitted to Communion, from which Mr Mitchell had suspended them until the matter was resolved. Miss Copleston reopened the school in 1878, but she decided not to allow the same girls to return to the school, repentant and reformed though they may have been. Chastened by the experience, she did promise herself to learn the Tswana language so that such misunderstandings might be avoided in future.

The account of this revolt is unusual and valuable because of the interaction between the missionary, Anglican hierarchy, African parents and students. When the parents agreed to have the girls taken into the school, they understood it to be a 'home', with Miss Copleston acting *in loco parentis*. Their complaints were not so much that she had taught them how to do laundry, but that her having the girls work for others represented a breach of faith. Miss Copleston had justified her actions in terms of being to the 'benefit of the Africans', yet the Africans themselves were not convinced. When they protested, through the girls' revolt and the parents' meeting, the missionaries were forced to listen.

This paper has been an attempt to describe briefly some of the forms which education for African girls took during the nineteenth century. Mission schools offer a privileged viewpoint for investigating issues of mission, gender and colonialism. Not only were schools often the centrepiece of mission stations and the African Christian community, but they also provided a focal point in which various elements of South African society came together to discuss the kind of education which would be offered to African girls and by extension the future roles of these girls. The relationship between African parents and girls, missionaries and colonial authorities, was not equal, but through various means, ranging from paying fees to rebellion, the Africans participated in shaping the form which the education took.

Most of the discussions about education for African girls revolved around the relative merits of academic and industrial education, and the importance of teaching girls to be 'domestic'. There does not seem to be adequate evidence to assert that the missionaries were training African girls only to become domestic servants to colonists; 'domesticity' involved creating Christian wives and Christian mothers as well domestic servants. The home life of Africans was of vital concern to the missionaries, who often equated a well-ordered home and family with Christianity, but the African home was also of interest to colonial authorities who wanted a stable frontier and workforce. The African home was also an area of concern to missionaries and colonists in different places and times in Africa; through the work of many scholars the basis of a comparative historical study of the concept of domesticity in Africa has been laid.[21]

Education for African girls was never 'only' about the 3Rs, but was also about defining and redefining what it meant to be an African Christian woman. Through looking at these schools, one can begin to account for the changing ideas of missionaries and Africans concerning what defined an African Christian woman, and the relationship between domesticity, gender, labour and race. These schools provide a valuable entry point into investigating the formation of African Christian communities in South Africa and the role of women in these communities.

Bibliography

Primary Sources

USPG Archives, Rhodes House Library, Oxford
    CWW: Committee for Women's Work
    E Series: Mission Reports
    D Series: Original Letters Received

Periodicals
    Bloemfontein Mission Quarterly Paper
    The Christian Express
    The Mission Field
    The Net
    Women in the Mission Field

21. For example, see D. Gaitskell and J. Cock for South Africa in the nineteenth century; D. Kirkwood on the Homecraft Village School in Rhodesia/ Zimbabwe, 1943–81; Sean Morrow on the Girls' Boarding School in Mbereshi, Northern Zambia, 1915–40; and Nancy Rose Hunt on the domestic training establishments for women in colonial Burundi, 1946–60. Taken together, these works could form the basis for a valuable study on the transmission of ideas of femininity and domesticity.

Secondary Sources

Cock, J. (1980) *Maids and Madams: A Study of the Politics of Exploitation*, Ravan Press, Johannesburg

Davenport, T. R. H. (1987) *South Africa: A Modern History*, 3rd edn, Macmillan Press, London

Davis, R. H. (1974) '1855–1863: A Dividing Point in the Early Development of African Education in South Africa', in *The Societies of Southern Africa in the 19th and 20th Centuries*, Vol. 5, University of London

———— (1969) Nineteenth-Century African Education in the Cape Colony, unpublished Ph.D. Thesis, University of Wisconsin

Dyhouse, C. (1981) *Girls Growing Up in Late Victorian and Edwardian England: 1880–1939*, Routledge & Kegan Paul, London

Etherington, N. (1988) 'Natal's Black Rape Scare of the 1870s', *Journal of Southern African Studies*, Vol. 15: 36–53

Gaitskell, D. (1979) 'Christian Compounds for Girls: Church Hostels for African Women in Johannesburg, 1970–1970', Journal of Southern African Studies, Vol. 6: 44–69

———— (1983) 'Housewives, Maids, or Mothers: Some Contradictions of Domesticity for Christian Women in Johannesburg, 1903–39', Journal of African History, Vol. 24: 241–56

———— (1984) 'Class Race and Gender: Domestic Workers in South Africa', Review of African Political Economy, Vol. 27/28: 86–108

———— (1988) 'Race, Gender and Imperialism: A Century of Black Girls' Education in South Africa', in Mangan, J. A., *Benefits Bestowed? Education and British Imperialism*, Manchester University Press, Manchester: 150–73

———— (1989) 'At Home with Hegemony? Coercion and Consent in African Girls' Education in South Africa Before 1910', unpublished paper, Berlin

Goedhals, M. M. (1979) *Anglican Missionary Policy in the Diocese of Grahamstown Under the First Two Bishops, 1853–1871*, unpublished M. A. Thesis, Rhodes University, Grahamstown

Hodgson, J. (1975) *A History of Zonnebloem College 1858 to 1879: A Study of Church and Society*, unpublished M A Thesis, University of Cape Town

———— (1979) 'Zonnebloem College and Cape Town: 1850–1870', *Studies in the History of Cape Town*, ed. by C. Saunders, Vol. 1, University of Cape Town, Cape Town

Hunt, N. R. (1990) 'Domesticity and Colonialism in Belgian Africa: Usumbura's *Foyer Social*, 1946–1960', *Signs*, Vol. 15: 447–74

Kirkwood, D. (1984) 'The Suitable Wife: Preparation for Marriage in London and Rhodesia/Zimbabwe', in *The Incorporated Wife*, ed. by H. Callan and S. Ardener, Croom Helm, London: 106–19

Marks, S. (ed.) (1987) *Not Either an Experimental Doll*, The Women's Press, London

Morrow, S. (1986) '"No Girl Leaves the School Unmarried": Mabel Shaw and the Education of Girls at Mbereshi, Northern Rhodesia, 1915–1940', *The International Journal of African Historical Studies*, 19, 4: 601–35

Purvis, J. (1989) *Hard Lessons: The Lives and Education of Working-Class Women in Nineteenth-Century England*, Polity Press, Cambridge

Schimlek, F. (1953) *Mariannhill: A Study in Bantu Life and Missionary Effort*, Mariannhill, South Africa

Van Onselen, C. (1982) *Studies in the Social and Economic History of the Witwatersrand 1886–1914*, Vol. 2, Longman, London

Walshe, P. (1970) *The Rise of African Nationalism in South Africa*, C. Hurst & Co., London

Webb, A. B. (1883) *Sisterhood Life and Woman's Work in the Mission Field of the Church*, Skeffington & Son, London

Willan, B.(1984) *Sol Plaatje: South African Nationalist 1876–1932*, Heinemann, London

8

The Elusive Christian Family: Missionary Attempts to Define Women's Roles. Case Studies from Cameroon

Fiona Bowie

Introduction

The monogamous family unit has for nearly 2000 years been regarded as the basis of Western Christian society, sanctioned by both Church and State. The desirability and sanctity of a single lifelong partnership has been taken as axiomatic, regarded as both the norm and as the ideal, even if an imperfect reflection of actual social relations. Church Fathers such as Augustine might have sought to justify the polygynous marriages of Old Testament patriarchs, but biblical exegesis did not present the same challenge to church teaching as the encounter with contemporary polygynists in the mission field. In Tropical Africa the insistence on monogamy has been a major stumbling-block to the widespread acceptance and practice of Christianity throughout the period of modern missionary endeavour. Among African Christians who have been baptised into one of the mission churches, church marriage remains the exception rather than the rule.[1]

When Christian missionaries were first confronted with polygynous societies in Africa, they assumed that conversion and monogamy would go hand in hand. Polygyny, and almost every facet of social life bound up with it, was regarded as morally inferior or downright pernicious, contravening Christian doctrine and ethics and offensive to the mores of a civilised society. To the Victorian mind polygyny was a symbol of the

---

1. The reasons for this have been discussed at length in Hastings (1973). Shorter (1978) also has some interesting observations on the lack of fit between Christian (missionary) and African marriage patterns (see esp. Ch. 6). For a brief historical survey of Christian attitudes to monogamy, particularly in the Western Church, see Dowell, (1990).

lascivious, debauched nature of the African. Few missionaries followed the example of Albert Schweitzer (1875–1965), who questioned the wisdom of doing away with an institution so deeply embedded in African social life.[2] A notable exception was John William Colenso (1814–83), Anglican Bishop of Natal, who sanctioned the baptism of polygynists without requiring them to divorce their second or subsequent wives. Colenso's leniency in this matter, together with his publications on the Old Testament (in which he questioned the historical validity of the Pentateuch), so shocked his contemporaries that he was accused of heresy and excommunicated by the Archbishop of Cape Town. He remained in Natal as the Judicial Committee of the British Privy Council ruled that he be permitted to retain the cathedral and the assets of Natal diocese.[3] The majority of missionaries, however, were as arrogant in their enforcement of monogamy as they were blind to the benefits offered by institutionalised polygyny (see Ekechi, 1970; Hurbon, 1969).

The association of polygyny with social, economic and moral values has lent it a strength which 150 years of missionary activity in countries such as Cameroon has failed to eradicate. The missionary churches have, of necessity, moved from a hard-line authoritarian approach to polygyny to a more pragmatic 'softly softly' stance, reasoning that fundamental structural changes in society will not happen overnight, and that time and economic forces may well be on their side. However, as the title of the paper suggests, the Christian family has proved an elusive concept. Much missionary effort has been expended in defining the roles of converts in relation to marriage and in controlling their sexual behaviour, in an attempt to encourage conformity with church teaching. The interplay of ideological and practical factors that have shaped missionary praxis become apparent at 'ground level', making it easier to identify specific attitudes towards women and the impact of mission activity upon their lives. This paper therefore uses case studies as a means of determining the dynamics of

2. Schweitzer (1961–3).

3. Reflecting on the Natal experience, the 1888 Lambeth Conference (the collective voice of the Anglican Communion) ruled that 'polygamy is inconsistent with the law of Christians concerning marriage'. A hundred years were to pass before the 1988 Lambeth Conference revised this decision and allowed polygynists to receive baptism, provided they promise to take no more wives. The compulsion to divorce existing secondary wives was removed (see Shorter, 1988: 173; Pobee, 1991: 803; Bowden, 1969).

mission policy and its effects on the lives of individuals within the mission sphere of influence.[4]

The Mill Hill Missionaries and the Christian Family

In 1922 the Society of St Joseph from Mill Hill in North London, commonly known as the Mill Hill Missionaries, were requested by the Sacred Congregation for the Propagation of the Faith in Rome to undertake missionary work in the Cameroons under British Mandate, and so fill the vacuum left in 1916[5] by the allied forces expulsion of German-speaking Roman Catholic missionaries.

The Mill Hill Missionaries, under a Scotsman, Bishop Joseph Campling, and his successor, the energetic and hard-headed Irishman, Bishop (later Monsignor) Paul Rogan, made their headquarters at Small Soppo near Buea on the side of the Cameroon Mountain. From here other permanent stations, both new and on the site of earlier missions abandoned during the war, were gradually opened throughout the territory. Each mission station had two or three European priests or brothers who would take it in turns to trek through the villages of the interior, instructing Christians and catechumens, administering the sacraments and settling disputes between church members. The catechists and local Christians were responsible for building and maintaining a house where a visiting priest could stay, and for providing carriers for each leg of the journey. The Mill Hill Missionaries aimed to cover a wide area, rather than concentrate their efforts on one or two sites, with the result that each outstation, left in the hands of a native catechist, was visited only two or three times a year, depending on its distance from the central station with its resident European missionaries.

The catechist, almost invariably male and often a native of the village in which he was posted, was frequently recruited while working on

---

4. The case studies on which this paper is based come from the Bangwa/Mbo areas of South West Province in the former territory of British Cameroons. Under British Mandate the Cameroons was administered as part of Nigeria's Southern Province, electing to join the Francophone Cameroons at Independence. The country is now known as the Republic of Cameroon.

5. The Mill Hill Missionaries were founded by Herbert Vaughan in 1866, as a missionary society of priests and brothers, to carry the Roman Catholic faith to the lands being opened up by colonial expansion. Their work in Africa started in 1895 in Uganda, followed by missions in Kenya, the Congo, Cameroon and the Sudan. Members of the Society are recruited from the Netherlands, the Tyrol (Italian and Austrian), Ireland, Scotland and England.

the coastal plantations to the south. His task was to teach Christian doctrine, according to his own understanding of it, prepare candidates for baptism and conduct church services. He saw to the upkeep of the mission buildings and liaised with the central mission station, trekking there each first Friday of the month to receive his small salary and report to the priest-in-charge. The catechists also acted as teachers, which involved giving elementary lessons in Christian doctrine, numeracy and literacy to small boys, a role which afforded the catechist, often the only semi-literate person in the village, considerable prestige. The medium of instruction was either the local language or, if the catechist came from a different linguistic group, pidgin English. English (or pidgin, which was widely spoken by men who traded or travelled for work across linguistic boundaries) had pre-dated and subsequently replaced German as the dominant European language in this part of the Cameroons.

The missionaries were well aware that a poorly instructed catechist, with only a basic primary education, working alone in the bush, was incapable of creating and sustaining a Christian community. They therefore sought to supplement the efforts of the isolated village catechists by removing some Christians and potential converts from their communities, encouraging them to establish Christian enclaves around the central mission station. For a period some priests even tried to encourage all Christians to form separate communities, cut off from the life of the village. Christian settlements were the source of much antagonism between the native Christians and the local chiefs, who considered, with some justification, that their authority had been undermined by the missions. This policy also brought the mission authorities into conflict with the British Mandate Government, whose administrative system, based on indirect rule, depended upon the authority of the traditional rulers being upheld (cf. Githige, 1982). The notion of self-contained Christian enclaves failed to take root, but separate settlements did become common for two groups of people whom the missions considered particularly susceptible to negative influences in their native villages. These were small boys attending school, who were kept under the eye of the mission until they could be baptised and admitted to the sacraments, and women.

'Sister Mammy' Settlements

In order to prevent Christian girls from living with their husbands before a church marriage could take place, the missionaries established 'sister mammy' settlements in or near the mission compound. Here women were obliged to spend some weeks or months receiving 'doctrine' and providing unpaid labour for the mission under the eye of a priest or catechist. By 1940 these sister mammy settlements existed at all the larger mission stations. There were continual reports and complaints of the catechists responsible for these settlements exercising sexual rights over the women under their care, sometimes with the knowledge of the European clergy.[6] Father Nabben, a Mill Hill priest writing in about 1940 from Mbetta, the chief mission station among the Mbo, commented that 'Getting mammies on the mission with belly [i.e. pregnant] is getting worse.'[7] All too often the women who had been brought to the mission to prevent them from living with their husbands, or husbands to be, until they were deemed ready for a church wedding became concubines of the catechist.

In a memorandum of 16 October 1930, addressed to the Resident, Buea (the senior British official in the territory), the District Officer (D.O.) of Mamfe, J. S. Smith, described the function of a sister mammy settlement at Baseng Mission in the following terms.[8] The settlement was on native land near the mission, technically under the control of the local chief, but in effect under the aegis of the priest-in-charge, Father Ham. The women, usually 60–70 in number, came and went at Fr. Ham's discretion staying in the settlement from a few weeks to a year or more. The women living in the settlement included those who wanted to learn 'doctrine' from a village with no teacher, women married to a 'pagan' who wished to remarry a Christian, and baptised women who were living with their husbands, to whom they had been married according to traditional custom, but who had not married in church. The concern of the missionaries was to prevent, as far as was in their power, any sexual contact between a woman and her husband or intended husband until both partners were baptised and married according to the rites of the Roman Catholic Church.

Marriage was, according to Bangwa and Mbo custom, a long process from betrothal at birth (for a woman) to the birth of her first child, with exchange of bridewealth forming an important element. The traditional procedures were regarded with suspicion by the missionaries who were troubled by the discrepancies between a Western Christian notion of marrige, based on a legal contract and enacted over a short period of

6. Illustrated graphically in Mongo Beti's novel *The Poor Christ of Bomba*, 1977, which is set in Fracophone Cameroon.

7. Father Nabben to Bishop Rogan, Mbetta Diocesan and Vicarate General Information Files.

8. File sd (1930)1.

time, and the African processual marrige with its complex social and economic ramifications. Whether they were regarded as more compliant, more in need of protection from family influence or more inherently sinful because of their gender, it was on women that the missionaries focused their efforts to reform African marriage.

The missionaries' desire to see marriages 'regularised' was not shared by the Native Authorities (that is the chiefs, the main organ of indirect rule) nor by the British District Officers. In the case of Baseng mission J. S. Smith considered it undesirable to have a community on village land which regarded itself as separate from village authority, and suggested that any woman wishing to join the settlement should personally ask permission of the chief, as any other 'stranger' who wished to settle on Baseng land would be obliged to do. The women would then be liable for communal labour along with the rest of the inhabitants of the village, and should not confine their activities to the mission. Father Ham, however, was anxious that the settlement should not be moved to the village a mile away. As J. S. Smith put it: 'he is aware that irregularities occur even when the women are living near the Mission, but the purpose of the Mission would be altogether stultified if the women were to live at a distance.'[9]

Apparently not all the women were there willingly, and there are reports of native women being 'rounded up' by the Fathers with the help of Yaunde natives, who acted as a kind of police force. In one case the priest responsible for such a round up, a young Dutchman named van Dal, was taken to court and charged, among other things, with 'deprivation of liberty', for taking a number of women and girls from Illoani village to Baseng against their wishes. It appears that the town elders consented to the girls going to Baseng, but that the girls themselves were not consulted and were taken under guard, to the extent of being escorted 'for the relief of nature'.[10] The Resident, Buea, described these settlements as 'a source of scandal and offence' and insisted that the women remain subject to the Native Authority and not under the absolute control of the Mission.[11] The British Administration, it must be said, was chiefly concerned with upholding the authority of the Native Courts, rather than with protecting the rights of individual women held against their will.

9. Ibid, para. 6.

10. Confidential memorandum from the Resident, Buea, to the Secretary of the Southern Provinces, Enugu, Nigeria, no.c6/1931, 14 May 1931, para. 19, file sd (1931)5. See also file sd(1930)5, Roman Catholic Mission, Baseng: Complaints Against.

11. Ibid.

The Authority of the Chief versus Mission Authority

In a report of mission activity among the Mbo, Bangwa and Mundani tribes in 1930[12] the District Officer of Mamfe outlined the attitude of local chiefs to the work of the Lutheran Basel Mission and the Mill Hill (Roman Catholic) Mission. The popularity of the respective missions depended largely on the degree to which they respected traditional attitudes towards women. The chiefs reported themselves satisfied with the Basel Mission and the work that it did. No woman was taken for religious instruction without the consent of her father or husband, and vernacular schools for small boys were well attended and popular. Education for girls was considered by the chiefs to be unnecessary, and in their view led to trouble. The District Officer concluded that there had never been any but cordial relations between the chiefs and Basel Mission, as the mission authorities did not go contrary to native customs.

Relations between the Roman Catholic Mission and the chiefs were not running so smoothly, and the District Officer suggested some of the factors responsible, in particular differences over infant betrothal and marriage, and the sanctity of the chief's wives. The mission and 'animists' started with diametrically opposed ideas, according to the District Officer. The mission demanded that everyone who sought refuge with them, including women, or who wished to attend their religious classes, should be free to do so. They also gave encouragement to women who wished to marry Christians, even if already married to someone else, provided that the new husband repay the bridewealth to his predecessor. The custom of infant betrothal ensured that every girl already had a 'husband' and was not therefore free to choose a partner for herself if she became a Christian. The Bangwa and Mbo insisted that unless their old customs and laws were obeyed, the administration of the country would become impossible. The District Officer noted that interest in the Roman Catholic Mission in northern Mbo (Nkinkwa) and Bangwa had actually declined, although the mission authorities denied that their own actions in alienating the chiefs were in any way responsible, putting the blame instead on the Administration for its 'prejudice and lack of support'.

Another frequent complaint was that the Fathers and their native catechists 'inveigled children and young girls under marriageable age into baptism and into becoming catechumens without the knowledge or consent of their lawful guardians'.[13] Despite the opposition of the chiefs, the District Officer, reporting on the missions in Mamfe Division, did defend

12. Report from the D. O. Mamfe c2/30/2, 11 June 1930. File sd(1928)2.
13. Confidential memorandum from the Resident, Buea, to the Secretary of the Southern Provinces, no.c6/1931, para. 18. File sd(1931)5.

the mission's right to give shelter to married women who had deserted their husbands for good reason, although the Native Courts and not the missions retained the right to settle disputes arising from such actions.

One of the main obstacles in the way of a Christian monogamous marriage was the bridewealth system, which involved a wide network of kin and future affines, all of whom had financial interests in a girl's marriage. As bridewealth payments started at birth, a woman who became a Christian could not be extricated from these obligations without considerable difficulty. The Catholic mission was accused by the chiefs and other male compound heads of converting their daughters to Christianity without their prior approval and of marrying them under the auspices of the mission without parental consent.[14]

Chief Fonwen and his Wives

These difficulties are illustrated in the case of an Mbo chief, Fonwen, and his wives, three of whom wished to become Christians. In 1924 the Chief and seven of his wives approached the catechist at Fonwen, a mission out-station of Baseng, and asked to attend catechism classes. After a year the Chief stopped going and forbade his wives to attend 'doctrine' or to say prayers in their houses. In 1928 three of these women took out a summons against their husband at Mamfe Native Court, complaining of cruel treatment. The court ruled that the women should return to their fathers who were to repay the bridewealth they had received for them. The women's fathers refused to take them back. One said that he would not take back a 'king's woman', one could not repay the bridewealth and it emerged that the third had not actually received bridewealth for his daughter, who was therefore living with the Chief voluntarily and not as a wife. The women sought refuge in Fonwen mission and were escorted to the main station at Baseng by Father Ham when he next visited their area.

The Chief and the District Officer were extremely annoyed with Father Ham, whom they accused of undermining the ruling of the Native Court. They ordered him to comply with the court ruling and to send the women back to their fathers. The mission argued that as catechumens the women had a right to mission protection. The case was finally settled in 1929 when the Mamfe Appeal Court upheld the original ruling and the women returned to their fathers who repaid the bridewealth.[15]

14. Minutes and extracts from a text written by the Resident and read to Mgr Rogan, 27 September 1931, para. 8. File sd(1931)5.

15. Confidential memorandum no.c5/1929, D. O. Mamfe to Resident, Buea, 27, 3, 1929. File sd(1928)4.

Another case illustrates the difficulties involved for women married to a polygynist who was converted to Christianity. Polygynists who became Christians were encouraged to choose one wife (they usually kept the youngest and prettiest) to marry in church, and to 'drive away' the others. If one of the wives was already a Christian she should be chosen, but if all wives of a polygynist were baptised Christians (a situation only arising in some Protestant churches) only one should remain with her husband, the rest being sent away from the compound (cf. Strayer, 1978: 79). The following case, concerning Buma, a native of Illo, Balundu, highlights the difficulties which faced all parties in such a situation.

Buma and his Wives

The case concerned a man who on becoming a Christian had sent away a wife, by whom he had had three children, so as to marry a second wife in church. In 1931 a Mill Hill priest, Father van Dal, was charged in Kumba Provincial Court with assaulting the man, Buma, for resuming cohabitation with his native ('pagan') wife. When called to witness on behalf of the Crown, Buma explained his situation: [16]

> I am a native of Illo, Balundu in Kumba Division and I am a Christian. About 5 years ago I married a wife by Native Custom and have 3 children of which 1 has died. About 2 years ago I married a wife in church by the R.C. Mission at Illo which I believe is not licensed for marriages. The Father Doeswyk told me to drive away my native wife and children although I was still fond of my wife. After about 1 year I sent for my wife and we three lived together my native wife and Christian one.... I know it is against Church law that a man has 2 wives and I anticipated some palava when the 1st accused [van Dal] came.

Potentially so distressing for those wives sent away without any status or means of support, and generally without their children who, when past infancy, would remain in their father's compound, such situations were resisted by converts. Polygyny retained its pivotal role in the society and monogamy was seldom accepted as an essential prerequisite for becoming a Christian.

---

16. Case at Kumba Provincial Court before D. S. Cook, D. O., on 24 April 1931. Rex v. van Dal and 6 others. See also confidential memorandum, D. S. Cook to Senior Resident, Buea, 29-4 1931, Kumba Provincial Court cases 40–44/31. File sd(1931)5.

Traditional Custom and Church Teaching

A quarter of a century later a Mill Hill priest in Mbetta (which became the central mission for the Bangwa and Mbo in 1936) was struggling with these same problems, trying to come terms with the contradictions inherent in the native and Christian views of marriage. He was anxious to determine the extent of the mission's authority, and to this end entered into a protracted correspondence with Bishop Rogan. Among other issues raised, Father Fitzsimons tackled the problem of marriage and bridewealth payments.[17] The young people in Bangwa and Mbo were often unable to marry quickly for various reasons. In some cases the family were slow in providing the necessary bridewealth, or the amount was too high (over £100 in the 1950s), or there were family quarrels preventing the exchange of bridewealth. In these cases the couple lived together without a full exchange of bridewealth (or a church wedding) and, if baptised, were therefore 'living in sin' and automatically excommunicated. Father Fitzsimons asked Bishop Rogan to clarify the regulations concerning bridewealth payments, and suggested that he be allowed to ignore the bridewealth, marry couples in church, and readmit them to the sacraments. Bishop Rogan's colourful reply to this question, based on his long years of experience in such matters, ran as follows:[18]

> But with regard to young couples, living together unmarried!!! If we simply marry them without dowry there is danger of dozens of sets of bans being called every week!!! Get parents or guardians of girls to agree to marriage in Church on part-payment of dowry... have witnesses to "witness" agreements and signatures.... Part... of dowry must be paid or there will be no "indissolubility": Parents would simply take the girl back saying the man had not been paid 'cargo'... "and the last state of both boy and girl will be worse than the first" – for the man will take another woman (although married to the first girl; and the girl will be given to another man, although married to chap 1...). And if we "ignore the dowry altogether" you will get dozens of weddings in church every few months.

Local customs of cohabitation were not the only topic on which Bishop Rogan held strong views. The missionaries thought it necessary to determine the behaviour of women as mothers, as well as their conduct as wives. In a letter to Father Kerkvliet, dated August 18 1941, Bishop Rogan responded to a comment of Father Kerkvliet's on the

17. Fitzsimons to Rogan, 14 July 1954. Diocesan and Vicarate General Information Files, Mbetta.

18. Rogan to Fitzsimons, 7 August 1954, ibid.

high infant mortality rate in the Bangwa/Mbo area with the following observations:[19]

> Sorry of course to hear that people are dying off but a great deal of that is their own fault. The remedy is in their own hands. They won't believe that. You mention one factor, – intermarrying. Then mothers should leave their pikins at home instead of tying them to their backs and humping them all over the country, – to dances, to farm, to bush. Babies need as much sleep as they can get. They cannot get it while being humped and bounced all day by mothers or by small girls toting them. Natives have an idea that babies must 'chop bobby' [breast feed] every ten minutes. Do not let people get into the "we want Sister for country, – Sister, Sister, Sister". The Sisters at Kumbo still have enough trouble trying to make the native mothers do what they tell them. And Fr. Figl, who is pretty frank and quick tempered and a DICTA-TOR, had to FORCE Christian mothers to adopt the cradle idea for babies. You will have to do the same. It will mean constant drilling in into them every trek; and in Central Mission...

Whatever the accuracy or otherwise of Bishop Rogan's theories of childcare and infant health, it is clear that religion and European culture were regarded by the missionaries as part of the same package. There was a tension between imparting Western patterns of behaviour, uncritically accepted as intrinsically 'Christian', and the encounter with local culture, which was by definition 'unchristian'. Any adaptation to African customs was regarded as compromise.

Questions of bridewealth payments ('dowry' in mission parlance) and Christian marriage were a source of much debate, highlighting the critical lack of fit between church canon law, missionary concerns and the realities of the pastoral situation. Father Fitzsimons advocated, for instance, barring from the sacraments Christian parents who had given their daughter in marriage to a 'pagan' or lapsed Christian. If, as was usually the case, the girl proved unwilling to desert her non-Christian husband, the parents should at least, Fitzsimons argued, return the bridewealth to the mission or Native Court as a sign of repentance.[20] He also noted that in one instance the mission 'dowry book' at Mbetta indicated that 56 people had received bridewealth for a particular girl, 46 of whom were Catholics.[21] As far as Fitzsimons was concerned these 'shady deals' over bridewealth dues were 'country fashion' and contrary to God's law. Accommodation to local marriage customs was regarded as political expediency and rejected by the purists as contrary

19. Rogan to Kerkvliet, 18 August 1941, ibid.
20. Fitzsimons to Rogan, 26 September 1954, ibid.
21. Ibid.

to Christian teaching. 'Does the Catholic Church take African marriage as such and sanctify it? Or does the Catholic Church first strip the African marriage down to the essentials as taught by the moralists?' was the question posed by Fr. Fitzsimons, with regard to bridewealth. In practice the Church found that it was unable to ignore the role of bridewealth in African marriage, although in theory marriage remained a sacramental act independent of bridewealth payments.

Another question raised by Father Fitzsimons in a letter to Bishop Rogan[22] was that of 'sacraments in *periculo mortis*'. A baptised Christian with several wives would, when dying, call for a priest to administer the sacrament of anointing. A Christian polygynist was officially barred from the sacraments, unless he first rectified his marital situation by sending all but one wife away. Fr. Fitzsimons argued that the only way to be certain that the man had rid himself of his surplus wives was to ensure that he had taken back the bridewealth he had paid for them. As it was impossible to arrange such complicated financial transactions at short notice, Fitzsimons reasoned:

> They should I think be refused the sacraments even *in extremis*, as we are trying to build up on a solid foundation the Church, and strike hard blows at the pagan habit of mind which many of our Christians still have. They consider it automatic that these men should be fixed up at the end, as they are important people usually, from the social point of view. As much as possible should be done for these men beforehand in the way of visitation, and instruction and warning while they are in health. But when serious illness comes, as it comes to all sooner or later, the same resolute stand should be maintained....I am not keen to budge an inch in such cases of wilful sinning, carried on for years.

Another point at which canon law and missionary theory parted company with the actual experience of life in Mbetta was over the question of infant baptism. Catholics were encouraged to have their children baptised as soon as possible, ideally within twenty four hours of birth, but did this hold in the case of those who, from a juridical Church perspective, were not validly married? As Father Fitzsimons lamented in a letter to Bishop Rogan:[23]

> I do not refer to the isolated case, but to Mbetta and Bangwa where it is practically a local custom that all young people must have intercourse before marriage. Christian parents encourage the young people, and then come afterwards to ask for Baptism. They deliberately prevent them from marry-

22. 1 September 1954. Diocesan and Vicarate General Information Files, Mbetta.
23. Fitzsimons to Rogan, 26 September 1954, ibid.

ing in some cases, because of the dowry. The young people talk a lot of nonsense about keeping the women in the house "to learn her fashion". When they do have a child, they have the cheek to stand up and say that God is responsible for the birth of the child.

Father Fitzsimons advocated postponing baptism until the couple had received a church wedding, a necessary course of action, he argued, if the Church was to be built on sound Christian principles of family life. In a similar vein, Fr. Fitzsimons offered his suggestions on how to tackle irregular Christian marriages.[24] As nearly all marriages were 'settling up cases', that is the couple had been living together (married according to traditional custom) for some time, they were not permitted a sung nuptial mass 'with all the white and flowers and band'. This, he concluded, would impress upon the people better than words 'that there is such a thing as Christian marriage, a Sacrament which stands on its own independently of marriage dowry and the various other payments which have to be made'. Fitzsimons had to admit that his policies had not materially affected people's behaviour, but had at least made them pause and think 'even if it is only that a queer chap has been put in charge of their mission' (ibid.).

Impotence and the Annulment of Christian Marriages

Mbetta parish was also troubled, it seems, by cases of impotence and consequent appeals for divorce and the annulment of Christian marriages. Through these cases the primary importance of children emerges as a source of tension between traditional African and Western Christian values. In one particular instance the father of a Bangwa woman married to an impotent man wrote to Bishop Rogan (in 1956) to further her petition for a divorce, pointing out the difficulties faced by a single woman in African society.[25]

My dear Lordship,

I send here my daughter, Sophena Nkeng, to see you about the above matter (a request for a divorce), the Rev. Fr. and I have fought the fight for several years and it is up to us to bring it to your decision.

My daughter is much worried because since 1950, when they married, they have not lived as husband and wife. There has been an internal strife between her and me and your failure to make things right soon may cause

24. Fitzsimons to Rogan, 26 September 1954. Ibid.

25. John Leke, Roman Catholic Mission, Foreke Middle, to Bishop Rogan, 15 December 1956, ibid.

her to take a wrong course.

I hope you will consider this matter very seriously because she has no place in the African Society if she remains in this state. It has been found out that the husband is unfit and we would like you to take the legal means.

I remain,
yours faithfully,
John Leke

Sophena and her mother visited Bishop Rogan in person several times between 1956 and 1958 in an effort to obtain the required divorce, but the bishop remained unmoved. What is striking, at a distance of over thirty years, is the persistence and attempted faithfulness to church teaching demonstrated by some Bangwa and Mbo Christians. It would have been much easier for them, a minority in their villages and far from a main mission station, simply to ignore such inconvenient aspects of church law, and return to the tried and tested customs and values of their neighbours. Some Christians did indeed develop their own unorthodox practices, based on traditional attitudes to women as property and the desire for children, regarded as one of life's greatest blessings. Referring to the case of Sopena Nkeng, Bishop Rogan expressed his displeasure at the current state of affairs among the Bangwa and Mbo, alluding to some of these practices, in the following letter to Father Fitzsimons:[26]

> Even "Christians" buying girls and hiring them out free to poor men but claiming the children and impotent Christians hiring out their Christian wives in the same manner so as to have children!!! And you can tell them from me that if we get any more impotence cases (the man knowing beforehand that he is impotent) I will make it compulsory for all men to produce a medical certificate before they will be allowed to marry for Church!!! ...of course Mbo- Bangwa- and Kinkwa countries are "off the beaten track", days away from the road; hidden deep in the bush: seldom in contact with a higher type of human being... BUT YOU CAN TELL THEM FROM ME THAT ALL FATHERS AND SISTERS AND DECENT NATIVES ARE SIMPLY DISGUSTED WITH THEIR VILE HABIT OF TRADING IN WOMEN AND GIRLS... The Church must fight "pagan country fashion" by constant propaganda. Really good Christian men and really good Christian women and girls will win out eventually. The old Christians still cling to many pagan customs. Constant ridicule of such 'unnatural' practices will stifle them eventually.

26. Rogan to Fitzsimons, 7 August 1954. See also Rogan to Altink, 18 August 1958.

Quite apart from Bishop Rogan's impatience with cases of impotence, church canon law did not favour a speedy resolution of Sophena's problems. Apparently 'Rome' demanded the evidence of two doctors before making a ruling in a case of impotence, and also stipulated that the matrimonial tribunal should meet at the place of the husband and wife, a condition totally impractical for a couple living in the isolated village of Foreke Middle. Bishop Rogan (ibid.) recounted a story in which a man was sent to the doctor at Mamfe, a town some two days' walk from his home village. The doctor diagnosed impotence. The man was then obliged to go to a doctor in Dschang in French territory (two days' walk in the opposite direction) only to be refused an appointment because he had come from the Anglophone side of the border. He was then sent him to Victoria (renamed Limbe) on the coast, where he disappeared without trace.

Disappointment or Indigenisation?

The Roman Catholic missionaries were trapped by a set of rules and assumptions as to what the Church should be like and as to how Christians should behave. The concern of a celibate clergy (or of religious sisters), and of the juridically minded hierarchy, to impose their control over what could be seen as private sexual mores, has been criticised in Europe as well as in the mission situation. Two factors, however, aggravated and exaggerated the clash between private behaviour and its public manifestations on the one hand and mission teaching on the other. In the African bush, particularly in a country such as Cameroon in which European presence was limited and communications poor, priests could operate their missions as a kind of personal fiefdom, relatively isolated from more liberal opinions developing at home. Secondly, the missionaries in the period described were still taught, in their theological training and by the societies from which they came, to regard African culture as intrinsically lacking in both its human and religious dimensions. Cameroonian Christians were expected to think and behave according to a Western model of Church which had little relevance to their own societies.

By the time of the Second Vatican Council (1962–5), after nearly forty years of missionary activity in the Mbo/Bangwa area, there were few families or individuals who conformed to Western conceptions of Christian morality. Pouring scorn on traditional practices, as Bishop Rogan had suggested, did not change people's behaviour so much as harden their attitudes towards the missionaries and towards the Christian faith. From the many thousands of boys, and handful of girls, baptised as children in mission schools, very few became the standard-bearers of (monogamous) Christian family values which the missionaries had intended.[27]

Strayer (1976: 5) suggested that 'The history of religious encounter must also include the theme of disappointment, early expectations subsequently unfulfilled'. This sense of disappointment was not limited to the missionaries. Early converts also felt that their expectations of Christianity fell short of what they had hoped. The missionaries had been seen as heralds of progress by those who welcomed them. Their educational efforts generally met with success, enabling Cameroonians to participate to a far greater extent in the dominant white society. Bangwa and Mbo ideas of progress, however, involved the possession of numerous wives and children, who would indicate status and provide economic and political support. The mission notion of progress, based on Western ideals of the monogamous family unit and adaptation to a Latinised Church, was antithetical to the native goal of building a powerful and populous community. This dilemma is illustrated in a Mbetta catechist's description of the differing reactions of the Fontem and Foreke people to Christianity in general and to monogamy in particular:[28]

> At first there was a Fontem man who refused to allow the mission to come to Bangwa. They saw the Church as a barrier to having many wives and as an impediment to progress – based on the number of children. The Foreke people accepted monogamy but the Fontem people did not, which is why Christianity is reaching Fontem only now. The Foreke people question the progress in Fontem. They reason that we who marry only one wife have less children and so there is not much progress. This has led the people to go back to taking many wives. There are very few people in Foreke now who are practising Christians. They feel they have been cheated – their old fathers accepted the new religion and depopulated the area. There are more women around than men as the men go to the towns. Women without husbands drift to the towns so that the total population is reduced. There are not so many women to give birth to children.

The accuracy of this assessment of Fontem's rapid growth (it has had a large, permanent mission presence since 1965)[29] and of Foreke's corresponding decline is less important than their perception of the situation. Monogamy is specifically blamed for depopulation and second-generation Christians are reclaiming a polygynous family structure rejected by their parents.

27. For the Basel Mission situation see Keller (1969).
28. Personal communication from Christopher Bebetta, 1981.
29. See F. Bowie, *A Social and Historical Study of Christian Missing among the Bangwa of South West Cameroon*, D.Phil Theses, Oxford, 1985.

This return to polygyny, which is widespread among second-generation Christians, a phenomenon by no means confined to Foreke, is not necessarily a rejection of Christianity as such. It has been argued that this is part of a natural process of inculturation. This is the position adopted by Ekechi (1970: 337), who argues that:

> To the missions, the return to multiple marriage by the converts was not only sad but signified that Christianity had made no appreciable impact upon the individuals involved. From the viewpoint of the Africans, however, the move was certainly a reaction *against* European acculturation. In looking at the so-called backsliding of the converts, it is more useful to look at it from the perspective of indigenizing Christianity rather than echoing the mission cliche that the African was inherently incapable of conforming to the teachings of Christianity.

The debate on the validity of polygyny and meaning of Christian inculturation has gathered momentum in the years following independence (and the Second Vatican Council), with both independent and historic Churches adopting differing views.[30] In the Bangwa area, however, Christian polygynists are often aware that through their compromise they have failed to live up to the teachings of the Church. When in 1979 a Roman Catholic priest, Father Celso Corbioli, visited Nkong, an isolated village on the Bangwa/Mundani border which had had little Christian contact, he found a man who had been baptised as a child in the primary school at Fossungo Down. He told Father Celso that he had 'passed all the sacraments' (by which he meant baptism, possibly confirmation, and Holy Communion) but had 'failed only in marriage' as he had two wives. When Father Celso returned in 1981, one of this man's wives had died and he asked to be married to the remaining wife in church. He was delighted that at last he had 'passed in all the sacraments' and he became Head Christian of his village (personal communication, 1981).

---

30. The Aladura Churches of Nigeria and Kimbanguist Church in Zaire, for instance, take opposing stands over the issue of polygyny. The Aladura Churches sanction polygyny, while the *Eglise de Jésus Christ par le Prophéte Simon Kimbangu*, as it is officially known, condemns the practice. The relationship between Christianity and traditional African culture is discussed in several of the articles in Fasholé-Luke et al. (1978).

Conclusion

Archbishop Desmond Tutu has written that:[31]

> Men became missionaries from all kinds of motives, most of which were undoubtedly beyond reproach. But they would have to be persons of heroic sanctity had they not been tainted by the arrogance which was the almost invariable concomitant of a dominant culture. Only the exceptional among them would realise that Christianity and Western civilisation were not coterminous; that the credal expressions and liturgical forms which the missionary brought with him were not to be confused with the eternal Gospel.

The development of an African christology, tackling questions of inculturation or contextualisation, is only just beginning.[32] Members of historic mission Churches will operate under different constraints from members of African Independent Churches, and no doubt the answers which emerge from African theologians and practical liturgists or Church officials will reflect the variety of historical and cultural experience among Christians. Archbishop Tutu speaks of the need for a 'radical spiritual decolonisation' in African theology (ibid.: 396), claiming that:[33]

> The worst crime that can be laid at the door of the white man (who it must be said, has done many a worthwhile and praiseworthy thing for which we are always thankful) is not our economic, social and political exploitation, however reprehensible that might be; no, it is that his policy succeeded in filling most of us with a self-disgust and self-hatred. This has been the most violent form of colonialism, our spiritual and mental enslavement, when we have suffered from what can only be called a religious or spiritual schizophrenia.

Africanisation of church hierarchies or indigenisation of liturgies will not of themselves correct the westernising impositions of past and present missionary activity. In relation to women and issues such as monogamous versus polygynous marriage a double form of colonisation has taken place. To European models imposed by the missions (and taken over in many cases by indigenous secular and religious authorities) one must add the dominance of male culture. To aim at a model (or models) of Church which takes account of women's experience is a task which has barely begun among the historical mission churches. African Independent Churches have in some cases attempted to find a more genuinely indigenous expression of faith which might entail, as in the

31. 'Whither African Theology?' in Fasholé-Luke et at. (1978: 364). See also article in Parratt (1987: 46–57).

32. See, for instance, Appiah-Kubi (1987).

33. Cited in Parrott (ibid: 47).

Aladura Churches, enabling women to play a more active role in line with their prominence in traditional society.[34] Whether monogamous Christian marriage will survive as a norm for some or all of the churches in Africa remains to be seen. African theologians are still, according to Archbishop Tutu (1987: 55), 'too much concerned to play the game according to the white man's rules when he is often the referee as well'. He concludes with the prophetic statement, relevant to practical pastoral problems such as Christian marriage, as well as to academic theology, that: 'It is only when African Theology is true to itself that it will go on to speak relevantly to the contemporary African – surely its primary task – and also, incidentally, make its valuable contribution to the rich Christian heritage which belongs to all of us' (ibid.).[35]

34. There have been numerous studies of the Aladura Churches. See, for instance, Omoyajowo, in Fasholé-Luke et al. (1978).

35. Speaking of Asian inculturation (not a term he favours), Aloysius Pieris (1988) points to the necessity of merging a cosmic (i.e. tribal) religion and a metacosmic religion (such as Christianity) if the latter is to put down institutional roots in a culture. He also stresses the necessity of forming base Christian communities, theologising out of their praxis of involvement with the society of which they are a part, if indigenisation of Christianity is to become a reality. These principles are equally valid in an African context.

Bibliography

Appiah-Kubi, K. (1987) 'Christology', in J. Parratt (ed.), *A Reader in African Christian Theology*, SPCK, London

Beidelman, T. O. (1982) *Colonial Evangelism*, Indiana University Press, Bloomington

Beti, M. (1977) *The Poor Christ of Bomba*, Heinemann, London

Bowie, F. (1985) *A Social and Historical Study of Christian Missions among the Bangwa of South West Cameroon*, D.Phil thesis, University of Oxford

Bowden, J. (1969) *What About the Old Testament?* SCM, London

Dowell, S. (1990) *They Two Shall Be One: Monogamy in History and Religion*, Collins, London

Ekechi, E. K. (1970) 'African Polygamy and Western Christian Ethnocentricism', *Journal of African Studies*, 3: 329–49

Fasholé-Luke, E., Gray, R., Hastings, A. and Tasie, G. (eds) (1978) *Christianity in Independent Africa*, Rex Collings, London

Githige, R. M. (1982), 'The Mission State Relationship in Colonial Kenya: A Summary', *Journal of Religion in Africa*, 13, 110–25

Hastings, A. (1973) *Christian Marriage in Africa*, SPCK, London

Hurbon, L. (1969) 'Racisme et theologie missionarie', *Presence Africaine*, 71: 35–47

Keller, W. (1969) *The History of the Presbyterian Church in West Cameroon*, Buea

Omoyajowo, A. (1978) 'The Aladura churches in Nigeria since independence', in Fasholé-Luke et al. op. cit.

Parratt, J. (ed.) (1987), *A Reader in African Christian Theology*, SPCK, London

Pieris, A. (1988) *An Asian Theology of Liberation*, T. & T. Clark, Edingburgh

Pobee, J. S. (1991) 'Polygamy', in *Dictionary of the Ecumenical Movement*, ed. Lossky et al., WCC Publications & the Council of Churches for Britain and Ireland: 802–4

Schweitzer, A. (1961) *On the Edge of the Primeval Forest*, A. & C. Black, London

Shorter, A. (1978) *African Culture and the Christian Church*, Geoffrey Chapman, London

Shorter, A. (1988) *Toward a Theology of Inculturation*, Geoffrey Chapman, London

Strayer, R.W. (1976) 'Mission History in Africa: New Perspectives on an Encounter', *The African Studies Review*, 19: 1–15

Strayer, R. W. (1978) *The Making of Mission Communities in East Africa*, Heinemann, London

Tutu, D. (1978), 'Whither African Theology?', in Fasholé-Luke et al., op. cit.

Tutu, D. (1987), 'Black Theology and African Theology – Soulmates or Antagonists?' In Parratt, op. cit.

Archival Sources

Cameroon National Archives Buea:
  sd (1928)2 Roman Catholic Mission, Mamfe Division
  sd (1928)4 Roman Catholic Mission, Interference with Native Courts
  sd (1930)1 Roman Catholic Mission, Kumba Division: Complaints Against
  sd (1931)5 Roman Catholic Mission: Interference with Native Courts

Diocesan and Vicarate General Information Files, Mbetta.

9

Mission Impact on Women in Colonial Kenya

Tabitha Kanogo

The early [mission] pioneers were often kindly despots, ruling their kingdoms with great firmness. (Bewes, 1953: 30)

The gospel . . . is, and was meant to be, a mighty revolutionary force; it is the sharpest sword ever laid to the heart and conscience of man. Much of the old Kikuyu way of life . . . was found to be incompatible with the Christian life. Changes were bound to come. (ibid.)

. . . the present need is for homemakers, and for this we need to train young girls of character who as Christian wives and mothers, and even teachers before marriage will by their knowledge of Homecraft be able to make a virtual difference in the standard of Kikuyu life. (KNA CMS 1/382)

Like a typhoon came western civilisation sweeping everything before it, or almost everything. It came with a rush and the tribal life of the Kikuyu reeled under the impact. (Bewes, 1953: 36)

Introduction

This paper seeks to analyse the experiences of Kenyan girls and women as they struggled to make sense out of the conflicts, contradictions, opportunities, limitations and the transformation created by their entry into mission stations. As with colonialism, the introduction of Christianity in Kenya had far-reaching effects on the indigenous people. Christian missionaries and colonial administrators shared the broad common goal of trying to transform the lifestyles of Africans. In many ways missionaries sought to restructure and redefine the social organisation of basic African institutions. They did not confine themselves to the spiritual realm; they interfered with all aspects of the day-to-day lives of those with whom they came into contact. The 'otherness' of

Africans provoked simultaneous revulsion and compassion; revulsion for the so-called heathen moral depravity and the cultural inappropriateness of the African experience, and compassion for a 'fallen' race, which must be redeemed from its low estate. The Christian gospel and Western civilisation were seen to hold the key to the big task ahead. To a large extent the anticipated restructuring presupposed the African social fabric to be a moral and cultural *tabula rasa*. Amidst a flurry of 'change agents', Africans became contested territory, African women not excepted. They too became entangled in a new and intricate set of relationships.

Missionaries and colonial administrators might differ in their specific backgrounds, personal experiences and sense of vocation. Ultimately, however, they shared a common culture, namely Western Christian civilisation, which in the nineteenth century was transplanted to distant lands, throughout the British Empire. The scenario in colonial Kenya was similar to developments elsewhere. On the one hand stood the colonial administrator with formulas for law and order, civil responsibility and greater economic productivity; on the other was the missionary expounding his or her version of more wholesome moral and social codes of behaviour, extolling self-reliance and advocating the adoption of wide variety of Western values and practices by Africans. However, the difference between the two, the missionary and the colonial administrator, was a fine one. Freund has argued that, except on rare occasions, missionaries

> did not oppose the essence of the colonial system: segregation, land alienation and migrant labour. Few if any missions challenged the political and economic imperatives of colonial dominations as opposed to specific policies and they usually accepted the racist aspects of it fairly easily. (Freund, 1984: 157)

Colonial government and missionary visions for Africans converged on many issues, including the need to introduce formal education, Western medicine and 'better' methods of agricultural production. They might not always agree on the means of executing specific tasks. However, at the end of the day, any differences between the administrator and the missionary were lost to Africans, hence the Kikuyu observation '*Gutiri muthungu na mubia*' (There is no difference between the administrator and the missionary). Both the missionary and the colonial official were perceived as enigmatic intruders whose presence turned the lives of Africans upside down.

Missionary struggles against recalcitrant groups resulted in appeals for protection from their mother countries. As pioneers into African lands, missionaries were said to blaze the trail for colonial occupation.

Their plea for territorial annexation anticipated the subjugation of indigenous populations by the colonial powers, supporting the missionaries' desire for 'peace', which was vital for their effective evangelisation. Indigenous men and women who found themselves drawn into the mission network were caught in a dialectical process, which sought to tear them from their past and to engraft them into new structures (Swantz, 1978: 145). Sandgren's observation (1989: 60) regarding mission belief that 'each decision to become a *muthomi* ('a Christian', 'a convert'; pl. *athomi*) was also a decision to reject the community' is contestable. For the *athomi* there were difficult choices to be made. However, more often than not, converts straddled contradictory systems. The dynamics of the period did not produce a clearly defined separation between the old and the new. Rather, a continuum throbbing with old and new forces was created. It is to that continuum of change and continuity that we now turn our attention.

Early Mission Encounters

By the second decade of this century there was a proliferation of missionary groups operating in various parts of Kenya (Oliver, 1965; Strayer, 1978). Earlier attempts to evangelise in the 1840s had been confined to the coastal area, where free ex-slave communities offered a nucleus around which mission work developed. As imperial penetration into the interior progressed, there was an influx of different missions. These included the Church Missionary Society (CMS), the Church of Scotland Mission (CSM), the African Inland Mission (AIM) and the Mill Hill Fathers, among others. Despite their individual idiosyncrasies, the various missions inserted similar irrevocable wedges into the host communities.

Two of the most influential missions were the CSM and the AIM. When the CSM established itself at Thogoto on the outskirts of Nairobi in 1898, African contacts with Europeans were still very limited. The only Europeans who had had any lengthy contact with Africans were the officials of the Imperial British East African Company operative in Kenya in the period 1888–95. They had managed to antagonise the local people wherever they encountered them. By not paying for goods sold to them, by seducing local girls, and by generally disregarding local power structures, the company officials unleashed the wrath of the indigenous population (Ochieng, 1985: 88–94). It was not always clear what the intentions of the next group of 'red' strangers might be.

Everything to which Africans were introduced at mission stations was foreign. They were presented with a new religion, Western medicine, literacy and new ways of dressing, among other things. Above all, however, missionaries introduced new philosophies of life based on a combination of Western culture and Christianity. At the mission station life was ordered differently. New values, different routines and social rhythms all served to accentuate the novelty; and African adherents, set apart from their kinsmen, were inducted into a different life pattern.

Genesis of Mission Girls

Many reasons have been advanced in an attempt to explain the failure of pioneer missions in getting catechumens and converts. By clinging to their value systems and religions, Africans were portrayed as having been responsible for the failure of early Christian missions. In reality, Christianity found itself pitched against a well-established social order whose fabric was difficult to dismantle. As an intruding force that sought to eradicate significant aspects of African cultures, Christianity was strongly resisted.

In Kenya, missionaries were not always enthusiastically received once it became clear that they despised many aspects of African cultures and practices (Nottingham and Rosberg, 1966; Welbourn, 1961). While children of collaborating functionaries were easier to recruit, the general population regarded missionaries with suspicion at best, and outright opposition at worst. They forbade their children to go to the missions. However, an unwanted orphan or a troublesome son might be offered or allowed to go to the mission station. Hence 'you did not remove a child from *ruru* (pasture) to send it to the mission'. Only unwanted children who were a liability to the family were free to go to the mission stations.

Thus the first generation of mission adherents comprised social misfits, the unwanted and vulnerable members of the society. There were, however, those who were motivated by the spirit of adventure and who ran away to mission stations. In most cases boys preceded girls, but in both cases those who pioneered entry into the missions constituted either the unwanted or abberant youth in society. Missionaries combing the countryside for possible catechumens might be offered the daughter of a dead relation. Likewise, an ill-treated orphan might escape to the sanctuary of the mission station. The former was the fate of the mother of one of my informants, who was given away to the Church of Scotland Mission in Thogoto before the First World War. She had lived in Muranga with her parents and when they died, relations had taken her in. Clearly, they had not relished the task of bringing her up. They were quick to offer the adolescent girl to the distant mission. Seemingly relieved of their responsibility, they did not check on her once although she lived to a ripe old age.

For most women, association with the missions involved more than a religious conversion; it also led to cultural and social transformation. The encounter permeated the whole of the adherent's life-style, creating new values, aspirations, role models and status symbols. All these were juxtaposed with the old order. However, as well as opening new doors, the encounter generated unprecedented conflicts and contradictions so that the loyalties of these girls were torn between familiar and well-balanced indigenous life-patterns and novel socio-cultural and religious structures, which sought to transform the adherents' lives along untrodden paths. In as much as the colonial government was to some extent concerned to preserve the social fabric of African societies, missionaries seemed bent on tearing them apart, thereby 'detribalising' church adherents. The missions' short-term solution to this conflict was to remove their wards from familiar 'pagan' surroundings to the safety of the mission. '*Mambere*', girls' boarding houses in mission stations in Central Kenya, became fermenting pots of female transformation. They also became centres of dissent. This scenario reproduced itself wherever the church was founded. At the AIM mission at Kijabe, Kikuyu girls attending school therein were described as 'wild black girls of the bush . . . thoroughly chained and enslaved by dark customs and superstitions of their tribal life' (Sandgren, 1989: 24). Missions were commited to freeing their wards from the hold of such 'evil' forces. The struggle was long and protracted.

A Look through the Window

The most noticeable and immediate changes in the lives of mission girls were external. As a first step towards the 'cleansing' of their wards, the girls were stripped of their traditional attire and jewelry. These were replaced with mission uniforms. Among the Kikuyu, those who had had their ear-lobes pierced and subsequently enlarged for decoration had them sewn-up in keeping with the prevailing spirit of Christian modesty. In their checked uniforms, the Thogoto CSM girls stood apart from their peers in the villages. They were cleaned-up, and all ochre and other decorations removed. Subsequent catechumens attested to the attraction of those uniforms and the 'cleaned-up' image of new recruits. A second-generation mission girl was nostalgic about the immediate transformation that such girls underwent. Reminiscing over the experiences of young girl catechumens, an ex-mission woman said, 'They cleaned you up, gave you new clothes and fed you. It was a home away from home.' It was, however, a different type of home. The girls underwent instruction which alienated them from village life. This, however, was not a chance development; neither did it go unchallenged. The inherent conflict was largely a product of insensitivity to, and in some cases complete rejection of, African beliefs and practices. Missions were averse to, and even scandalised by, what was acceptable as standard local practice among various Kenyan societies. Initiation ceremonies, especially female circumcision, polygamy, payment of 'dowry' and divination, among other customs, were termed pagan and therefore incompatible with Christianity. This attitude, together with certain aspects of mission doctrine, irritated, and in some cases angered, both mission charges and their parents and thus created a tense situation which made the success of the work difficult. By confining their newly acquired charges to the mission stations, missionaries hoped to protect and wean them from these so-called evil practices.

They were particularly protective of girls and women whom they perceived as being especially vulnerable. For this reason, pioneer missions insisted that all female catechumens must reside within mission compounds. This drastic physical relocation of girls was in many ways indicative of the more radical and challenging changes that they were to encounter. Like colonialism, Christianity in some ways was about the drawing of new boundaries and the redefinition of values, loyalties and life-styles. Significantly, it was also about straddling seemingly mutually exclusive social structures and institutions. It was one dynamic continuum of conflicting loyalties.

Removed from their familiar socio-cultural milieu, the girls soon became misfits in their own societies. Not allowed to participate in the various cultural festivities and everyday social activities, they became increasingly alienated. Members of their peer groups and kinsmen began to hold them up to ridicule and to treat them as incomplete members of the society since they had not undergone some of the vital rites of passage. As part of the assimilation process, the girls themselves began to question certain cultural practices within their own societies. That, however, did not entail the abandonment of all aspects of their culture. More often than not, they were torn between antagonistic factions in various controversies. Catechumens fluctuated between two systems, the old and the new, each driven by a desire to appropriate their absolute allegiance.

The Female Circumcision Controversy

One of the most protracted and traumatic conflicts emanating from missionary attempts to redefine the life-patterns of their wards revolved around the issue of female circumcision, clitorodectomy. Quoting medical reasons, but possibly more disenchanted with the festivities which preceded the surgery, missionaries, led by the CSM and the AIM, declared that female circumcision was incompatible with Christianity. It was argued that the surgery was extremely drastic and that it created large scars which made childbirth excruciating. The lives of the expectant mother and that of the child were said to be in great danger. This controversy hinged upon an institution that was deemed central to a people's social organisation. Missionary attempts to persuade the community to stop female circumcision resulted in a massive abandonment of the missions.

By the 1920s missionaries had managed to attract an increasing number of converts who wished to attend their schools. Education was rapidly perceived as a new vehicle for social mobility. The Government's failure to provide formal education reinforced mission monopoly of educational facilities (Anderson, 1970). When the missions began in 1929 to insist that children of people who supported female circumcision would not be allowed to attend their schools, a crisis of an unprecedented magnitude was unleashed. This brought all the simmering misunderstandings and misinterpretations of African culture and Christian doctrines to the fore.

While missionaries focused on the actual operation, the Kikuyu saw clitoridectomy as the culmination of a long process of socialisation, and cultural identification (Kenyatta, 1961). The surgery itself was merely an external physical act, which sealed an intricate rite of passage that transformed girls into women. The spiritual and personal maturation surrounding the whole process was irreplaceable. The controversy tore the Church assunder. Mission adherence fell by over 90 per cent. Parents withdrew their children from schools rather than give up the rite. The parting of ways seemed inevitable. What did all this mean to mission girls, especially for those of them who had not undergone circumcision? The *muthirigu* song which condemned both Christianity and colonialism at the height of the female circumcision controversy best summarises the ridicule and contempt in which such girls were held. They were seen to symbolise the ultimate in an unprecedented assault on Kikuyu social fabric. Their rejection of the rite jeopardised an age-old paradigm of societal organisation. To the wider Kikuyu community, the dismay at the girls' betrayal of traditional values was reflected in the diminished status of mission girls. In the words of the *muthirigu* song:

> Irigu you are not costly;
> only seven dogs and you marry in church.
> (Sandgren, 1989: 177)

The whole concept of womanhood was at stake. What did it mean to be a twenty-year-old female in a mission station in 1929? In Kikuyu society, such an uncircumcised female never graduated to the status of a woman. She remained *kirigu*, a novice in the art of womanhood. In this respect, her juvenile traits were protrayed in the *muthirigu* song thus:

> And to know that it is really bad,
> it (*Kirigu*) will urinate in the bed and say that the bed has become cold.
> (ibid.: 178)

The marriageability of such 'women' became questionable. Even their personal hygiene was said to fall short:

> Smell, smell, smell
> I have smelt uncircumcised
> girls passing nearby.
> (ibid.: 180)

No woman, unless a mission convert herself, would want an uncircumcised daughter-in-law. Neither did men outside the mission fold consider marrying such women. In more ways than one, Christian girls were considered inadequate. This was largely expressed in perjorative terms: *Irigu ni iranunga'* ('uncircumcised girls stink'), they wet their beds and they cannot perform a host of tasks which ordinary women would find easy to execute. This socio-cultural battle was extended to the political arena where such girls were seen as 'collaborators' in the pursuit of Christian as well as colonial domination. District Commissioners, who were in reality the eyes and ears of colonial regimes, were accused of having unsanctioned liaisons with mission girls reinforcing the view that the latter were colluding with the agents of colonialism and Christianity. They were also seen to embody all the vices associated with the Euro-Christian community.

One of the most common allegations levelled against the girls was that they practised prostitution. This allegation was probably rooted in the fact that mission stations had both young men and women in their custody. Although the two sexes were housed in separate dormitories, the fact that they lived away from the supervision of elders perpetuated the belief that anything could happen in such 'unregulated' conditions. Unsanctioned sexual practices ranked high among the various possibilities. Hence missions were seen as 'hot-beds of prostitution'. Tension and suspicion continued to simmer between those within and those outside the mission stations. They belonged to two opposed camps linked by kinsmen and women operating across the divide. *Gichambanio*, 'mutual vilification', was rife.

Furthermore, the girls were said to be exceptionally lazy and hence unsuitable for the day-to-day work of village women. It was believed that within the confines of the mission they did not have to undertake tedious tasks which characterised the lives of ordinary women in the villages: the long hours of agricultural labour, fetching water and gathering firewood which occupied the lives of village women. Although mission girls had to grow their own food, it was said that theirs was a less rigorous life. The reality, however, was otherwise. For example, at Githumu mission in Muranga, which was located at the top of a hill, girls had the unenviable task of fetching water from a river at the bottom of the hill, which was the only source of water in the immediate vicinity. To meet the station's needs, the girls had to make several trips. The ten-gallon barrels in which the water was carried made the exercise particularly difficult and unpopular. For that reason 'Many of the girls considered this work forced labour and a number left the mission rather than endure it further' (Sandgren, 1989: 61).

The theme of forced labour provided a significant rallying point in early political mobilisation in Kenya. With regard to female forced labour, Harry Thuku, who was in the vanguard of anti-colonial struggles in the 1920s, had earned for himself the title 'Chief of women' for opposing the forced recruitment of women. Missionaries were accused of reviving forced labour, a situation which mission girls as well as the wider community resented. Suggestions by the local Christians that a pump be installed to replace the girls' labour at Githumu was opposed by the missions. The expenditure was deemed unnecessary 'when able-bodied people were available to do it' (ibid.). Even when the local church followers offered to finance the installation of the pump, the missionaries remained adamant and interpreted both the women's and the community's idea about the pump as a challenge to their authority. This episode, one among many, illustrates the fact that life at the mission stations was not a bed of roses. There was hard work to be done, and conflict over this existed even between missions and their adherents. At another level, women's self-assertion over the issue of the control of their own lives was not limited to the water issue alone. They had to grapple with more conflict-generating changes such as marriage.

Marriage

As a result of the growing chasm between mission and non-mission people, there was an increasing tendency for missions to encourage their girls to marry Christian boys. Such marriages did not always have the support of the parents of the couple involved and resulted in protracted conflicts. The missions, however, did not hesitate to officiate in marriages where parental consent had not been granted. In order to protect themselves and the newly married couples from parental harassment after the wedding, churches sought the approval of local District Commissioners, the High Court and their own councils.

Conflict over the marriage of mission girls embraced wider social concerns relating to the patriarchal control of women and the circulation of wealth among elders. It also had to do with the control of older women over younger ones. Mission interference in and regulation of the marriages of mission women and men threatened established local authority structures. This elicited opposition from all manner of people. For example, in Kisii, as in other parts of the country, missionaries became involved in the 'dowry' (bridewealth) issue and sought the co-operation of the Government in limiting 'dowry' so that:

> If one gives more cows as dowry and the girl leaves or the marriage *shauri* (affair) is in any way dissolved, the husband has a right only to the return of the official dowry: he forfeits all right to any additional cows he may have given (Bogonko, 1981: 17).

Around Thogoto, parents were wary of losing 'dowry' once their daughters entered mission stations; in general, the novelty of the mission life provided much room for speculation regarding the marrigeability of such girls. The presence of elderly spinsters among the mission staff created a fear that girls might not get married. It was also argued that the Christian marriages which did take place were arranged by the missionaries, thus denying the catechumens the right to choose their partners. The result was said to be 'marriages which quickly broke asunder for lack of bases' (ibid.: 16).

Missionaries were said to be insensitive to problems that might arise from such 'fragile' marriages, and they were reluctant to listen to arguments brought against them. In general, such marriages were believed to generate embarrassing social relations between the families thus united. For example, the mothers of mission girls were said to suffer loss of respect as a result of allowing their daughters to embrace the Christian religion which reduced the social worth of their daughters. Elderly women did not get their due respect from non-Christian sons-in-law. The situation was captured thus:

Mother of a Kirigu (uncircumcised girl) if we meet
Greet me with Mbembe (Muthirigu).

For I am not your *Muthoni* (in-law)
Your *Muthoni* is NGUI (a bitch or conflict). (Sandgren,
1989: 77)

Nothing could have been more insulting than for an elderly woman
to be in such a predicament. Mothers with sons of a marrying age were
equally anxious lest their sons should choose to marry mission girls
whom the wider society considered to be 'half-baked'. In general, then,
it can be said that the conversion of a girl to the Christian religion might
result in the social alienation of her family and of that into which she
married. Some of the non-mission boys were aware of their mothers'
anxieties and sought to assure them that they would not bring such mis-
fortune upon them. Mission girls, the non-Christian men argued, could
only be married for ridicule and exploitation. They did not make good
wives. Sandgren has documented various versions of the *muthirigu*
song which is quoted below to illustrate what some of the non-Christian
men thought about mission girls.

Mother do not worry,
do not worry yourself
for I am a Kikuyu
and I cannot change religion.

IRIGU are not costly;
only seven dogs and you marry in church.

I would not marry an uninitiated girl
For an uninitiated goat
    (portion of ears and tail cut off)
I will buy one
For my mother
Who is old now

She can fetch firewood
for her.

I will buy (marry) one (an uninitiated girl) to make me
some stockings,
After making the stockings,

I will send her away.
Smell, smell, smell
I have smelt
Uncircumcised girls
Passing nearby.

To be sure she is foolish.
When I ask for a tie she brings a rope.

To be sure she is foolish.
She gives a one-week-old baby maize.

To be sure she is naughty,
Whichever home she goes
She climbs castor oil trees.

To be sure she is naughty,
She urinates in the bed,
And says it is another kind of wetness.
The D.C. (District Commissioner)
Is bribed with uncircumcised girls
So that the land may go.
(Sandgren, 1989: 177–82)

Mission girls were caught in a trap as they continued to oscillate between two cultural types: one familliar, the other an unknown novelty. Attempts to combine elements of the two met with vehement opposition. In one case a girl sought to persuade Catholic missionaries to agree to her father's insistence on what the missionaries considered to be an exhorbitant dowry. She was disappointed with the unyielding attitude of the missionaries and threatened to leave. Despite this threat, they remained adamant: 'Father Doyle is firm. She threatens to throw up religion; a stupid girl' (Bogonko, 1981: 16). Where neither the missionary nor the local communities were willing to budge, the girls found themselves in a difficult situation and in many cases, as the bridge between the protagonists, they paid the price.

While reasons for the break-up of marriages were diverse, what irritated local communities was the fact that missions gave refuge to women experiencing marital problems; this led the local community to accuse them of colluding with the women to rob men of their wives 'although the men had paid dowry'. The Seventh Day Adventist Mission in Kisii was accused of 'encouraging mission girls not to be sold into slavery' (Bogonko, 1981: 17). This was in reference to the inflated bridewealth that a father might ask a prospective son-in-law to pay. This particular mission had gone a step further than the others by defining the number of livestock that should be given as 'dowry' for their girls.

By giving asylum to troubled wives, the mission was said to interfere with ethnic and traditional authorities, which would otherwise have dealth with marital problems. In patriarchal societies where the payment of bridewealth perpetuated the circulation of wealth among elders, broken marriages might necessitate the partial or complete refund of the bridewealth. This could result in material loss to the girl's father. The intervention of elders, even where it contradicted the wishes of either parties in a shaky marriage, was, within certain limits, final. In this respect then, the missions provided a safety-net for women caught in such a predicament. This displeased local power-brokers. Agwada, a local assistant chief in North Bugirango, argued that a number of *Gusii* men had 'been deprived of their wives by the Roman Catholic Mission in Nyabururu and were unable to get them back' (Bogonko, 1976: 19). A situation had arisen in which the question of the control of women was at stake. The missions and local elders were locked in a conflict that was to last much longer than anticipated.

For women, the missions provided an escape from overbearing husbands and kinsmen. To the wider community, however, they were seen as asylums for girls and women who had broken societal mores by transfering the mediating role in family disputes to external institutions. In so doing, they disobeyed their elders and husbands. Likewise, in so far as the village patriarchs were looked upon by the Government as the custodians of the society's values and authority, the women who escaped to the missions were portrayed as disobeying government authority. The recurrent colonial quest for the control of the native was complicated by the arrival of the missionary. The control of young men and women was contested by colonial administrators, missionaries and local authority hierarchies. At times colonial administrators concurred with local African allegations regarding the negative influence that missions had on African youth. In this vein, the Kisii District Commissioner in 1932 noted that mission villages were 'night clubs for young men and girls who not only escaped from tribal and parental authority but repudiated all obligations' (KNA: DC/KSI/I/3: 9–10).

The question of polygamy was of particular concern to the missionaries. While acknowledging that polygamy as a social institution had a legitimate role in 'traditional' societies, it was considered undesirable for Christians. In Kenya, the campaign for its eradication was linked with attempts by missionaries to promote 'the emancipation of girls'

(Holding, E.M., 1961: 64). Polygamy and the authority of the clan over the family were perceived as a hindrance to the development of 'Christian relationships between husband and wife'. A gradual reorganisation of family sturcture with Christian nuclear families as the ultimate goal was initiated, starting with the catechumens. For this purpose the Church of Scotland Mission established its first girls' dormitory in 1909 at Thogoto 'mainly as a protection against unwelcome marriages to heathen husbands, mostly polygamisst [sic] and also to prepare wives for our mission boys who as time went on were getting more and more beyond the status of the raw native' (KNA:EDAR, 1928: 68). The rejection of polygamy plunged the girls into innumerable problems. Family and church loyalties were in conflict. The crisis of marriage in colonial Kenya was exacebated not only by the imposition of alien moral codes, but also by rapid social change.

In all these developments women and girls found themselves victims of a male power struggle. They also had to contend with sanctions from older non-mission women, especially mothers-in-law. The mission girl thus became both ward and 'victim' of all parties involved in the struggle.

Self-reliance

In order to feed themselves and contribute towards their upkeep, mission girls were allocated individual plots on which they grew different food crops. These plots were reputed to have been more productive than village plots as the former were cultivated according to strict agricultural methods taught to catechumens by the missionaries. The girls were allowed to sell the crop surplus and to keep the proceeds. At Thogoto, they boosted their income further by collecting firewood, which found a ready market in the mission stations. In this way the girls could earn a steady income for themselves. However, although this cash nexus proved an additional attraction for girls, it generated conflict in those situations where missions themselves tried to raise money by utilising the labour of the catechumens. At another level, mission wards were opposed to the stress on manual labour at the expense of formal education (Sandgren, 1989: 224). Hence the notion of the mission as an avenue for economic independence was also subject to conflict. All the same, informants lauded improved methods of farming introduced by missionaries, and the girls themselves became agents of change, transmitting newly acquired knowledge to their villages. It has been asserted that Protestant missions were more rigorous than Roman Catholics in ensuring that better husbandry was practised in the villages. This change in production is said to have been equalled by mission obssession with cleanliness.

The economic independence accorded to the girls was closely tied to the idea of self-reliance, which informants agreed was a major 'doctrine' on mission stations. As one informant observed, 'the mission station gave us all general knowledge including needlework and self-reliance. One was taught to organise oneself'. This military type of regime was widely acknowledged by ex-mission informants who implied that mission-trained women were better organised, cleaner, more efficient and productive than their non-mission kinswomen. Whether that claim was generally true is debatable. What is clear, how- ever, is the fact that shifts in priorities as a result of the mission encounter became evident. Daily social rhythms changed. For example, Saturdays were deemed to be cleaning days while for the village girls Saturdays were ordinary days when routine domestic chores were undertaken. Shifts in patterns of child-care, diet, dress and food production among other things, were evident. Mission girls were introduced to new philosophies of life which were in some respects far removed from their past experiences. Thus, once they embraced Christianity, they adopted a fair amount of Western culture which alienated them further from their kinsmen. The latter considered some of these new practices as 'foolishness'.

In general, individualism seems to have crept into the lives of cate-chumens quite rapidly. Females, like their male counterparts, delayed parenthood as they pursued general and sometimes specific training for a variety of careers. While the choice of marriage partners became dependent upon new variables, including the suitor's religious affiliation, acceptance of Christian weddings and other such new ideas, many mission women found it difficult to relate to non-mission men. More importantly, marriage in general became increasingly optional. This was especially so for girls who had had a long association with missionaries which tended to set them further apart not only from the wider community, but from the world of men as well.

At a glance, the society's perception of mission girls was ambivalent. The girls were regarded with a mixture of ridicule, suspicion and esteem. Part of their ambiguous status emanated from the girls' seclusion on mission stations. This tended to create an aura of mystery around their lives. They were deemed aloof, a characteristic which was traced back to mission overseers who were said to be extremely severe in their dealings with their wards and the wider world as well. At Thogoto mission, one such 'no-nonsense' woman was said not to hesitate to mete out corporal punishment to offending parties, male or female. Thus, the physical and social isolation perpetuated the myth of their 'otherness'.

For those who mingled with the wider community in the course of their duties, their newly acquired skills, including teaching, nursing and preaching, tended to reduce their social distance while at the same time inflating their social standing. To some extent their commitment to work, foreign to the society from which they came, removed them from the daily rhythms of other villagers who thus perceived them as different and in some cases as 'proud'. A case is cited of one girl who was among the first generation of ardent mission pupils. She travelled far and wide evangelising and advocating Christian marriage. She stood out as a unique representative of the more forceful of the mission girls. She is reputed to have looked down upon most prospective suitors whom she referred to as *'nguci'* (scab). In her estimation, these people were unworthy of her. When she did get married eventually, her contemporaries were taken aback. A male contemporary saw the marriage as 'an act of the grace of God'. Left to herself, she would have continued to turn away her suitors. It was said that God had intervened on behalf of her husband-to-be.

We have already alluded to an ambiguity in attitudes towards mission girls. In many respects, this ambivalence was indicative of the plethora of social changes that society itself was undergoing. Like the mission girls, society itself was straddling Western Christian and African traditional cultures. The transition was not easy. Old practices and values were juxtaposed alongside new expectations in a rapidly changing socio-economic milieu. A fluid and tense situation was emerging. Within institutionalised worship, breakaway churches abounded as accusations of cultural imperialism and domination were levelled against missionaries (Welbourn, 1961; Nottingham and Rosbreg, 1966). The female circumcision controversy only encapsulated a crisis which attained a public dimension. More often than not, girls encountered conflicts that were mediated at the personal and family levels, occasionally creating deep wounds that took long to heal. Simultaneously, new opportunities were created through contacts with mission stations. It was a mixed bag, offering wide possibilities and unprecedented pitfalls. Some of these contradictions were played out within mission stations.

Early Mission Training

It is now apparent that up to the early 1950s missionaries were concerned to enhance the so-called 'domestic' attributes of women in various fields of training. In Kenya, at the beginning of their careers, the missionaries were keen primarily to inculcate ideals relating to cleanliness, proper housekeeping and a general aptitude in housecraft, including sewing, cooking and child-rearing. Academic training was given secondary attention, as it was anticipated that the majority of girls would get married as soon as they left the mission. Nor were parents keen on the idea of their daughters going to school. This was initially looked upon as a loss of vital labour. While the general missionary view was that there was no need to 'burden' the majority of the girls with academic training, there was a small minority who did not agree with this general principle. Commenting on the state of girls' education in Central Province, one of the CMS strongholds, it was observed in 1935 that:

> Though for sometime to come most of our girls in CMS will leave school to be married, there are already a few, and these are increasing, who want an outlet in nursing and teaching for two to three years between school and marriage. (KNA CMS 1/382)

Once the society had realised the social and economic benefits of formal schooling, an insatiable demand for education developed. This desire permeated girls in mission schools; however, they had to contend with the myopic missionary views on girls' education. In retrospect, the educational policies that prevailed in colonial Kenya were reminiscent of the situation in Victorian England a century earlier. The belief that there was 'no need to trouble girls with any more education than they were already receiving, for it might tempt them to try and enter professions of a higher station than the order of the world will permit them to engage in' (Borer, 1976: 228), summarised nineteenth-century sentiments on female education in Britain. Here girls who received lessons in 'English, French, dancing, musick [sic] and all kinds of needlework' (ibid.: 184) might be considered well instructed. Twentieth-century missionaries in Kenya were themselves convinced that their primary duty was to train women to be better wives.

In evaluating the CMS projections for girls' education among the Kikuyu in the 1930s, it was observed that:

> ... the present need is for homemakers and for this we need to train young girls of character who as Christian wives and mothers, and even teachers before marriage will by their Christianity and knowledge of Homecraft be able to make a virtual difference in the standard of Kikuyu life. (KNA CMS 1/382)

This concurred with Bewes' summary of the initial missionary rationale for establishing girls' schools of which he said:

> The chief purpose of these schools was to bring the girls to Christ and to help them towards the building up of real Christian home-life. The recognition that Christian education had wide implications was to come later (Bewes, 1953: 34).

It was considered necessary, as in nineteenth-century Britain, to channel career-oriented mission girls towards less intrusive careers, those that did not threaten male aspirations. The teaching profession was contested terrain. The observations of one missionary in the 1930s gives a lucid insight into the feminisation of the kind of education that mission girls received. The missionaries argued that:

> In order not to overlap or spoil the field for men teachers, these girls might be trained for kindergarten work for the small children, and for our schools to teach sewing, knitting, housecraft and simple nursing. (KNA CMS 1/382)

The government was in full support of this one-sided training for girls. For example, a 1932 Inspector of Schools' report on a CMS school at Kabete complained that 'the curriculum of the girls is much too literary . . . further periods should be allocated to sewing and knitting.' The inspector was convinced that the literary education given to girls would be 'of little practical use when these girls become women'. He did not anticipate that some of them might desire waged employment after leaving school. Public space to a large extent remained male territory. For women, the place of honour was in the kitchen – or was it? The apparent dichotomy between marriage and career created a scenario where those who anticipated female entry into waged employment were discouraged by situations where European women were considered 'pretty useless and always would be so as long as their thoughts are taken up with marriage'. It was argued that as soon as such a woman 'gets down to a bit of work, she gets married' (KNA CMS 1/350). Neither the administrators nor the missionaries anticipated a different model for African women.

In this respect, it could be claimed that missionaries were instrumental in slowing down the pace at which women entered professional occupations. For Kenya, this was an early indication of the conflict between career and motherhood. Where women were admitted to public sector employment, they only occupied the lower levels of the job hierarchy. Hence in an answer to the question 'What is to be the role of women teachers?' the Christian Council of Churches suggested that in general women should not be given the academic training available to men. Rather, they should be trained to teach elementary pupils, 'which is an excellent preparation for the work of bringing up their children' (KNA CMS 1/136). They would also be expected to teach homecraft subjects.

For their part, the girls did not always conform to the missionaries' preconceptions. The missionaries in consequence found it necessary to review periodically their strategies to accommodate those 'who wanted an outlet in nursing and teaching for 2 to 3 years between school and marriage'. The need to provide training for such girls was acknowledged. What the missions had not bargained for, and what eventually transpired, was the fact that a group of career women who sought to combine domesticity with careers emerged. There were, too, women who did not intend to marry and who wished to embark upon full-time careers. For those of either category who went into teaching and nursing, mission schools and hospitals provided ready employment.

Mission influence did not come to an end once the girls had completed their training. The continuation of a strongly protective attitude towards their girls created further setbacks. The missionaries were apprehensive about sending them to work in secular institutions. Neither did they welcome the idea of girls working away from their homes. Their conviction about the need for close supervision bordered on the absurd. They emphasised the need for the girls 'to return home at the end of trainig to be safe to teach in schools near their homes' (KNA CMS 1/350). Ideally, girls taught or worked as nurses and lived in mission schools and hospitals, respectively. Where this was not possible, the missions vetted arrangements for alternative accommodation prior to allowing 'their' girls to take up any teaching or nursing jobs in non-mission institutions. Thus, in 1948, a number of trained female teachers were without jobs 'because it has been impossible for their missions to post them to schools near their homes or at schools where accommodation is available' (KNA CMS 1/136).

The ratio between male and female teachers was unequal in the extreme. Sometimes this created ironical situations. The story is told of one woman who upon embarking on a teaching career found herself being addressed as Mr Rachel. In her area, the term Mr was used to address all teachers and for a long time, all the teachers were male. As the only female teacher, she was an anomaly and the local people used the only title they knew for addressing teachers. This was in the 1940s. More significantly, Rachel broke the tradition by combining her teaching career with marriage. She taught from 1943 to 1964, when she retired.

Without belabouring the point, it is apparent that the nature of girls' training was sexist in its emphases. Up to the mid-1930s, the curriculum at the CMS boarding school for girls at Kabete comprised domestic science, agriculture, and classes for baptised girls who were being trained for village preaching and Sunday school teaching. The Christian Council of Kenya (CCK), an 'umbrella' body representing various missionary groups, expressed limited aspirations for girls. Its major concern revolved around the girls role in the improvement of the standards of domestic and family life. Thus:

... If the education given to the mass of the girls effects an awakening of the mental life, and gives a knowledge of Homecraft subjects, CCK would be happy. For that reason, child welfare, cooking, nutrition and housewifery are the important subjects. Sewing, while of real educational value, cannot rank in importance with these other subjects from the view point of raising the standard of living in the villages. (KNA CMS 1/136)

In conclusion, the council observed that it would not be satisfied with a standard of education which excluded the teaching of these subjects to the majority in the schools. By the end of the 1930s, therefore, the missions were agreed that while a few girls should be given general training 'similar to that of men' (KNA CMS 1/136) and that they could be accommodated at mixed centres, the majority of girls would be given training with an obvious bias in homecraft and practical subject; and the missions underestimated the girls' ability to cope with those subjects that were considered academic.

Training in other professions followed a fairly similar pattern. An appreciable number of mission girls were trained as hospital orderlies, nursing auxiliary and midwives in mission hospitals and some qualified as nurses. However, even the medical profession was affected by the traditional 'myopia' regarding the academic potential of girls. For that reason, the latter were largely channelled into the lower levels of the medical profession.

Conclusion

Nevertheless, the modest training that mission girls received was quite dramatic by comparison with that of their coevals who remained within the traditional system. Working away from home, being financially independent, and aspiring to ideals which had not formed part of their background, was not an easy transformation. For most of these girls, the mission encounter opened new horizons that offered choices heretofore unknown.

In general, they themselves were perceived as agents of change in the fields of agriculture, education and health, where they sought to practise their newly acquired skills. Freund argues that mission girls were significant in the acceptance of new commodities, crops and commerce. Once they left the missions, girls and women disseminated the new skills, tastes and services to those with whom they interacted.

To a large extent, these girls could claim some measure of freedom from the social constraints imposed by their kith and kin. Trained nurses and teachers, they no longer depended on their families for a livelihood. Even modestly educated girls stood a better chance of getting such jobs as were available in rural and urban areas. These included domestic service for European families, especially in the urban areas. In other respects, mission training created opportunities for leadership for its graduates. For women, these included positions in church-related organisations such as the Mothers' Union and Women's Guild.

In retrospect it is possible to underestimate the effects of missions on girls and women. The transformation of their day-to-day patterns of life was striking. As one informant observed, 'once a mission girl, always a mission girl'. To a large extent this statement had little to do with religious conviction. Some of the girls gave up religion with the passage of time. Rather, the phrase referred to women's commitment to external attributes of mission contact. As well as the overriding concern for self-reliance mediated within new contexts, there developed an almost obsessive regard for mission-defined cleanliness and planned cultivation. The latter was especially geared towards the production of a marketable surplus. There was, too, a general adherence to the more overt teachings of the missions. This entailed the condemnation of such institutions as polygymy and alcohol consumption.

By breaking away from the firm hold of their immediate families, mission girls had the opportunity to evolve their own social and power structures within which they sought social mobility. Learning was not restricted to the classrooms. By watching the *bibis*' (female missionaries and the wives of missionaries) changing fashions, they could employ their new skills of cutting-out and sewing. By making clothes for sale some of them realised a degree of financial independence. Despite the limited nature of these opportunities, contact with missions enabled an increasing number of women to move further afield in pursuit of public careers. Their new skills gave them latitude to explore new horizons. Their pioneering status, however, was in many respects unenviable. Balancing as they did between two cultures, mission girls were among the first people who paid heavily for the conflicts and contradictions that characterised the attempt to establish a *modus vivendi*. They were the crucible within which change was mediated.

Bibliography

Anderson, J. (1970) *The Struggle for the School*, Nairobi Publishers

Bewes, T.F.C. (1953) *Kikuyu Conflict: Mau Mau and the Christian Witness*, London Publishers

Bogonko, S.N. (1976) 'Christianism and Africanism at the Cross-roads in Kenya, 1909–1940', Conference paper, Kenya Historical Association, Nairobi Publishers

_____ (1981) 'Catholicism and Protestantism in the Social and Political Development of Kenya' , Conference paper, Eastern Africa Historical conference, Naivasha, Kenya

Borer, M. R. (1984) *Willingly to School: A History of Women's Education*, London Publishers

Freund, B. (1984) *The Making of Contemporary Africa*, London Publishers

Holding, E. M. (1961) *Christian Impact on Meru Institutions*, R.H. Mss., Afr. r.191

Kenyatta, J., (1962) *Facing Mount Kenya*, London, 2nd ed.

K. N. A. Kenya National Archives.

Nottingham, J. and Rosberg, C. (1966) *The Myth of Mau Mau: Nationalism in Kenya*, York

Oliver, R. (1952) *The Missionary Factor In East Africa*, London Publishers

RH Mss. Rhodes House Library unpublished manuscript, Oxford

Sandgren, D.P. (1989) *Christianity and the Kikuyu: Religious Divisions and Social Conflict*, New York Publishers

Strayer, R. W. (1978) *The Making of Mission Communities in East Africa: Anglicans and Africans in Colonial Kenya, 1875–1935*, London Publishers

Swantz, M. (1978) 'Church and the Changing Role of Women in Tanzania', in Fasholé-Luke, E. W. et al., *Christianity in Independent Africa*, London Publishers

Welbourn, R. B. (1961) *East African Rebels*, London Publishers

_____ and Ogot, (1966) *A Place to Feel at Home*, London Publishers

10

Mary Ann Cooke to Mother Teresa: Christian Missionary Women and the Indian Response

A p a r n a   B a s u

Coming out as I did to the lowest of the low, my ardent desire was, and still is
to teach the Bible to the many who had none to care for their souls, leaving
the few in higher life to others. (May Ann Cooke)

I wanted to be a missionary, I wanted to go out and give the life of Christ
to the people . . . In Skopje in Yugoslavia, I was only twelve years old then

. . . It was then that I first knew that I had a vocation for the poor. (Mother Teresa)

Introduction

'If it were not for the help and encouragement given by Mrs Macphee
and her husband, I would never have passed my Matriculation examination and gone on to college,' so wrote my grandmother, Lady Vidyagauri Nilkanth (1876–1958), the first woman graduate of Gujarat.[1] Mrs
Macphee was the Lady Superintendent of the Mahalakshmi Teachers'
Training College in Ahmedabad and her husband was the Principal of
the Church Missionary Society school in the city. Vidyagauri finished
her primary schooling at the Maganbhai Kanyashala the oldest girls'
school in the city, and wanted to continue her education but could not do
so as there were no girls' high schools since girls left school by the age
of nine or ten to be married.

Social Reformers and Missionaries

Vidyagauri's mother's and husband's families were intimately involved
in the social and religious reform movements of Gujarat. Her grandfa-

1. Vidyagauri Nilkanth, *Forum*, Ahmedbad, 1956.

ther, Bholanath Sarabhai (1822–86), was brought up as a devout Hindu and was deeply religious, performing his daily *puja* with great pomp and ceremony. In 1855, Ranchhodlal Chhotalal, the founder of the first textile mill in Ahmedabad and who belonged to the same caste as Bholanath, lent him a copy of Dr Blair's sermons. This had a profound impact on Bholanath, who began to lose faith in traditional Hindu beliefs and rituals, in idol worship and superstitions. In 1872, together with Mahipatram Rupram Nilkanth (1829–91) and a few others he founded the Prarthana Samaj in Ahmedabad. Like the Brahmo Samaj of Bengal, the Prarthana Samaj rejected idol worship, preached monotheism and was influenced by many features of Christianity such as congregational prayers on Sunday. Both Bholanath and Mahipatram not only changed their religious views but were also convinced of the necessity for social reform. They became opponents of child marriage, advocates of widow remarriage and champions of women's education. Thus Vidyagauri received full support from her mother's as well as her husband's family for continuing her education. But as there was no high school for girls, Mrs Macphee made arrangements for holding special classes for Vidyagauri and a few other girls at the Mahalakshmi Training College. Mr Macphee also came over and taught the girls.

Mahipatram, as a teacher in government schools and later as a principal of Mahalakshmi Training College, naturally came into contact with missionary teachers. His wife, Parvatikunvar, was interested in women's education and in the training of women as teachers and nurses and this brought her into touch with women missionaries working in these areas. As reformers they were ostracised by orthodox Hindus. Mahipatram crossed the sea, went to England, thereby defying caste rules, and was excommunicated from his caste. Since there were not many Prarthana Samajists in Gujarat, these reformed families formed links with reformers in other parts of India. The main enemy for them at this time was Hindu orthodoxy and in this battle they regarded the British Government as well as Christian missionaries as their allies. When the Scottish missionary Alexander Duff opened his school in Calcutta in July 1830, the influential social and religious reformer, Rammohun Roy, came in person during the first few days to smooth the path of the teachers and to clear away the deep suspicions that lurked in the minds of many. While the conservatives in Indian society opposed the missionaries on both the evangelical and social reform fronts, the tiny liberal element opposed only the evangelical front and actually emulated their social reform involvement. As Gopal Krishna Gokhale once said, as far as women's education was concerned, Indians were indebted to the English for showing them the way.

Missionaries' Views on Indian Women

Christian missionaries were the first to put women on the agenda of Indian social reform. They drew attention to the low social status of women in India and criticised customs such as *sàti*, female infanticide, child marriage, enforced widowhood and the denial of formal education to women. Charles Grant summarised the missionary attitudes at the end of the eighteenth century when he wrote that Indian women's state was one of subjection and seclusion, to be commiserated with and to be improved if possible.[2] British administrators and scholars shared the missionary perceptions regarding the backward and degraded nature of Indian society, particularly of its women, and highlighting this was one way of establishing the moral superiority of the rulers and justifying colonial rule.

The State of Women's Education in the Early Nineteenth Century

While Hindu *shastras* (scriptures) did not forbid women's education and in fact there are *shlokas* (verses) which not only permit but enjoin women to seek education, by the early nineteenth century, women were by and large denied access to formal education and strong and deeply rooted prejuices against women's education had developed. Women's education was considered to be unnecessary, dangerous and unorthodox. It was believed that an educated woman would become a widow, that she would indulge in romantic intrigue and be unfaithful, that no man would marry an educated girl.[3] Education would spoil feminine qualities and bring disgrace upon the family. Girls were very useful in the house and parents thought that they would forget and despise their ordinary household duties if they learnt to read and write. Educated girls were also less likely to submit to their parents' choice of husbands. Woman's role, it was widely believed, was to look after the house, where she could, by her virtue and chastity, devote herself to her husband and family. For such a role formal education was not necessary. 'A woman's intelligence does not rise higher than her foot, her rightful place was to serve her family.' 'Start with founding a high school for girls', said Bal Gangadhar Tilak, 'and it would soon lead to women running away from home'.[4] It is therefore not surprising that when the

2. Charles Grant, 'Observations on the State of the Morals of the Asiatic Subjects of Great Britain', 1792, Parliamentary Papers, 1812–13, Vol. X.

3. William Adam, *Reports on the State of Vernacular Education in Bengal, 1835–38*, ed. Ananthnath Basu, Calcutta, 1941.

4. *Kesari*, 28 September 1887, 25 October 1887.

Governments of Bombay and Madras undertook inquiries into the state of indigenous education in the 1820s, in the reports received from the Collectors, Judges and Commissioners there was little mention of female scholars attending any of the common schools of the provinces.[5]

William Adam, a missionary who was deputed by Lord William Bentinck to undertake a survey of education in Bengal in the 1830s, also noted that in Rajshahi district, as in other parts of Bengal, female education was practically unknown because of the superstition that a literate girl would be widowed shortly after marriage. So great was the anxiety to prohibit daughters from learning to write that when a sister, in the playful innocence of childhood, is observed imitating her brother's attempts at penmanship, she is expressly forbidden to do so.[6]

Adam found that the only literate women were courtesans, *Vaishnavis* (followers of *Vishnu*) and daughters and widows of *zamindars* (landowners). Courtesans and dancing girls in the service of Hindu temples were taught to read and write so that they could compose poems, write letters and provide intelligent conversation and companionship to men who could not obtain it at home, as respectable women were denied education. Margaret Wilson, on her arrival in Bombay, also noted that education was considered a proper accomplishment for dancing girls but neither 'desirable nor decorous for a woman who was expected to maintain the least respectability of character.'[7] *Vaishnavis*, who did not marry and wandered around preaching the cult of *Vaishnavism* were also literate. The *Vaishnava* religion in Bengal, with its stress on the equality of man and woman among other things, provided room for women from different segments of society: widows of *kulin* Brahmins (a Brahmin sub-group) who had nowhere to go, women who wanted to escape from prostitution after having been seduced by their lovers, prostitutes who after becoming old had lost their occupation, or outcastes aspiring to a higher status. There are references in contemporary records of women in villages, widows, married and unmarried women deserting their homes to join a *Vaishnavite* monastery. Here, religious norms allowed them greater freedom and access to education. They were mainly versed in *Puranic* literature which they in turn taught

5. R.V. Parulekar, *Survey of Indigenous Education in the Province of Bombay, 1820–1830*: 6–11. The Madras Reports have been reprinted in Dharampal, *The Beautiful Tree: Indigenous Education in the Eighteenth Century*, New Delhi, 1983.

6. Willim Adam, *Second Report on the State of Vernacular Education in Bengal*, ed. A. Basu, 1861: 187–311.

7. John Wilson, *A Memoir of Mrs. Wilson of the Scottish Mission*, London, 1937: 195.

to upper caste girls in *Vaishnav* families. Women in the Tagore household had been taught to chant verses by *Vaishnavis* from the beginning of the nineteenth century. Necessity often overruled prejudice, and in Bengal, larger *zamindars* (landowners) taught their daughters to read and write and to maintain accounts so that they would be able to protect and manage their *zamindaris* or estates. Many of the estates, according to Adam, were managed by literate widows.

Child marriage prevented girls from going to school. The giving of a daughter in marriage was considered a religious duty by Hindus and parents became extremely anxious to marry their daughters before they reached puberty. Because of early marriage, girls were deprived of the joys of childhood and if they became child widows, life was an accumulation of miseries and humiliation. Denial of formal education was only one of the many discriminations they faced in a society where the dice were heavily loaded against them.

The Coming of Christian Missionaries

It was no part of the East India Company's original policy to introduce Western education in India. This is not surprising since the Company was primarily a trading corporation interested in making profit. It did not allow Christian missionaries to operate within its territories lest their activities arouse the hostility of the indigenous elites. It was only after considerable pressure from missionary groups in Britain, particularly the Evangelicals, led by the Clapham Sect, that Parliament and the company agreed to include a clause in the Charter Act 1813 allowing Christian missionaries to enter India. Evangelicals such as Charles Grant argued that the spread of Christianity was necessary to remove ignorance and superstition and this could be done by introducing English education which would at the same time also create a class of Indians loyal to British rule. Neither the Company nor the Indian intelligentsia were, to begin with, interested in women's education. The earliest effort to promote women's education was by Christian missionaries who undertook this risky venture, despite strong opposition, mainly for proselytising but also on humanitarian grounds. They felt that education was an important means of influencing people and it would be particularly useful if women could be converted to Christianity. Apart from this, many missionaries felt that education alone would help women to oppose customs like child marriage, *sàti* and enforced widowhood. One of the reasons for the degeneration of Indian society was said to be the low status accorded to women, and missionaries emphasised that education would not only improve the position and status of women but would lead to the regeneration of India. As James Wilson of the Scottish Missionary Society said, 'I am more and more convinced that in seeking for the moral renovation of India, we must make greater efforts than we have yet done to operate upon the female mind . . . . In India it is the stronghold of superstition. Its enlightenment ought to be an object of first concern with us.'[8]. His wife, Margaret Wilson, who was a pioneer of women's education in western India, believed that the general state of native society could never be improved while women's education was neglected since women's ignorance was the source of all corruption.[9]

Day Primary Schools

It is difficult to discover who took the first step towards women's education but all missions were convinced of its importance. It seems to have sprung up simultaneously in Bengal and Madras around 1820. Mrs Traveller, the wife of a missionary of the London Missionary Society, opened a school for Eurasian girls at Vepery in May 1819, but there were no Indian girls among her pupils. Robert May, also of the LMS, started a school for girls at Chinsurah in Bengal in 1818. The Baptist missionaries at Serampore were determined from the start that education should be accessible to girls and in 1819 they enlisted the support of several English ladies of Calcutta to form the Calcutta Female Juvenile Society in an attempt to make some organisational provision for girls' education. This was followed by the establishment of a Native Female Society at Serampore. At Serampore, under the eyes of a respected teacher, several Hindu girls sat in a classroom separated from the boys by a mat partition. This experiment was not, however, extended because of the fear of arousing opposition of the local population.[10]

William Ward, one of the Serampore Baptist Missionaries, during his visit to England in 1820, addressed an open letter to the 'Ladies of Liverpool and the United Kingdom' in which he drew attention in vivid and exaggerated terms to the Indian women's 'state of ignorance and superstition', which he claimed had 'no parallel in the history of tribes the most savage and barbarous'. After giving examples of infanticide, child marriage and above all *sàti*, Ward urged his 'countrywomen' to put an end to the sufferings of Indian women by helping to educate them.[11] The

8. M. D. David, *John Wilson and his Institutions*, Bombay, 1975: 31.

9. Wilson, *A Memoir* London, 1837: 83.

10. David Potts, *British Baptist Missionaries in India, 1793–1833*, Cambridge, 1967: 123.

11. In Potts, ibid.: 123

British and School Society of London, in consultation with Mr Harrington of the Calcutta School Society and William Ward, both of whom then happened to be in England, opened a subscription for a school mistress to be sent out to India. The London Society had written to the Calcutta Society about sending an 'eminently qualified lady for the purpose of introducing a regular system of education among the native female population'. The lady the Society had in mind was was Mary Ann Cooke.

Mary Ann Cooke, who arrived in Calcutta in 1821 and subsequently married the Church Missionary Society's Rev. Isaac Wilson, can be regarded as one of the first missionary women to have come out to India especially to promote girls' education. She was supposed to set up a school for girls in association with the Calcutta School Society but because of the opposition of some Indians and lack of funds, was unable to do so. She therefore started a school under the auspices of the Church Missionary Society with the splendid title The Ladies Society for Native Female Education in Calcutta and its Vicinity. The foundation stone of the Central School was laid on 18 May 1826 on the eastern corner of Cornwallis Square, Calcutta and a brass plate bore the inscription: 'Central School for the Education of Native Females founded by a Society of Ladies which was established on March 25, 1824, Patroness – Lady Amherst; Superintendent – Mrs.Mary Ann Wilson.' Mrs Wilson, together with her husband, started the school in 1828 with 58 girls. By 1829, the daily attendance was between 150 and 200. In 1836, Mary Ann Wilson had 30 schools under her supervision which were attended by nearly 600 pupils. The curriculum included reading, writing, spelling and needlework. The girls' school texts included the Acts of the Apostles, St Mathew's Gospel, Bible history and Pearce's *Geography*. James Long visited the school and noted that 'great success had been . . . obtained in the instruction of females through the indefatigable exertions of Miss Cooke' (now Mrs Wilson).[12] Bishop Heber who visited the school was also most impressed by Miss Cooke' efforts. He set out the principles on which her work was based: 'not to attempt in any direct way the making of converts, but to give as many Indian females as possible, an education of a useful and moral character; to enable them to read the scriptures; and to leave them in short, in such a state of mental cultivation as will enable them in after life to choose their religion for themselves'.[13] Apart from the Central School, the Ladies Society and the CMS had several schools in Calcutta and other towns of Bengal

12. James Long, *Handbook of Bengal Missions*, London, 1848: 413.
13. *Life of Reginald Heber*, by his wife, London, 1830, Vol. II:187.

which Mrs.Wilson supervised. Missionary women opened schools in Nadia, Burdwan, Krishnanagar, Khulna and as far away as Benares and Allahabad.[14] Mary Anne Wilson noted, that

> I believe our female schools are doing much in a general way towards bringing us better acquainted with the Hindus; and not only are the prejudices against teaching females giving way, but a very decided preference is now manifested in favour of the object. The parents of children are chiefly poor, and always ignorant.[15]

Women missionaries also played a significant role in laying the foundations of girls' education in Bombay. On her arrival in Bombay in the late 1820s, Margaret Wilson, the wife of the Scottish missionary James Wilson, took up the education of women as a challenge and established six day schools for girls.[16] She learnt Marathi and Hindustani so that she could teach through the vernacular and herself translated Rollin's Ancient History into Marathi.[17] By 1832 her school had 176 girls; she supervised these schools personally and was convinced that she was serving God:

> I take the entire superintendence of the school and consider that this affords me a most valuable opportunity of conveying a knowledge of divine truth to the females of India. I feel that every increase of occupation brings with it an increase of happiness, and I see in this arrangement a wonderful illustration of the goodness of God. Had I contemplated at a distance the number and variety of duties which now devolve upon me, I should have been appalled at the prospect; but instead of lessening they greatly add to my enjoyment.[18]

By the 1850s, there were nearly 200 pupils in Margaret Wilson's school and after her death, her sisters Anna and Hay Bayne continued to run the school.[19] The efforts of Margaret Wilson and her colleagues influenced Major St Clair Jameson who appealed to the women of Scotland to help their sisters in India. This led to the starting of the 'Ladies Society for Female Education in India' which supported girls' schools in Bombay, Poona and other cities.

---

14. Priscilla Chapman, *Hindu Female Education*, London, 1839. J.Long, *Handbook of Bengal Missions* 1848; J.A. Richey, *Selections From Educational Records, Pt II, 1840–1859*, Calcutta, 1922.

15. Long, *Handbook* 1848: 415.

16. S. Mookerjee (ed.) *The Wilsonian, 1832–1957*, Bomby, 1957: 20.

17. M. Weitbrecht, *The Women of India and Christian Work in the Zenana*, London, 1875: 176.

18. ibid.

19. M. D. David, *John Wilson and his Institutions*, Bombay, 1975: 31–2.

Thus all the Christian missions opened day schools for girls where reading, writing, arithmetic, environmental education, general knowledge, tailoring and knitting were taught. In some schools music also formed a part of the curriculum.[20] Pupils in most mission schools were drawn mainly from the very poorest and the lower castes. William Adam, who conducted a detailed survey of the state of education in Bengal in the 1830s, reported that mission schools became popular among the Bagdis, Muchis, Bauris, Doms, Haris, Tantis, Chandals, Kurmis and other low castes. Mary Carpenter, though, states that in Poona twenty-five little Brahmin girls attended the mission boarding schools as day scholars.[21] Margaret Wilson appointed Brahmin teachers to attract pupils from this high caste.[22] But as soon as any conversion took place, girls were immediately withdrawn and often the school was forced to close down.

Many of the mission schools, particularly in the villages and remote areas were extremely primitive. There were no desks, bookcases or libraries. An ordinary house would be rented, some cheap matting procured and a *dai* or woman servant engaged to call the girls. Wooden slates, chalk and a blackboard were the only pieces of equipment. The teacher had a few books but not enough for each child to have one. Girls' schools were usually taught only up to Class VII, as girls left after that to get married. Absenteeism and dropping out were very common as girls from poor families were needed at home to look after younger brothers and sisters as well as to help with household work. Mission schools often gave money and offered prizes for regular attendance. In many cases a copy of the Bible and some clothes were given once a year to attract and retain pupils. In Bengal, peons known as *hirkara* were employed to fetch absentee pupils from their homes. By 1854, there were about 7000 girls at schools run by missionary societies; the majority of pupils were native Christians but there were also Hindu girls from high castes.[23]

College Education

The number of girls' schools increased and their quality improved after 1857 following the Education Despatch of 1854, which recognised the importance of girls' education and also offered grants-in-aid. Initially, the missionary societies limited their work to elementary schools but

21. Mary Carpenter, *Six Months in India*, Vol.I, London, 1868: 113.
22. Wilson, *Memoir*, 1837: 235.
23. *Report of Indian Education Commission*, 1883: 11.

later on, they devoted the greater portion of their energy and resources to secondary and collegiate education. In Bombay, the Wilsons established a High School and College, which was later named after them. Wilson College was the first arts college to admit women. The first two girls to join the College in 1866 were two Parsis, Ratanbai Ardeshir Vakil and her sister Mehrbai. Ratanbai specialised in French and was elected a Fellow of Bombay University in 1890. From then until her death five years later, she taught French in Wilson College. Mehrbai studied medicine.[24] In 1897–8, twelve girls were studying in the College, of whom seven were studying for the Preliminary Examination, three for the Intermediate and two for the B.A. Over the years a large number of women graduated from the College. Chandramukhi Basu, one of the first two women graduates of Calcutta University, and the first woman graduate of Bombay University, Cornelia Sorabji, were both Christians. Chandramukhi had studied at the American Presbyterian School at Dehra Dun from where she had appeared for her matriculation examination of Calcutta University in 1878.

Isabella Thoburn was the sister of the American Methodist, Bishop James Thoburn, who was in the North Western Provinces (UP). Until the 1870s, American missions did not send out unmarried women to India as they considered them to be 'helpless creatures' incapable of coping with Indian conditions. It was, therefore, wives of missionaries who did the work of educating Indian women. Bishop Thoburn, however, thought otherwise. A Methodist Women's Foreign Missionary Society was established in 1870 in the United States and this sponsored Isabella Thoburn's trip to India. Upon her arrival in Lucknow, she started a primary school for girls with six pupils. Gradually the school expanded and in 1886, two girls, Leelavati Singh and Shourat Chuckerbutty, passed the matriculation examination of Calcutta University. Isabella then decided to open college classes for women. The Methodist Society in the United States was not very enthusiastic about this and was unwilling to fund the venture. But Isabella went ahead with her plans. Shourat's mother donated 500 rupees and college classes were started with three pupils. Isabella believed that if India were to progress and her women be emancipated, it was necesary to educate and train women who could be leaders. She appealed for funds in America emphasising that India needed women teachers and doctors. Known as the Women's Christian College, it was renamed Isabella Thoburn College after the founder's death in 1901. This was the first women's Christian college, not only in India, but in the whole of Asia.

Isabella did not lose sight of the Christian basis of the college. Money had been raised in America to carry the Christian faith to the women of India and the aim was conversion through education. Chapter worship, Sunday church and religious instruction were a vital part of the curriculum. But Isabella wanted to attract women from higher castes and elite families who could be trained as leaders. There was a belief by this time that if a few from the top stratum of society could be converted, Christianity would percolate down to the masses. As Leelavati Singh, one of the first graduates from the College and later its first Indian President, wrote, it was to accomplish this aim of developing leadership qualities that the college was founded. 'My college taught me to love India . . . [Isabella] planted true patriotism in me . . . I learnt about the glories of the past...I perceive the tragedies of the present . . . I know the future lies in our hands, yours and mine.'[25]

Isabella Thoburn College was followed by the opening of the Women's Christian College in Madras and Kinnaird College, Lahore. In 1932, Christian missions ran twelve of the twenty arts colleges for women and of the 2,966 women attending colleges of all kinds, 726 were Christians.[26] In the early years, in Christian women's colleges, all the teachers and most of the pupils were Christians. But soon these colleges drew pupils from elite Hindu and Muslim families. In 1932, two in every three non-Christian families who sent their girls to college preferred to enroll them in Christian institutions.[27]

Orphanages and Boarding Schools

A second important agency for encouraging girls' education were missionary orphanages and boarding schools, which were established all over the country and generally supervised by wives of missionaries. Mrs Charles, the wife of the Senior Chaplain of the Scottish Church in Calcutta, brought together a few orphan girls and fed, clothed and educated them at her own expense. When she left India, the orphans were transferred to Mrs MacDonald, wife of Rev. John MacDonald. A Society of Ladies was formed in Scotland for the promotion of female education in Calcutta and in 1840 Miss Laing was sent to superintend these orphans. As the number of orphans increased, she was joined by anoth-

25. F. Nichols (ed.), *Isabella Thoburn Who Went to India, Collection of her Reminiscences by her Friends and Admirers*, Women's Foreign Missionary Society, 1929: 96.

26. *Progress of Education in India, 1927–32*, Vol. I: 185–9.

27. ibid.

er Scottish woman, Miss Saville. The manner in which some of these orphanages were founded and attracted pupils can be gleaned from the following extract about an orphan home conducted by Mrs Wilson:

> One widow, through the pressure of poverty, desired to be freed from the burden of maintaining her daughter, another, having a child at the point of death with cholera, brought her to the school in order to get medicine, and on her recovery, made her over to those who had been instrumental in saving her life, a third girl having embraced Christianity, and been cast out by her relatives, sought and found refuge in the central school; others having been left destitute by the death of their parents, had recourse to the same refuge. Thus in various ways, a considerable number of destitute children were brought under the care of Mrs.Wilson . . . .[28]

The main objectives were clearly spelled out by her:

1. The object of the school shall be to afford support and Christian instruction to destitute native girls, particularly widows and orphans.
2. The school shall be placed under the charge of a committee, consisting of Mrs Williams, Mrs Wilson, Mrs Money and Mrs Webb. Mrs Wilson was to act as general superintendent . . .
3. The children admitted shall be decently clothed, and a small sum shall be allowed for their food.
4. When relatives are disposed to take proper charge of the girls, they shall be allowed to lodge with them; and when the case is otherwise, and the girls are particularly destitute, some arrangement shall be made for their board.
5. When the girls have made a certain progress in reading, they shall be instructed in female work. Encouragement shall be given to such of them as may be disposed to become *ayahas* (maid-servants) to acquire the requisite knowledge and practice.[29]

These orphanages and boarding schools run by different mission societies provided shelter for destitute children during famines and epidemics and also for children from the poorer sections of society and child widows. They provided a minimum education and often some vocational training such as lacemaking, embroidery, needlework, knitting, dressmaking and weaving. The idea behind this was to make the pupils self reliant and enable them to earn a livelihood and be economically independent. Some of the orphanages trained pupils in agriculture and industrial work.

28. Richey, *Selections,* 1922: 42.
29. Wilson, *Memoir,* 1922: 334.

The *Zenana* System

The *zenana* system of home education was the third important agency of missionary education for women. The importance of *zenana* education was reflected in Wood's Despatch of 1854 and in the Hunter Commission's Report of 1882, both of which recommended that *zenana* teaching be brought under a comprehensive educational system and assisted through grants-in-aid. The Hunter Commission expressed the view that for the education of girls of better classes who did not go to school, a system of domestic instruction was needed: 'Actuated in many cases by religious motives, *zenana* teachers have brought some measure of secular instruction into the homes of those who would otherwise have been wholly debarred from it. We see no reason why the secular instruction imparted under the supervision of ladies worthy of confidence should not be recognised and assisted, so far as it can be tested by a proper inspecting agency.'[30] Girls from upper caste/class families did not go to schools because they often practised *purdah* and young girls left school to get married. These problems were to some extent solved by the development of the *zenana* system. Popular lore attributed the invention of *zenana* education to a Mrs H. C. Mullens who, it was said, 'opened the *zenanas* at the point of her embroidery needle.' (An Indian gentleman admired slippers she had embroidered for her husband and invited her to teach his wife this art.) Helen Montgomery is adamant that Mrs John Sale actually began this practice when she gained access to the inner compartments of a gentleman's home in Jessore.[31] Indian elites wanted their women to be educated and they regarded *zenana* education as acceptable and it was particularly common among the *bhadralok* (gentry) families in Bengal. Rev. Fordyee and Mrs Mullens succeeded in getting access to some of the leading aristocratic families of Calcutta. Keshub Chandra Sen and Debendranath Tagore both employed missionary women to teach the women in their houses. The first successful teacher associated with this system in Bengal was Mrs Togod who learnt Bengali and taught her pupils in this language. She taught, among others, Kailashbasini Debi, wife of Kissory Chand Mitter.[32] In 1871, there were more *zenana* pupils in Bengal than in the other six Presidencies put together.

30. Report of the Indian Education Commission, 1882:.542–3.

31. Geraldine Forbes, 'In Search of the Pure Heather: Missionary Women in Nineteenth Century India,' *Economic and Political Weekly*, 28 April, 1986.

32. Malavita Karlekar, *Voices From Within: Earley Personal Narratives of Bengali Women*, New Delhi, 1991.

Popularisation of *zenana* education created a demand for female teachers willing to work in India. Here missionaries took the lead. Wives of missionaries had been active in setting up schools and in domestic education. Single women started coming out from England in the second half of the nineteenth century. Until then the choice for them was limited to either staying at home or seeking employment as governesses or companions. Therefore, when opportunities became available to travel abroad as teachers, it was not difficult to find educated young women of a religious bent ready to accept the challenge.

In Bombay, the first Society to promote *zenana* education was the Society for the Promotion of Female Education in the East, which initiated this work in 1842 by sending women from England to teach Parsi ladies. A training school and home for *zenana* teachers was established in north-west India. The Society was founded in 1834 by an American missionary, Rev. David Abeel, who had appealed to single women to help in converting the heathen. The Ladies Association for the Promotion of Female Education among the Heathen, which was closely associated with the Society for the Propagation of the Gospel, was established in 1866. Its aim was to promote female education and it invited applications from young women who had 'a love of adventure, a sense of dullness or friction at home, a desire for change or for a means of livelihood'.

When Keshub Chandra Sen visited England in 1870, he addressed a meeting of the Victorian Discussion Society. In his speech, he appealed to English women to do all in their power

> to effect the elevation of the Hindu women . . . . The best way in which that help can be given is for some of you to embark on the grand and noble enterprise of going over personally to that great country . . . . At the present moment a thousand Hindu houses are open to receive and welcome English governesses, well-trained, accomplished English ladies, capable of doing good to their Indian sisters, both by instruction and personal example.And what sort of education do we expect and wish from you? An unsectarian, liberal, sound, useful education . . . an education calculated to make Indian women good wives, mothers, sisters and daughters. Such an education we want for our ladies, and are there no feeling hearts in England capable of responding to this exhortation and invitation?[33].

The rhetoric of Keshub had an electrifying effect on Victorian women. Annette Akroyd, a Unitarian, was not present at the meeting but heard about it and was deeply moved. Her father had died recently leaving her with a 'blankness and dreariness inexpressible'. She had been educated at Bedford College, was not married and was undecided about what to do as the options were limited. She therefore came forward to

---

33. William H. Beveridge, *India Called Them*, London, 1947: 84–5.

answer Keshub's call, met him several times and decided to go to India. She arrived in Calcutta in October 1872, and the next year opened a school for girls, the Hindu Mahila Vidyalaya. She taught Keshub's wife at home, though later differences of opinion developed between her and Keshub over the kind of education to be given to women.

Zenana teachers taught reading, writing, letter composition, ordinary accounts and often music, needlework, embroidery and darning. Missionary women were interested as this gave them an opportunity to enter the inner recesses of an Indian home. They insisted that the Bible and simplified stories from the Scriptures should form part of the teaching. Indians did not mind this as long as efforts were not made at conversion. Gradually, the missionary women satisfied themselves that secular education was better than no education at all and that they were planting 'seeds' that would grow later. Examinations were held behind the *purdah* in the homes and suitable rewards were given to those who passed. The missionary women usually described the women in the *zenana* as stupid, listless, shy, indifferent and apathetic to learning. It was the men who usually decided whether or not their wives or daughters were to be educated or not and often the women may not have been interested. But this was not always so. Women like Kailashbashini Debi and Bamasundari held, like the missionary women, that the panacea for those in *purdah* was education and a non-ritualistic, secular way of life. We do not know enough of what these Indian women thought of the missionary women.

Teacher Training Schools

As there was a prejudice against men teaching girls, the need for women teachers both for schools as well as for *zenana* education was soon felt. Mary Carpenter, the daughter of a Unitarian priest who had been a friend of Raja Rammohun Roy and Dr Joseph Tukaram, visited India four times during the 1860s and 1870s. In 1867 she toured the whole of Bombay Presidency extensively. She was keenly interested in women's education and felt that the lack of trained women teachers was one of the reasons for its slow progress. She suggested the opening of training schools for women teachers, and as a result three such schools were established in Bombay, Poona and Ahmedabad. When Mary Carpenter visited Calcutta in 1869 with a scheme for promoting women's education Manomohun Ghosh was one of her most ardent supporters. She proposed the establishment of a Brahmo normal school[34] to train

34. Brahmo Samaj, a society founded by Rammohan Roy (1772–1833) in 1828 promoted worship of one God and rejected 'idol worship' or popular Hindu devotion.

women teachers for girls' schools, and she urged them to expand the usual home economics programme by offering additional subjects that would stimulate women's curiosity and develop their minds. During her first two trips to India, she met Brahmo Samaj leaders in Calcutta and urged them to help extend American and English efforts to emancipate the women of India. In 1932, five of the seven teachers' training colleges for women in British India were Christian institutions and over 100 of the 157 students were Christians.

Medical Education

Christian missionaries were often required to provide medical care. The Baptist missionaries at Serampore were compelled to treat the sick, though neither Carey, Marshman nor Ward had any professional medical training. As early as 1810, the Baptists obtained a volunteer doctor, William Jones, who was accompanied by a Miss Chaffin to whom belongs the honour of being the first missionary nurse.[35] Mary Warburton Booth who lived and worked in Gorakhpur in the United Provinces, began as a teacher but was forced to do medical work because of lack of hospitals and doctors.

It was only in 1835 that Lord William Bentinck, largely due to the urging of Alexander Duff, established the Calcutta Medical College where for the first time Indian students could study western medicine and surgery. Christian missionary women also realised the need for women doctors as Indian women would not go to male doctors, especially for childbirth. A pioneering effort in this direction was made by Miss Clara Swain, who belonged to the Methodist Episcopal Church of America. She began her work in Bareilly in the United Provinces but later moved to Bombay. Due to her efforts, by 1887, seventeen girls were studying at the Grant Medical College, Bombay, of whom two were matriculates working for a degree, while the others were awarded diplomas and certificates.[36]

Hospitals exclusively for women were also established in the Bombay Presidency. The first such hospital was opened in Poona by the Church of Scotland. In 1892, St Margaret's Hospital was opened and a similar hospital was started at Kolhapur by the American Presbyterian Mission. Missionaries helped to train women as doctors, nurses and midwives. Among the women who studied medicine in western India

---

35. Potts, *Baptist Missionaries,* 1967: 65.

36. Margaret Balfour and Ruth Young, *The Work of Medical Women in India,* Bombay, 1985: 16.

were Anandibai Joshi, Annie Jagannadhan and Rukmabai. Anandibai Gopal (Joshi) graduated in 1886 from the Women's Medical College at Philadelphia. She returned to India and was appointed to take charge of the women's ward of the Albert Edward Hospital at Kolapur. Unfortunately, she suffered from tuberculosis and died in 1887 before she could take up her assignment. Annie Jagannadhan went to Edinburgh School of Medicine in 1888 and obtained the triple qualification of the Scottish College in 1892 and was appointed house surgeon in the Cama Hospital. But like Anandibai, was unable to pursue her career because she too died of tuberculosis in 1894.

Rukmabai was educated in a Free Church Mission School and afterwards as a *zenana* pupil. She was an accomplished and clever girl who had been married in infancy to Dadaji Bhikaji, a delicate and consumptive husband. When in 1887 she refused to join him and consummate the marriage, he filed a suit in the Bombay High Court for the enforcement of conjugal rights. The Court ordered her to join her husband but she refused. One of Rukmabai's friends in Bombay, a CMS missionary, daughter of the Bishop of Carlisle, encouraged her to appeal to the British public and the Bishop published her pathetic letter in *The Times* of 9 April 1887. Rukmabai went on to study medicine at the London School of Medicine in 1889 and returned to India in 1895. She took charge of the women's hospital in Surat, and in 1918 was selected for the women's medical service and at the same time received the offer of appointment as Medical Officer in charge of the *zenana* state hospital in Rajkot, which she accepted.

The Indian Response

Missionary efforts for women's education were like a drop in the ocean; while they were limited to relatively small numbers they nevertheless reached remote areas and sections of the population like the low castes, untouchables and tribals in whom neither the colonial rulers nor the Indian intelligentsia were interested. Most of the missionaries came from the lower-middle and working classes, from families of tradesmen and artisans, often described as the 'aristocracy of labour'. Reaction to the missionaries varied. The early social reformers like Rammohun Roy were influenced by them and befriended them. Rammohun wrote a tract on the 'Precepts of Jesus' and praised the ethical teachings of Christianity. This was true of reformers in western India also. But as nationalist sentiments became stronger and hostility to foreign rule increased, Christian missionaries were viewed with increasing suspicion as handmaidens of colonial rule. Reformers like Swami Dayananad Saraswati, the founder of the Arya Samaj, who was active towards the end of the nineteenth century, bitterly criticised the missionaries, though the Arya Samaj copied many of the features and programme of the Christian missions.

The higher castes were suspicious of the missionaries' activity and feared conversion. The literature of the period reveals a great deal of hostility to missionary activity but this was written by the literate upper castes. The view of missionaries from below was different from the view from the top. A low caste social reformer like Jyotiba Phule in Maharashtra, who was an ardent advocate of female education, viewed missionary activity with favour as mission schools admitted children of all castes as well as girls. Women who were given an opportunity to go to school for the first time by the missionaries also had a different perception. Vidyagauri Nilkanth, for instance, was full of gratitude to Mrs Macphee. Ramabai Saraswati, a remarkable woman widowed at a very young age, found the Hindu attitude towards women and widows totally repugnant. She was attracted by the Christian teachings on the equality of sexes and the opportunities for education and training that missionaries gave to women. Her contact with Christian missionaries in Poona took her to England where she was baptised in Wantage parish church. On her return to India, she founded Sharda Sadan, an organisation for widows, and a school for day scholars. The main objective of Sharda Sadan was to make young widows economically self sufficient by training them as teachers, housekeepers, nurses and midwives. Particular attention was given to moral education, good manners and home management. Besides the usual subjects, sewing, embroidery, knitting and clay modelling were also taught. Ramabai faced stiff opposition from orthodox Hindus as well as social reformers when it became known that some of the girls in Sharda Sadan had been converted to Christianity. Although she was often dubbed a 'demon', widows and young girls continued to enrol themselves saying, 'Let her be a demon! We don't mind. At least she looks after us well. That is enough for us . . . '[37] Undaunted by the hostility shown towards her, particularly by the Poona Brahmins, Ramabai established Mukti Sadan, a salvation home for the women victims of the famine which broke out in the Central Provinces in 1896. At Kedgaon, 30 miles from Poona, she started a new colony and in addition to Mukti Sadan opened a Rescue Home, called Kripa Sadan, which within three years had 300 inmates. Similarly when

---

37. Devdutt Narayan Tilak, *The Brilliant Lady of Maharashtra:Ramabai Saraswati,* 1960: 231. See also Ramabai Ranade, Ranade, *His Wife's Reminiscences,* trans. Kusumvati Deshpande: 222–3.

famine broke out in Gujarat in 1900, Ramabai personally sent twenty of her Sisters to rescue women affected by the famine and soon her institution had around 1,900 inmates.

Christian missionaries helped to reduce the historic prejudices against women's education by starting schools and colleges, providing domestic instruction and emphasising the need for professional education, particularly for the training of teachers, nurses and doctors. Contrary to missionary belief, the education of women in India was not entirely novel. Even in the early nineteenth century there were quite a few educated women among the higher castes, but they were educated at home. Lower caste girls often went to the village schools until they were nine or ten years old. However, a lack of girls' schools and a reluctance to send girls to those that did exist made the missionaries' efforts important. Not only did they educate girls who might perhaps have otherwise remained illiterate, but they stimulated Indian interest. Gaurmohan Vidyalankar's *Strisiksha Vidyalankar*, published in 1822 by the Calcutta School Book Society, advocated women's education and was perhaps more effective than missionary efforts in this direction. But it was the work of missionaries which precipitated Indian interest in women's education.

The missionary example was emulated by Indian social reformers, both men and women. In 1863 the Brahmo Samaj established the *Bamabodhini Sabha*, an association for women's education. The same year it started publishing *Bamabodhini Patrika*, which organised a correspondence course for girls known as *antahpur shiksha* or education for women at home in their secluded sphere. A number of social reformers started educating their wives at home. One such example was Ramabai Ranade, the wife of Justice Madhav Govind Ranade, who was educated first at home by her husband – in fact he began teaching her on their wedding night – and later by Miss Herford, a Christian woman who taught her English. Inspired by the work of missionaries and particular-ly by Ramabai Saraswati, she founded the *Seva Sadan* in Bombay in 1908 and a year later a similar institition in Poona, where under her personal care and guidance there were classes for adult women, industrial classes, a girls' hostel, a teacher training college, a girl's high school, a nursing school and a medical department. The *Seva Sadan* became more than an institution, it became a movement. Similarly, in some towns of Gujarat *Vanita Vishrams* were started for educating girls who had been withdrawn from school after marriage. Many women who studied in missionary schools started schools for girls. The number of girls actually affected by Christian missionary education was admittedly small. It was, however, the missionaries who, in spite of the limitations of their work, demonstrated that Indian women were capable of better things and who in the long run stimulated in women themselves the desire to improve their lives.

A new type of family and a new woman were emerging among the liberal intelligentsia in the latter half of the nineteenth century. Missionaries contributed to creating and popularising this new role model of the educated woman who introduced into the home, order, thrift and cleanliness and who ran the house in an efficient manner. She was no longer in *purdah* and could venture outside the home. She could go to school, accompany her husband to public entertainments, join women's associations and do charitable and philanthropic work, which was the natural extension of her nurturing, maternal role. She was a good mother and wife, a companion to her husband but also socially responsible.

Although the Raj was religiously neutral, the fact that Great Britain was a Christian country and that missionaries enjoyed the active sympathy of a large number of British officials, naturally helped the expansion of Christian missions. The government conceived its role as largely neutral and left education and social services to private agencies. Through their humanitarian work among the wretched, the poor and the oppressed, exemplified in the magnificent work of Mother Teresa, missionary women have made on impact on India. Mother Teresa began her life in India as a teacher in the Loreto Convent School in Calcutta. But then she felt an inner call to give up teaching and go out into the streets to serve the poorest of the poor. She went to Patna for three months to the American Medical Missionary Sisters for an intensive training course in nursing and after returning to Calcutta opened her first slum school with five pupils. She chose to live in the slums of Calcutta amidst all the dirt, disease and misery. Initially, she faced a great deal of opposition and even death threats because it was felt that she was converting the dying and the orphans whom she rescued from the streets. But when people began to see the good she was doing for all, regardless of caste or creed, there was widespread appreciation for her selfless service and dedication.

Women missionaries, like all Christian missionaries, were implicated in the colonial policies of the British. Through their educational activity and their emphasis on the superiority of Western learning through the English language (a belief they shared with Macaulay, Mill and a large number of liberals and Utilitarians) they helped the Raj in its efforts to dominate the Indian mind, both culturally and intellectually.

Missionaries did not succeed in their original aim of conversion. The Church in its proselytising activity was an object of suspicion and hostility. In the schools and colleges started by missionaries from the late nineteenth century onwards for the children of the elite, the majority of students were non-Christians and not many converts came from them. Through those schools, however, some Christian ideals, such as the belief that the way to God lies through the service of humanity, the ideal of *seva* (service), percolated through national life.

Bibliography

Adam, William (1861) *Reports on the State of Education in Bengal,1835–38*, ed. A. Basu (see p.190), Calcutta

Albuquerquie, Teresa (1985) *Urbs Prima in India, An Epoch in the History of Bombay, 1840–65*, Bombay

Balfour, I. Margaret and Young, Ruth (1929) *The Work of Medical Women in India*, Bombay

Basak, N. L. (1976) *History of Vernacular Education in Bengal,1800–1854*, Calcutta

Beveridge, W. H. (1947) *India Called Them*, London

Carpenter, Mary (1867) *Addresses to the Hindus*, Calcutta

_____ (1868) Six Months In India, Vol.I, London

Cowan, G. Minna, (1912) *The Education of the Women of India*, New York

David, M. D. (1975) *John Wilson and his Institutions*, Bombay

Forbes, Geraldine (1986) 'In Search of the Pure Heathen: Missionary Women in Nineteenth Century India', *Economic and Political Weekly*, 28 April

Fuller, Marcus, B. (1984), *The Wrongs of Indian Womanhood*, New Delhi, [1900]

Ingham, Kenneth (1956) *Reformers in India*, Cambridge

Karlekar, Malavika,(1991) *Voices From Within, Early Personal Narratives of Bengali Women*, New Delhi

Laird, M. A.,(1971) *Bishop Heber in Northern India*, Cambridge

Mishra, Lakshmi (1966) *Education of Women in India*, Bombay

Mohar Ali, Muhammad, (1965) *The Bengali Reaction to Christian Missionary Activities,1833–57*, Chittagong

Mookerjee, S. (ed.) (1957) *The Wilsonian,1832–1957*, Bombay

Mote, H. V. (1972) *Vishab Sharda, Vol. I, 1897–1947*, Bombay

Neill, Stephen (1966) *Colonialism and Christian Missions*, London

_____ (1985) *A History of Christianity in India,1979-1858*, Cambridge

Nilkanth, Vidyagauri, (1956) *Forum*, Ahmedabad

Oddie, G. A. (1979) *Social Protest in India*, New Delhi

Parulekar, R. V. (1950) *Survey of Indigenous Education in the Province of Bombay, 1820–30*, Bombay,

Potts, E. David. (1967) *British Baptist Missionaries in India, 1793–1833*, Cambridge

Richey, J. A. (ed.) (1922) *Selections from Educational Records*, Pt II, 1839–1854, Calcutta

Sharp, Henry (ed.), *Selections from Educational Records*, Pt.1, 1793–1839, Calcutta

Tilak, Devdutt Narayan (1960) *The Brilliant Lady of Maharashtra-Pandita Ramabai*, Nasik

Weitbrecht, M.(1875) *The Women of India and Christain Work in the Zenana*, London

Wilson, John (1837) *A Memoir of Mrs. Wilson of the Scottish Mission*, London

11
Does Christianity Empower Women? The Case of the Anaguta of Central Nigeria

Elizabeth Isichei

Introduction

The suggestion that Christianity can empower women seems implausible to many Western feminists. Some have concluded that Christianity is irredeemably patriarchal and have moved to a post-Christian position, Mary Daly being perhaps the most celebrated instance. Feminists who remain Christians have tended to stress the silencing, marginalisation and oppression of women in earlier and contemporary churches. In the Nigerian context, a colonial official's report on an Igbo community in the 1930s made the interesting point that Christianity reinforced its traditional patriarchal values (Vaux, 1936: paras 62–6). But, it seems to be much more generally true in Africa that women experienced Christianity as empowering. It gave them a place on which to stand, from which they could bypass or challenge male-dominated sacred worlds. Truth is always complex however, and sometimes Christianity paved the way to new forms of marginalisation.

The focus of this paper is the way in which Christian mission has affected women among the Anaguta of central Nigeria, who have adopted Christianity only since the 1950s. They are a very small ethno-linguistic group, numbering perhaps 5000 who have, until very recently, resolutely evaded the impact of the Western world despite living very close to the modern city of Jos. Originally, as Map I shows, they lived in five settlements (*upana*) in the Naraguta and Shere Hills. During this century they have migrated either to Jos itself, or to Maza valley or to the plains north of the city which Anaguta call Hwoll, Kunga or Babale. Each Anaguta woman identifies herself as a member of a particular descent group (*tibiri*) and *upana*.[1] At the end of 1983, I attended the installation ceremony of the

1. Anaguta history and social structure are analysed in Isichei (1991a and b).

Map I: The Anaguta and Urban Jos

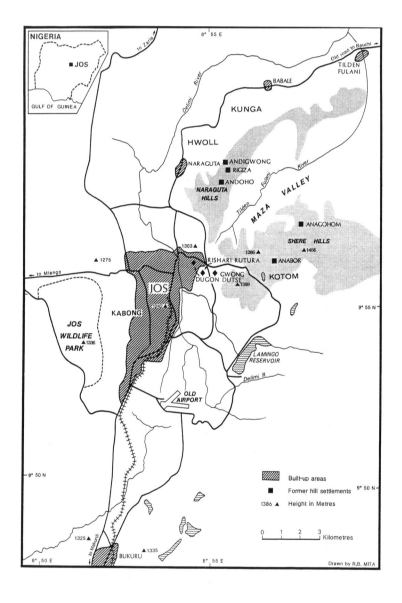

Ugomo (District Head) of Rigiza, the most recently settled of the five *upana*. A group of women sang, in a mixture of Eguta and Hausa, with much gusto and many repetitions:

> *Ujah ugadu, sarauta gado.*
> *Sarakuna mu yabi Yesu.*
> 'Rule is an inheritance.
> Rulers we are praising Jesus.'

Several months later I met with a group of women to record traditional songs. Among the Anaguta as among other northern Nigerian peoples, notably the Hausa, women traditionally sang songs of protest while grinding grain, a socially sanctioned vehicle for expressing discontent, especially with husbands (Isichei, 1983: 2242). I was told that Anaguta women no longer sing these songs, partly because of the introduction of mechanical grinders, and partly because of the impact of Christianity, which has they claim (improbably, to the cynical observer) led to greater marital harmony. A male singer, Ita Tua, a very considerable creative artist, sang grinding songs with alacrity, turning them into a vehicle for his own reflections on life (Isichei, 1984: 1170–1). The women chose to sing something very different:

> Christ [*Uwyang*, God] had died, has risen because of us.
> Our hearts are white.

When women did sing traditional songs their content tended to marginalise rather than empower women. The wedding song, Izara, runs:

> If you marry Yongol
> You must buy her oil
> For she has a rough skin.
> If you marry Zara
> you must buy her camwood
> For she has a black skin.

I was told that this means that women are insatiable and grasping in their demands. It was sung with energy and good humour, as was a song which belonged to moonlight courting, *Iyarwa*:

> If you want a young girl come and take me.
> If you want beauty, who will get me?

At the time, I found all this deeply perplexing and disconcerting. Years later, I begin to understand it. The building-blocks of our understanding must come from an analysis of traditional Anaguta religious and social concepts and structures.

The Anaguta World[2]

At the heart of the Anaguta world lay the secret-sacred. Surounded by larger neighbours, they believed that safety lay in invisibility. The traditional Anaguta hero is one who can make himself (sic) invisible. A favourite proverb states that the Anaguta are a basket of water. This has understandably been taken as mirroring a perception of demographic decline (Diamond, 1972: 362). But its meaning is in fact quite different – that the Anaguta survive and flourish when they flow or become invisible, like water.

The realm of the secret-sacred was entirely dominated by elderly men, who were believed to be sorcerers. They held specific offices which were exercised in particular ritual contexts, and for most of the time lived the life of ordinary farmers – though treated with healthy respect by others for their reputed supernatural powers.

In this world of the secret-sacred, women were almost entirely excluded. None of the sacred offices was held by women. A women's spokesperson, the *ambatuga* (mother of women) communicated with the senior men through a male official, *Itatuge*. *Banduma*, an elderly man, had ritual responsibility for women's work parties and their associated dances.

In modern times, regular women's meetings are held; their antiquity is unknown. They are held at the level of the *tibiri* and *upana*, as well as for the entire Anaguta community. The women of each *upana* have an

2. The major source for what follows is fieldwork conducted between 1983 and 1985. It was financed by a research grant from the University of Jos. B. P. Ateka was my main research assistant among the Anaguta. He also collected his own oral texts, given *in extenso* in his Special Project in History. The women's songs were recorded in early 1984; the group was headed by Jumai Garba and Jumai Bulus. Ita Tua sang in duet with Tasha Djang; both played the *burma* (thumb piano). Adrian Collett and I did independent research on the Anaguta. Collett, an anthropologist, worked in Andigwong while I was abroad on sabbatical. I am happy to place on record my esteem for his excellent study, and especially his continuing concern for the Anaguta.

Pius Pam acted as my research assistant among the Berom of Du, Forom and Zawan in July and August 1977, and also translated the Hausa autobiography of Toma Bot for me.

acknowledged leader, *Ambatuga*, and meet on the third Sunday of each month – 'We have discussions and finish with dances'. It is probable that these meetings, and the multiplication of *Ambatuga* title holders, are recent innovations.

Only older men could visit Anaguta shrines; the name of the most sacred could not be spoken in women's presence. Women could not visit the traditional burial grounds, even if a woman was being buried. The High God, *Uwyang*, was remote. Religious life was dominated by three spirit cults, all of which excluded women. *Andugubishe* were audible, invisible spirits in the sacred grove *upeinpein*, near Anabor (Map I). *Anaburr* were also heard but not seen. They manifested at night, singing through a voice disguiser. One of their functions was to discern and accuse witches. Women stayed inside while they sang, placating the spirits with gifts of beer and food.

The ritual associated with *Jankai* (Red Head), representing the third spirit cult, was introduced from peoples further east, perhaps in the nineteenth-century, and a *Jankai* wears a helmet of red abrus and a billowing gown. Women could not join the cult or learn its secrets, as most men did. Among some central Nigerian peoples, such as the Amo, a woman could be punished by death as a result of an encounter with *Jankai*. In communities such as the Buji and Anaguta, women could watch the masked representatives of *Jankai* from afar on certain occasions. One of *Jankai*'s chief functions was to denounce witches. Men voluntarily submitted to its flogging, which was thought to confer fertility. *Jankai* played a major role at the male initiation ceremonies, which ended in around 1930. Interestingly, although *Jankai* is not thought of as female, it 'was regarded as the female version of *Anaburr*'.

Women have internalised these values to a striking extent. Collett's valuable study bears independent testimony to the conservatism of older women. He describes how he was showing a video which included scenes of an Anaguta cemetery. Two women callers were shocked, and made a great show of averting their gaze (Collett, 1984: 116).

In many parts of Africa, women are empowered by spirit possession cults which enable them to voice demands and grievances which are not otherwise readily expressed (Lewis, 1971; Boddy, 1989). The Anaguta have a possession cult, intended to cure spirit sickness, which is peculiar to women (Collett, 1984: 124–7). It is similar to the Hausa *bori* cult, and it is not clear whether it is a relatively recent import, like *Jankai*, or whether it is part of an ancient heritage. It has a therapeutic effect on individuals, but no general impact on society as a whole, unlike the male masking cults.

Anaguta women and men have a deep-seated fear of witchcraft. In pre-colonial times, witches (*akiri*) were dealt with in various ways.

They could be forced to consume sasswood (which they would vomit if innocent), or they would swear their innocence on the thunder shrine, *Aradu*. Someone who swore falsely was struck by lightning. I was told that the word *Ambatuga*, mother of women, has connotations of witchcraft, but there seems little difference between the astral powers reputed to the witch and those attributed to titled men, and witchcraft accusations seem to be levelled as much against men as against women.

Fertility has always been a dominant Anaguta concern, and infertility is a deeply felt affliction. The death of children was often attributed to witches. Women would leave their home and even join another ethnolinguistic group to escape witchcraft:

> When someone was sick, and it was believed to be the effects of witchcraft, he was taken to the next village to hide from the effects of the witch. In this way Anaguta were given hospitiality among the Buji and vice versa. Frequent loss of children by a mother may make her seek refuge in the neighbouring group when she became pregnant. (Ateka, 1985: 108)

The fear of witchcraft threads it way through Anaguta songs. The sacred song, *Uzoto*, the most sacred of them all, includes the line: 'We hate a witch and all her evil deeds' (Isichei, 1984: 1171).

A different song, which, like *Uzoto*, I recorded from a group of Anaguta women, ran:

> Witch you must hide.
> God [*Uwyang*] will avenge me.
> *Uwyang* shall come.
> Witch, you must kneel in your yard.
> *Uwyang* shall come [repeated]
> Witch, you must hide.
> Witch, you must kneel.

When asked why only women are subject to spirit sickness, Anaguta women point to all the many duties of their lives and the strain these engender (Collett, 1984: 125). Like many other African women, they found that colonialism added greatly to their burdens. Anaguta men continued to follow a policy of invisibility, of evasion, managing to avoid working in the tin mines, or on public work projects. Older men still say that it is unworthy of a human being's dignity to work for another, and are reluctant to sell grain. The men of other ethnic groups were forced to earn wages to pay taxes, and purchase small luxuries such as matches and sugar which, in time, became necessities. Among the Anaguta cash income was earned by women, who sold first firewood and then other commodities as well – mangoes and leaves for wrapping bean cakes, *moi moi*, in the Jos market.

A group of Anaguta women told me about the contemporary economic pattern of their life. They sell guavas, which are first purchased on the tree: 'Our husbands sell, they don't give us free'. 'I buy carrots and sell them. I buy them on the farm. I am not strong enough to farm. I buy them from Miango and Rukuba women.' 'We buy and sell mangoes.' '*Atili* [*canarium*] grows in our home town. Men get it and I buy from them.' I asked about the relative economic contributions of husbands and wives: 'A man who is strong gives his wife money to buy food. If he is not strong, with a large family, the woman feeds them alone'. 'We get corn from the man. Woman has no right over corn . . . . Benniseed and spinach and beans are grown by the women.'

Anaguta women could not inherit land or property, nor leave it to their daughters. But as Amadiume's important study of the Igbo women of Nnobi reminds us (Amadiume, 1987), the theory of ownership and inheritance may differ greatly from actual usufruct. Diamond studied the Anaguta in the 1950s. He believed that women's economic importance had led to a new balance of power within the family: 'in periods of intense cultural disorganisation . . . when the worldly status of males declines . . . families become mother-centered. To a certain extent this has occurred among the Anaguta. Women, by supplying cash, even in minute quantities, shield their husbands and are thereby valued in a new way' (Diamond, 1972: 478). There was and is, however, a clear discrepancy between their economic importance which extends to other spheres (products gathered by women, such as wild leafy vegetables and edible fungus, still form an important component of daily diet), and their exclusion from the realm of the secret-sacred, around which all Anaguta life revolves.

The Advent of Christianity

By 1922 Jos had Baptist, Anglican and Catholic churches (Fremantle, 1921). In 1925 an 'African church' with 118 adherents is recorded as well (Lonsdale, 1925: 223). The Sudan Interior Mission (SIM) and Sudan United Mission (SUM) established missions in Jos, and the Assemblies of God founded a station at Rahama. The Seventh Day Adventists, established in 1932, opened a mission at Jengre which had a considerable impact on the Amo and Buji, but not on the Anaguta, despite their close cultural ties with Buji. Since about 1970 a considerable number of prophetic Aladura-type churches have grown up in Jos. The Catholic church in Jos, like its counterparts in Kaduna and Zaria, was established initially to meet the needs of southern migrants. A Catholic mission was also established in the Berom village of Zawan.

The Anaguta came late to Christianity, although they were surrounded by various forms of Christian influence. They remember: 'The initial reaction of the Anaguta to the preaching of Christianity was that of indifference. They showed little interest because the first preachers used Hausa, which many of the Anaguta could not speak. Besides, anyone who tended to be attracted to Christianity was mocked as a lazy man' (Ateka, 1985: 159).

When Diamond conducted his fieldwork in the late 1950s, there were 'perhaps a dozen nominal Christians among them . . . . There is a single Christian family, that of the Anaguta pastor who holds Sunday services in an extraordinary hut in his compound . . .' (Diamond, 1972: 459).[3]

However, between 1960 and 1980 the Anaguta turned to Christianity in significant numbers. This was clearly part of a wider trend. In 1960, COCIN (The Church of Christ in Nigeria) had 5,644 members and 474 local congregations with 452 evangelists and 18 pastors. By 1980 there were 50,000 church members, 1,500 local congregations, 1,500 evangelists and 150 pastors (Anon., *The Church of Christ in Nigeria*, 1980). This dramatic expansion probably reflects the impact of grassroots, indigenous leadership and, above all, the spread of Western education, so readily equated with Christianity.

The Missionary Presence

The Anaguta lived on the margins of two Protestant mission spheres of influence. The missions had much in common with each other and were briefly united. The Sudan United Mission, founded in 1904, and the Sudan Interior Mission, founded in 1914, were both interdenominational and strongly evangelical with a remit to work among 'pagan' peoples on the edge of Islamic expansion.

The Sudan United Mission's radical demands, which included permanent monogamy and the renunciation of local beer and dancing, made the adoption of Christianity difficult for the Anaguta. The first male Bercom converts remember how they could not obtain wives and had to pound their own grain. Toma Bot, one of the two Forom pio-

---

3. I interviewed that pastor, Nyampi, in late 1983, shortly before his death. He and his brother, Chai, were converted by an unpaid Berom evangelist, Dajang, from Du. Nyampi learned to read the Hausa Bible, but not to write. His little church still stands.

Map II: The Missionary Presence in 1921: Major Mission Stations

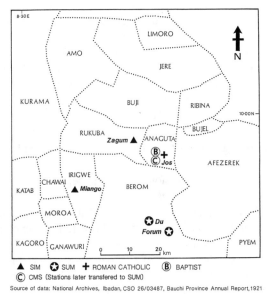

SIM ▲   SUM ✪   ✚ ROMAN CATHOLIC   Ⓑ BAPTIST
Ⓒ CMS (Stations later transfered to SUM)

Source of data: National Archives, Ibadan, CSO 26/03487, Bauchi Province Annual Report, 1921

Map: III The Missionary Presence in 1950: Major Mission Stations

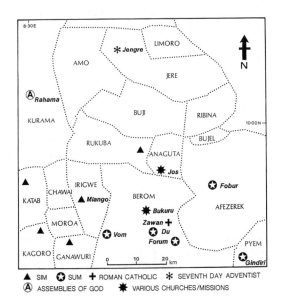

SIM ▲   SUM ✪   ✚ ROMAN CATHOLIC   ✳ SEVENTH DAY ADVENTIST
Ⓐ ASSEMBLIES OF GOD   ✸ VARIOUS CHURCHES/MISSIONS

neers, relates how he married the first Forom woman Christian, Tin, in 1922: 'I learnt that my wife suffered a lot but remained in the Christian faith. That was why I married her' (Bot, n.d.). Such converts often acted as unpaid evangelists, either to other communities within their own ethno-linguistic group, or even to peoples outside it.

The Sudan Interior Mission, founded by Canadians, was established west of the Anaguta, in the area popularly called 'southern Zaria' (Katab, Kagoro, Chawai and Moroa, shown on Maps II and III, form part of this area). The SIM station closest to the Anaguta was among the Rukuba.[4] The Anaguta feared and disliked the Rukuba – the only neighbouring people to whom they were hostile, stereotyping them as ferocious canibals. Not surprisingly, the Rukuba mission did not impinge in any way on Anaguta life.

Both the SUM and SIM missions in Nigeria became, in due course, autonomous, indigenous churches, changes symbolised by new names. In 1948, the SUM mission, in what is now Plateau State, had joined EKAS (*Ekklisiyar Kristi a Sudan*), part of a loose fellowship of churches. In 1975 it became EKAN, 'Nigeria' replacing 'Sudan'. It is alternatively known as COCIN (Church of Christ in Nigeria). On 1 January 1977, the British branch withdrew from Nigeria, although it continued to supply funds and some workers to COCIN. It is now called 'Action Partners'. In 1954 the SIM became ECWA (Evangelical Churches of West Africa).

Although the preponderant Anaguta affiliation is SUM, they belong, as the Ujah told me when I began my research, to 'all kinds of churches', reflecting the choices available in urban Jos. Only three Anaguta are Muslim. One should not, however, conclude that the Anaguta are *either* Christian *or* traditionalist. The whole-hearted, exclusive adherence to Christianity is probably exceptional. Both supernatural worlds coexist at least to some degree in most Anaguta hearts. For the first Anaguta Christians, conversion offered no material benefits. If anything, it led to social deprivation and isolation. The modicum of education the SUM and SIM offered was too little to lead to clerical or teaching jobs – a policy both missions later regretted. Futhermore they offered little in the way of material inducements, and conversions were few.

---

4. Established in 1914, it made little progress for many years. There were very few Rukuba Christians in the 1930s; by 1964 it was estimated that there were between 400 and 500, 5 per cent of the Rukuba population (Muller, 1976: 23).

Largely as a result of the Second World War, but partly also due to increasing land shortages,[5] there was a dramatic change from the late 1940s on. The hunger of the young for education, widened opportunities and salaried employment benefited the missions as becoming a Christian seemed synonymous with entering the modern world. Essays written in Hausa by the first generation of Anaguta school children in the late 1950s mirror with poignant clarity the Anaguta mind at that time: 'We are very primitive . . . Africans used to wear leather [i.e. the leather kilt traditionally worn by Anaguta men]. Then white men invented a better way, that is why Africans started to go to school . . . . The use of education is when someone is educated he will get a good job . . . God created heaven and earth, Adam and Eve, and the whole world' (Diamond, 1972: 446–54). But for most Anaguta, the education available to them was too little and too late. At the time of my field work in the mid-1980s, they had produced only three graduates. The prizes which independence brought eluded them, and their songs reflect a sense of bitter chagrin and loss. Ita Tua and Tasha Djang, asked for a song of their own composition, responded:

> Ita Tua: I wish I could read.
> Djang: Father made a mistake by not sending me to school.
> Ita Tua: I would have known how to read.
> Djang: One cannot live from the hoe these days . . .
> Ita Tua: I start my song always in tears.
> Djang: Father asks what's the matter.
> Ita Tua: I always tell him I have back ache.
> Djang: I continue weeping for the world is hard.

There is no better image of the bankruptcy of the Anaguta's policy of invisibility than the fact that an article entitled 'Who owns Jos?' (Plotnicov, 1972) does not mention the Anaguta at all. Neither are they mentioned in Maxwell's history of the SUM, though he worked on the Jos Plateau from the inception of the mission there until he retired in 1934 – yet he mentions equally small groups, such as the Pai, Gerkawa and Montol. They do not appear in Boer's history of the SUM (Boer, 1979),

5. This was acute among the Berom because of their expanding population and, in particular, because of the destruction of much of their best farmland due to tin mining. It first became an issue with the Anaguta in the 1980s, largely as a result of the sale of land to urban developers and speculators. A few, having sold all their land, have actually been forced to return to their original hilltop settlements.

or in Grimley's history of church growth in central Nigeria (Grimley and Robinson, 1966).

Today, most Anaguta are at least nominal Christians – the main exceptions being some older male officeholders. One of these told me of his wish to become a Christian; he felt that his ritual obligations precluded it. Kauda, old and blind, told me poignantly that his sightlessness was the obstacle – an indication of the evangelical emphasis on Bible-reading. For women, Christianity offers a world of ideas and values independent of the male-dominated sphere of the traditional Anaguta secret-sacred, reinforcing the economic independence they have forged for themselves this century. It may also exercise therapeutic functions which are more effective than spirit possession rituals, now performed infrequently. Women's songs make it clear that Christianity is perceived to be at the opposite pole from witchcraft, which is feared and hated. They make it clear, too, that one of Christianity's chief attractions is the prospect of eternal life it offers, valued perhaps especially in a society where the death rate among children is high:

> God has brought us here.
> A world with death is a cheat . . .
> The world is to be feared.
> The world disturbs me.
> Let God unite us all with His love.
> Let God unite us all with His love.
> Let God divide those with hatred.
> Love is from God.
> Ruling is difficult.
> If you wish to repair you are blamed.

Significantly, this song was sung partly in Hausa, the language of church services, and was called, simply (in Eguta) song of Anaguta, *Irmah Iyah Anaguta*. Chai, an early convert, told me, perhaps with an implied rebuke:

Talking about Christianity is different from talking about history . . . . When Christianity came, it said, when somebody dies, he does not die but goes somewhere to stay. That there is a day when God will call him. That is why I became a Christian. For me, before, when you die you just rot. But when you die you do not rot. Your spirit [*rai*, heart] goes somewhere. If that is the case, I will go somewhere. If that is the case, I will follow. So that when I die my heart will be taken somewhere and rest.

Marriage Patterns

No area of missions-related change has affected Anaguta women's lives more profoundly than that of marriage customs. The Anaguta, like most of their neighbours on the Jos Plateau and in Southern Zaria, had a complex (and possibly unique) system of primary and secondary marriage (Smith, 1953; Muller and Sangree, 1973; Muller, 1976, 1980). The details vary greatly from one people to another, and what follows is a generalized reconstruction, before we focus on the Anaguta experience.

The basic pattern is that a woman contracts a primary marriage and up to three or four secondary marriages. There is no divorce, and she can return to any of her partners. This system, sometimes called serial polyandry, coexists with polygyny: men may have more than one wife at a time, though not all succeed in doing so. Typically, first marriages are arranged in infancy, and involve an exchange: the family which acquires a bride must also provide one, and inability to do so may dissolve the partner's union.

Serial polyandry does not necessarily contribute to a woman's happiness. Sometimes she must leave a husband with whom she is happy at the insistence of a male guardian eager for more bridewealth. Among the Rukuba, she must leave her children behind. Significantly, secondary marriages are less frequent among them (Muller and Sangree, 1973). Wives often change residence (and spouse) in an attempt to avoid the sickness or death of their children – believed to be the effect of witchcraft which can only operate locally (Sangree, 1974: 263). Nevertheless, men's competition to obtain and keep wives undoubtedly works to the latter's advantage, and women have a socially sanctioned variety of sexual partners unknown in the Western world.

The number of secondary marriages which could be contracted was limited by what was socially acceptable – usually three to four. Different peoples abandoned the practice of secondary marriage at different times – sometimes by a gradual transition, sometimes by a specific decision. The Gerkawa, a small people in the Benue valley, did so in 1931; exchange marrige gave way to marriage with bridewealth (Middleton, 1931: para. 18). The reason given by Gerkawa elders was that wives were becoming increasingly difficult to obtain – presumably because women rejected exchange marriage. The Kagoro took such a decision in 1951 (Smith, 1960: 146), and the Irigwe in 1956. The Kagoro decision had a long history. In 1931 it was noted that Christian women were rejecting marriages arranged for them in infancy (Middleton, 1931: para. 109), and insisting on a husband of their own choice.[6]

Traditional Anaguta society had strong matrilineal elements. In such societies, which are as male-dominated as patrilineal ones, kinship is primarily defined in the female line. Studies from many parts of Africa, including Ghana and Zambia, have recorded the decline of matrilineality this century (Douglas, 1969; Meek, 1931: II, 189). Different explanations have been suggested for the decline. It has been pointed out that it is a concomitant of increasing differentials in wealth. A man who creates, for instance, a flourishing cocoa farm tends to leave it to his sons, not his nephews. Undoubtedly, it also reflects the absorption of Western and mission values about 'normal' family patterns.

Anaguta Marriage Changes

Traditionally, marriage for Anaguta women did not preclude other sexual relationships. In general, they showed a striking lack of concern with the identity of the biological father, which was perhaps linked to their great emphasis on fertility, so that all children were welcomed. Various outsiders have commented on this freedom with disapproval. A colonial official minuted in 1914 that Anaguta women were 'exceedingly promiscuous in their sexual intercourse. The system of "free love" is carried to the most extreme point and very little claim appears to be recognised on the part of a man to a woman' (Stobart, 1914: para. 31). Diamond wrote, with reference to the 1950s, of 'their involved and "promiscuous" sexual arrangements before and after marriage' (Diamond, 1972: 369).

The first, or primary, marriage was negotiated, usually by mothers or grandmothers, in early childhood. The marriage was solemnised, with considerable ceremony, when the girl was in advanced pregnancy. 'The biological paternity of the child is of little social importance; a girl may have several affairs, or spend several months living with a paramour' (Diamond, 1972: 471). Primary marriage depended on the exchange of

6. The substantial literature on primary and secondary marriage has generated a controversy as to whether these systems, reconstructed from the past, have been systemised in a way which may do violence to an ever-changing reality (Sharpe, 1983; Muller, 1984). The questions asked are valid ones of far-ranging significance, though they cannot be explored in the context of this paper. Especially relevant, however, is the issue of whose perspective these reconstructions represent – are they indeed 'the ideal property of chiefs, elders and household heads rather than of subordinate men and women'? (Sharpe, 1983).

real or classificatory sisters. Its weakness was that if one of the marriages involved in the exchange broke down, usually because of childlessness, its partner union also came to an end, even if it was a happy one. In these circumstances, the woman's child joined the household of her brother, and became a co-heir there. Men vied to attract women to their compounds in secondary marriages; when one succeeded, his mother announced his triumph with an ululation.

A woman could have several secondary husbands and was free to leave the one she was living with to join another, or to return to her father's home. Often, such moves were due to the sickness or death of a child, which were attributed to witchcraft. But 'a women who develops a reputation for moving too capriciously will be held cheaply' (Diamond, 1972: 472).

There was a third type of marriage – Berom girls, often from Du, were obtained in early childhood, in exchange for grain or horses. They were brought up as Anaguta, and became wives – prized for their reputation for fertility and strength in farming. Berom wives were not free to contract secondary marriages and if one left her husband a refund of the bridewealth could be requested.

Sexual unions were forbidden between groups which had a joking relationship, *apari*. This existed between specific Anaguta descent groups (*tibiri*), all of which were exogamous, and between the Anaguta as a whole and the Buji and Akashi. The Akashi were of Afezerek origin, but had been accepted as Anaguta and spoke Eguta.

The Ambatuga of Kinga (a modern Anaguta settlement) described traditional marriage in this way:

> In the past a girl must be pregnant in her father's house before she is married. There was no sanction against sexual relations between a boy and a girl in love, who were yet to be married, when a girl had been promised in marriage in the traditional way . . . . If she has the baby at home, it is for her parents. The intending husband must try hard to marry her during the pregnancy . . . . When a boy was in love with a girl . . . he would invite his friends who would waylay the girl and carry her to his home. He would sleep there till morning. There would be ululation and roads leading to the house would be swept by the women in the compound. If the parents of the girl approved of the marriage, she would be left there . . . . A man could steal away a woman from her husband through secret love . . . . When he succeeded there would be ululation and he would tell the man that he had stolen his wife. Usually the man would come and fight for his wife with a stick called *ubandi*. (Ateka, 1985: 81,2)

Two elements of this account are striking: it speaks consistently of love, and there is no deception. In theory, a man could have several wives at once, but this seems to have been very rare. Divorce did not exist, and a wife could return to any husband at any time. Anaguta women were never given in marriage to outsiders. The general ambience was undoubtedly one in which women were sought after and courted, and in which men strove to acquire wives and retain them. This is reflected in the following song which tells of a lonely and depressed man's unsuccessful attempt to win back his wife, who has left him. He laments:

> I've had misfortunes since I was born
> and the whole thing was my own fault.

But the wife will not go back to him – implicitly, because of childlessness:

> 'I've always had bad luck in your home.
> I have got no son in my house.' (Isichei, 1984: 1170)

This is the context in which the courting and marriage songs with which we began this paper must be understood.

Diamond described the Anaguta as: 'a society in transition from matrilineal to patrilineal descent' (Diamond, 1972: 473). Collett's study of the Anaguta is subtitled: 'the making of a patrilineal ideology'. There were certainly strong matrilineal elements in their traditional culture – the fact that children stayed with the mother, or her brother, when a marriage dissolved, and the inheritance rights of a sister's son, *wazoho*. Diamond also cites 'sacred medicine bundles . . . passed down through the mother's line' (ibid.).

In modern Anaguta society the traditional system of primary and secondary marriage has been replaced by marriage with bridewealth, and the matrilinial element is disappearing. The *apari* prohibition is weakening, and Anaguta sometimes marry Buji. This is partly, but not wholly, due to Christian influence. The way in which premarital sexual unions were not only permitted but were regarded as a necessary prelude to marriage, the sanctioning of serial polyandry, and the way in which a primary marriage ended if its partner union was dissolved were all clearly incompatible with traditional Christian morality. Missionaries, moreover, took it for granted that the 'normal' family was one in which children were reared by their biological parents, and not by their maternal uncles. More basically, these Anaguta changes may reflect a tendency among the Western educated to condemn their own culture unanalytically as 'pagan'. However, this condemnation, in areas such as marriage, seems not to have been incompatible with an emphasis on cultural revival in music and dancing. (I attended a re-enactment of the traditional marriage ceremony, *rhigisau*, performed in this spirit.) They may well have absorbed certain Western assumptions that matrilineal systems and serial polyandry were primitive and archaic. Diamond described the Anaguta as 'urban primitives'. Murdock, in a celebrated Africa-wide survey, published in 1959, singled out the Jos Plateau as: 'a cultural cul-de-sac characterised by a series of interesting archaic traits ranging from widespread, complete nudity to certain utterly unique marriage practices' (quoted in Muller, 1980: 362).

There have been other factors at work. The most obvious social function of the primary and secondary marriage system was to unite various sections of an ethno-linguistic group with an intricate web of marriage bonds, thus avoiding conflict. Its most obvious dysfunction was actual or potential hostility between rival husbands. The colonial government, by establishing an external legal force, helped to eliminate physical conflict, but the basic dysfunction then loomed larger. Not surprisingly, colonial authorities were uniformly hostile to serial polyandry.

Collett suggests that Christianity weakened the position of Anaguta women: 'the status of Tiv women is said to have declined after the abolition of sister exchange . . . . Christianity in Nigeria may well reinforce the inequality of women rather than the reverse. The teaching that the first woman was created from Adam's rib is frequently cited as unassailable proof that woman is inferior to man' (Collett, 1984: 279). He also provides interesting evidence about the decline of matrilineal elements in Anaguta and, in particular, the erosion of the inheritance rights of the *wazoho*, sister's son. There are several reasons for this. The escalation of urban land values has made inheritance a question of crucial importance. Matrilineal systems create problems when marriages are contracted outside the ethno-linguistic unit, as is becoming increasingly common.

Conclusion

Much Anaguta life revolved around the secret-sacred from which women were excluded, with the exception of a spirit possession cult. In the colonial period, women earned new economic importance, providing the cash income which was needed to pay taxes, and shielding Anaguta men from the need to enter the modern economy. There was a contradiction between their economic importance, and their exclusion from what was regarded as of crucial importance, the religious life and rituals of their society. The Anaguta gradually adopted Christianity from the 1950s onwards, despite much opposition from traditional guardians of the secret-sacred, because it was seen as inseparable from education, and perhaps because it seemed to offer a cognitive map more appropriate for the modern world. It had come to be perceived that their policy of avoiding the impact of modernity led only to poverty.

Women's songs reflect a strong sense of identification with Christianity. This may be because it seemed congruent with their new economic role. What the songs stress, however, is the promise of eternal life, and protection from witchcraft. In so far as Christianity provided a world of the sacred from which women were not excluded, it empowered them. The serious preoccupation with eternal themes contrasts with the self-mocking flirtatiousness of traditional courting songs. As among other Nigerian peoples, church institutions, such as women's meetings, were modelled on existing structures. The churches may well have helped preserve the tradition of women's meetings by giving them a clear focus for discussion and action.

In some African societies, Christianity inspired women to mount a frontal attack on male-dominated areas of traditional religion. In 1950 a group of Christian Igbo women in Aguleri attacked a masked figure and removed his mask – an action punishable by death in pre-colonial times (Isichei, 1980: 72). A less radical challenge was recorded on the Jos Plateau (south of the area discussed in this paper) in 1938, when SUM women converts in Kamwai refused to run away and hide when the *dodo* (masked figure) appeared (Pembleton, 1938: 4). Nothing of this kind occurred among Anaguta women, who seem to internalise traditional values to a high degree. The only known occasion when Anaguta women acted together on a religious matter was in *support* of a traditional male ritual – the circumcision and initiation ceremonies from which they were excluded. These came to an end in around 1930, apparently because a ritual blunder was thought to have caused the death of a titled elder. In the words of an oral text: 'When Wabura and Kashang stopped circumcision women came to challenge them. They came naked'. There is a fascinating parallel with studies of nudity as a form of women's protest in other parts of Africa (Van Allen, 1972; S. Ardener, 1975). One further instance of women's corporate action was recorded in the late fifties:

> when all woodcutting was prohibited in the forest reserve, the women marched down from the hills and assembled before the courthouse in a silent, formidable and dense mass, unnerving the chief and council, all of whom made speeches pledging sympathy; and similar demonstrations took place when it was rumoured that women were going to be taxed in the Northern Region. (Diamond, 1972: 476)

Matrilinial structures are being replaced by patrilineal ones, and a complex system of serial polyandry has given way to marriage with bridewealth. It is possible that the decline of exchange marriage has diminished women's autonomy. It is clear that traditional courtship patterns, mirrored in song, meant that women were cherished and pursued, and men often experienced rejection. The decline of these patterns may well be experienced by women as a loss. It also seems likely that oppressive myths, such as the traditional interpretation of the story of Eve and Adam, have reinforced patriarchical tendencies which were always inherent in some aspects of Anaguta society.

The complexities and ambiguities of the data are apparent. There is no single clear answer to the question – did Christianity empower or marginalise Anaguta women? Their most passionate concern is not with power but with life, and with protection from evil, given human form as the witch. At a time when some Western theologians are questioning traditional dogmas relating to the Resurrection, heaven and the eternal life of the individual soul, Anaguta women internalise the fundamentalism of the missionaries, and sing with joy and conviction.

> *Uwyang* has died, has risen because of us.
> Our hearts are white.

Bibliography

Amadiume, I. (1987) *Male Daughters, Female Husbands, Gender and Sex in African Society*, London

Ardener, S. (1975) 'Sexual Insult and Female Militancy', in S. Ardener (ed.), *Perceiving Women*, Dent (first published in Man, 1973)

Ateka, B. P. (1985) Interviews collected for his Special Project in History, B A, University of Jos, and given *in extenso* there

Boddy, J. (1989) *Wombs and Alien Spirits: Men, Women and the Zar Cult in Northern Sudan*, Madison

Boer, J. H. (1979) *Missionary Messages of Liberation in a Colonial Context: A Case Study of the Sudan United Mission*, Amsterdam

Bot, Toma T. (n.d. but before 1977), *Tarihin da Toma T. Bot*, Hausa manuscript

Collett, A. (1984) 'The Making of a Patrilineal Ideology: A Study of Continuity and Change in Social Organisation among the Anaguta of Northern Nigeria', SOAS PhD

Diamond, S. (1972) 'The Anaguta of Nigeria; Suburban Primitives', in J. H. Steward, *Three African Tribes in Transition*, Urbana (reprint)

Douglas, M. (1969) 'Is Matriliny doomed in Africa?', in M. Douglas and P. M. Kaberry, *Man in Africa*, London: 121–36

Fremantle, J. M. (1922) Bauchi Province Annual Report, National Archives, Ibadan, CSO 26/09506

Grimley, J. B. and Robinson, G. E. (1966) *Church Growth in Central and Southern Nigeria*, Grand Rapids

Isichei, E. (1980) *Entirely for God: A Life of Michael Iwene Tansi*, Ibadan and Basingstoke

_____ (1983) 'Hausa Women's Songs', *West Africa*, September: 2242. This paper reports the research of Fatima Othman

_____ (1984) 'Anaguta Songs', *West Africa*: 1170–1

_____ (1991a) 'Change in Anaguta traditional religion', forthcoming in *Canadian Journal of African Studies*, 34–57

_____ (1991b) 'On Being Invisible: An Historical Perspective of the Anaguta and their Neighbours', forthcoming in *The International Journal of African Historical Studies*, 513–556

Lewis, I. (1971) *Ecstatic Religion*, Harmondsworth

Lonsdale, P. (1925) Bauchi Province Annual Report, National Archives, Ibadan, CSO 26/2/12537/III

Maxwell, J. L. (n.d., c.1952) *Half a Century of Grace. A Jubilee History of the Sudan United Mission*, London

Meek, C. K. (1931) *Tribal Studies in Northern Nigeria*, London, 2 vols

Middleton, H. Hale (1931) Plateau Province Annual Report, National Archives, Ibadan, 12601/IX

Muller, J. C. (1980) 'On the Relevance of Having Two Husbands: Contribution to the Study of Polygynous Polyandrous Marital Forms on the Jos Plateau', *Journal of Comparative Family Studies*: 359–69

_____ and Sangree, W. H. (1973) 'Irigwe and Rukuba Marriage: A Comparison', *Canadian Journal of African Studies*: 27–57

Pembleton, E. S. (1938) Plateau Province Annual Report, National Archives, Ibadan, CSO 26/2/12601/XII

Plotnicov, L. (1972) 'Who Owns Jos? Ethnic Ideology in Nigerian Urban Politics', Urban *Anthropology*: 1–13

Sangree, W. (1974) 'The Dodo Cult, Witchcraft and Secondary Marriage in Irigwe, Nigeria', *Ethnology*: 261–78

Sharpe, B. (1983) 'Headpanners and Dredgers: Theory in Plateau Studies', *Africa*: 84–91

Smith, M. G. (1960) 'Kagoro Political Development', *Human Organisation*: 137–49

Stobart, S. E. M. (1914) 'Anaguta and Jarawa Tribes of Bukuru District: Reassessment Report', National Archives, Kaduna, Josprof 257/1914

Van Allen, J. (1972) 'Sitting on a Man: Colonialism and the Lost Political Institutions of Igbo Women', *Canadian Journal of African Studies*: 165–81

12

Catholic Missionaries and Andean Women: Mismatching Views on Gender and Creation

Sarah Lund Skar

Introduction

In this paper I try to explain the failure of missionary activity in a Runa village in Peru's southern highlands.[1] This is despite the evangelising presence of the Church in the area during the past 400 years. I will argue that this impasse arises out of a fundamental divergence of beliefs about the relationship between women and men between Runa and the Catholic Church and its missionaries. The latter convey ideas which are at odds with Runa beliefs as embodied in their religious practices, kinship system, and indeed, in the language itself.

Because I knew the Roman Catholic missionary priests resident in a neighbouring town well, there has been a personal reason for struggling with these issues. Yet the shared interest between anthropologist and priests concerning the understanding of Runa society and culture was often confused because of the vast discrepancies in our points of departure. One of the most frustrating and difficult themes in our discussions

1. The fieldwork (1976–7) on which this paper is based was financed by the Norwegian Social Science Research Council. Later work in Peru (1980–1, 1984, 1986) funded by the Swedish Research Council contributed to my deeper understanding of Runa culture. I am indebted to both these institutions. This paper has been presented in an earlier version for two workshops; the one in Oxford of which this volume is a result and another in Oslo on Gender Identity and Morality. I want to thank the participants in both groups for stimulating discussion which encouraged me to continue with the work. Let me also acknowledge the editors and Joan Burke for valuable criticisms some of which have been incorporated in the subsequent rewritings of this chapter. However, it must be noted that I alone am responsible for this final version.

has been that of gender, an area of concern largely implicit in the Runa cultural context and consistently overlooked or defined out of the discussion by the priests. Nevertheless an exchange of views over the years has been stimulating and a source of creative impetus.

This paper starts with a discussion of some of the general issues involved in the evangelisation process, and then moves on to present ethnographic material from Matapuquio. The relative detail afforded to the ethnography is necessary for any understanding of the fundamental gap in communication between the missionaries and the villagers. My purpose is not to arrive at a conclusion as to whether Matapuqenos are truly Christian or not. Nor is it my intent to trace the syncretic interplay between Roman Catholic religious beliefs and traditional Runa worldviews. My focus is placed on the cultural confrontation between these two traditions and especially the conflict which arises out of their opposed views on women. Far from being a minor issue, I find this to be a crucial indicator of fundamental differences in the orientation of held beliefs as to the nature of the universe and the place of women and men in it. The fundamental difference between Christian monotheism and the principle of duality which generates the Runa cosmos is one which cannot be resolved by some kind of syncretic compromise. Though cultural change implies a change of values at many levels, a process which is far from simultaneous or in complete conformity, nevertheless the area of changing gender identity is a profound indicator of transformations and continuity.

Catholic Missionary Work in Peru

From the year 1532 when Francisco Pizarro landed on the coast of Peru and began his campaign to conquer the Incas, missionaries have been actively seeking to convert the indigenous populations to Christianity. Forty years after that first landing, when the final Indian resistance was subdued with the execution of Tupac Amaru I, the systematic evangelising work effectively began. As an administrative arm of the Spanish Crown, the Church made its entry into every level of colonial life. Today active missionary work continues, as does the debate as to the extent to which Christianity has truly been accepted by the indigenous peoples of the highlands.[2]

From the outset of their long history of missionary work in Peru, Catholic missionaries of the colonial period were eager to document the

2. For early church models of conversion in Peru, see Sabine MacCormack (1985: 443–66).

process of religious transformation. Thus we are left with a rich legacy of chronicles of pre-hispanic religion as well as pastoral reports and memoranda to the Spanish King. These documents give us at least a partial picture of the evangelising process during this early period. At the culmination of the grand campaign to eradicate idolatry in the mid-1600s, according to churchmen the indigenous populations were basically Christianised (Casaverde Rojas, 1970: 139). This conclusion has been generally accepted until modern times. In the 1920s with the emergence of the Indigenista Movement and its focusing of political consciousness on indigenous problems, and later with the emergence of an academic preoccupation with Andean culture in the fields of ethno-history, archaeology, and anthropology, this conclusion has finally been called into question.

Anthropologists writing on religious aspects of contemporary Runa life have by no means given us a uniform picture. However, over the years they have touched on many themes and certain threads of continuity seem to be emerging. Mishkin (1946: 462), for example, states that Runa religion is essentially a form of Catholicism, characterised by a jumble of non-integrated ideas, beliefs, and practices. He goes on to state that the Runa recognise 'God' as one of several in the first order of supernatural beings, but he questions whether they recognise a single Supreme Deity (ibid.: 463).

Much academic attention has also been focused on the Runa fiesta cycle, the most overt form of religious expression in many communities and the topic of extensive description and analysis (Manguin, 1954; Stein, 1961; Doughty, 1968). An important theme in much of the writing on the fiesta cycle has been that of the syncretism of two religious traditions. Importance has been placed on establishing parallels between the Incaic and the Catholic calendars and in demonstrating that many important feast days roughly coincided (Vallee, 1972; Isbell, 1978).

There is an assumption in much of this writing (see, for example, Arguedas, 1956) that there is an official religion, that is Catholicism, and a local religion, Runa, which exist side-by-side, each fulfilling their respective functions in a symbiotic relationship in which integration into the larger Christian community is carefully balanced against the maintainance of local traditions through the worship of local gods. This interpretation mirrors and, indeed, seems to me to fit too perfectly with the pre-Conquest situation in which official religion, focusing on the worship of the Inca, functioned to integrate a far-flung empire while the local cults were tolerated and even encouraged by the state as a way of placating newly conquered peoples. It seems much too simplistic to suggest that the 'official' Inca religion was merely replaced by that of the new conquerors' Christianity and that the local religious traditions continue more or less intact (see González Martinez, 1985: 748).

Another interpretation, in which the small highland towns are viewed as the centre of Catholic beliefs and practices while the country-side remains basically 'pagan', is a theme which merits more careful consideration (see Albo, 1976: 174; and Sallnow, 1987). In such a situation, religious beliefs and ethnic boundaries separate and give articulation to the opposed groups of the *misties*[3] or hispanisicised town-dwellers and the Indians in the countryside. In such a view, the Christian God is most concerned with the welfare of those with Spanish cultural affinity, while the traditional gods of the countryside watch particularly over the Indians. A similar juxtaposition is found in Wachtel's (1977) analysis of the evangelising process of the early colonial period where he emphasises a situation of dysfunction between two opposing worlds in which acculturation of the dominated into the culture of the conquerors was negligible.

The theoretical development in anthropology, which has gone beyond the compartmentalising of social phenomena into categories such as religion, politics and economics, has freed us to approach the study of religion as a cultural system (see, for example, Geertz, 1973) and as a consequence has resulted in a much more fruitful examination of Runa culture in all its varied aspects. From much of this work we are able to identify certain Andean ideals which are fundamental to their views of the nature of society and the universe. Two points which par-ticularly mark the contemporary discussion on continuity in the Andes are those of verticality and duality (Pease, 1981: 112).

Unlike the Western concept of space, which is based on the contrast-ing notions of the vertical and the horizontal, the Andean view is domi-nated by the vertical (Murra, 1972). Vertical space is as much a symbol-ic universe as a physical one and is experienced in a social setting imbued with religious meaning (Bastien, 1978). The mountains and slopes are inhabited with guardian spirits, which the Runa believe pro-tect them and nurture them like a parent does its child (Allen, 1984: 153). With such a perspective the spatial designation of upper (*hanin*) or lower (*urin*) has multiple signification far beyond a simple physical description of relative position on a vertical slope.

3. The term *misties* or *mestizo* are used in the cultural sense to indicate people of the town who are integrated into the dominant Peruvian culture, but with some affinities with the Runa culture of the countryside.

Space is intertwined with time in the Runa concept of *pacha* (Skar, S., 1981; Bouysse-Cassagne and Harris, 1987; Kaarhus, 1987, etc.). *Pacha* translates roughly into earth/world and epic time (Lira, 1982; Perroud and Chouvenc, 1970) and is personified in the Runa deity of Pachamama, Mother Earth.[4] Pachamama is the generative force in the world, and all living things not only come from her but also return to her at death. The past, the present and the future all are born and return to the Pachamama (Gow, 1982: 5).

Many authors have pointed out for us the fundamental importance of space in Andean perceptions ot their universe (Bastien, 1978; Urton, 1981) but an equally important principle in their vision of the cosmos is that of duality. In Runa thought, existence is based upon complementary opposition (Platt, 1976). All living things come in pairs of opposites which are reciprocal and complementary and are often defined in terms of sexuality (Isbell, 1976). All forces of nature have their opposite forces with which they exist in balanced harmony. Pachamama as source of fertility and central female principle articulates with male deities such as the sun (*Inti*), the sky (*Pachakemag*) and the mountain ancestors (*wamanis*) (Mariscotti de Gørlitz, 1978: 193–205). The social ideal is the merging of opposites (*tinkuy*) within a greater whole to give balance and proportion to the world.

Social space is also organised to express this principle of the merging or coming together of opposites. Most Runa villages are divided into two, with an upper section called *hanin* and a lower part called *urin*. Many such divided villages have a moiety organisation, which incorporates the basic distinction between upper and lower as the organising principle in most aspects of social life (Skar, H., 1982). It is the balanced interplay between these two village halves which generates social life, just as it is the harmonious relationship between a paired man and woman which creates and perpetuates family life.

The Village as Sacred Landscape

Matapuquio is a small community (*Comunidad Campesina*) of about 1200 people typically located on a steep slope above the Pincos River in the Province of Andahuaylas, Apurimac. As described in many monographs from the southern highlands (Skar, H. 1982; Sallnow, 1983,

---

4. Tristan Platt (1976) writes about the dual nature of this earth divinity among the Macha of Bolivia. There the earth is referred to as female, Pachamama, during August–September and is called Father Earth, Pachataytay, during Carnival.

Brush, 1977) the villagers' houses are scattered up and down the slope, with the highest dwellings being situated at about 3800 metres above sea level and the lowest borders of the village lying at about 3000 metres. There is no central plaza in Matapuquio nor are there any shops, marketplace or roads. It is an isolated village, a day's walk from the nearest commercial centre of Huancarama, where one can shop and take passage on a truck to the bigger towns, another day's journey away. In Huancarama there is a church (founded c. 1590) with two resident Roman Catholic priests, members of the Society of St James. Mata-puquio is among the villages which these priests are supposed to include in their parish work, but for at least the past decade the relation-ship between the village and the Church has been very poor.

This in part may stem from earlier relations with the bordering *hacienda*, Pincos, where most villagers had to work in order to be allowed to use their traditional *laymi* lands in the heights for pasturing animals and planting tubers. In 1973, Pincos had become a co-operative expropriated under the land reform legislation, but for generations prior to expropriation the *hacienda* had been run by the Trelles family. There was a chapel at the *hacienda* and villagers related how the *hacendada* required that they should attend mass. In this context the missionary contact with Matapuqenos was highly coloured, not only by the element of Runa subjugation[5] associated with the *hacienda* in general, but also by the connotation the *hacienda* area had with pollution and danger for women. Runa women living at Pincos were assumed to be prostitutes living an idle life far removed from the upright ways of village women, who worked, as they should, in the fields and pastures further up the slopes.

To say mass in the village of Matapuquio, the priest must first be invited by the village leaders (*varayoqkuna*) and they are under obliga-tion to inform the villagers and make certain that people come to the chapel at the appointed time. Also a meal should be prepared for the priest before his return trip to Huancarama. Unlike many of the other villages in which masses are said fairly frequently, Matapuquio was especially anxious to have the priest come on only two occasions during the year: to celebrate the village's saint's day, Santa Rosa, on 30 August and later, in the spring, to pray for the coming of the rains.

I shall return to these two occasions later. To my knowledge individ-ual masses for the dead were never requested and between themselves

---

5. See Sallnow (1983) for a discussion of how Catholic devotion and ecclesi-astical power were mobilised in establishing the legitimacy of local estates in the sierra.

the priests often expressed disillusionment about the relative lack of devotional fervour and religious understanding demonstrated by the villagers in contrast to other communities in their parish. The attitude of these missionaries reflects important changes to the Church's emphasis on the personalisation of the relationship between the individual and God. There is a real effort being made by certain groups within the Church to move away from the preoccupation with a set of outward observances towards a concern for a deepened, more inward spiritual life (Christian, 1972: 181).[6] It is the foreign missionaries who are some of the most dynamic in this regard insisting on instruction and a heightened degree of understanding before receiving such sacraments as marriage or adult baptism.

One might ask why it should be necessary in a Catholic country like Peru to have to bring in foreign missionaries at all, since the Roman Catholic Church has had a virtual religious monopoly there for 400 years and more. And yet there is a chronic shortage of priests; a situation which is by no means a recent development but rather symptomatic of the Church throughout Latin America. This weakness stems from the Church's great reluctance to admit non-Europeans to the priesthood (Neill, 1975: 506–7).[7] Though the Roman Catholic Church continues to enjoy the status of state church in Peru, it has had to face increasing pressures from evangelical Protestant groups, which have been allowed to work in Peru since the 1920s (*Mission Handbook*, 1976: 519).

The Catholic priests in Huancarama are in a difficult position. Through conviction and Anglo-American tradition, they are demanding more of their congregations in terms of understanding the Christian message. This requires a much greater personal investment from their point of view. They expect more of their mission yet they are hopelessly understaffed for the number of outlying villages which they cover in their parish. Perhaps it is easy to understand then that when communication between a congregation in an outlying parish such as Matapuquio and the priests breaks down, the priests concentrate their efforts on other parishes where their attentions are needed and fervently requested. Because of a long series of episodes in which the village has demonstrated its preoccupation with the performance of church rituals while

6. This distinction is a crucial one and points up the great discrepancy between faith or authority and reason as discussed by MacCormack (1985) in much of the Church's approach to missionary work. See also Pagden (1982).

7. In 1985 the first local Peruvian priests were ordained in Abancay at the seminary run by the local bishop, the long-term plans being to free the Church of the liberal missionary presence.

failing completely to convey a sense of seeking a deeper understanding of the faith, Matapuquio for the time being has been more or less written off by the priests as spiritually superficial.

However, from the anthropologist's point of view, the everyday life of Matapuqenos was filled with ritual activity which revealed their deep sense of religion and emphasised their reverence for the natural surroundings and the rhythms of the day and seasons. In traditional households, prayers are offered at daybreak; requests for protection throughout the day for all the members both human and animal are made to an entire pantheon of gods. This includes supplicating the Christian God (Dios Taytay), Christ (Jesu Kristu, el Señor), the saints (Santukuna), the *apus* (gods) of the mountain peaks overlooking the village and then, particularly, that *apu* controlling the household's pasturelands, and Pachamama.

On those days when work parties are held (whether *ayni*, *ayuda* or *faena*; see Skar, H., 1982), alcoholic drinks are always an important aspect of the group effort. In the context of group drinking, a small libation is always poured on the ground for Pachamama, an act (*tinkay*) with little ceremony but never omitted (see Irarrazaval, 1988: 15). Throughout the day, Runa pass by numerous sacred places; for example, where water springs from the mountain or where boulders (*illa*), believed to be living growing forces, stand out on the slope. Precautions must be made to avoid insulting or disturbing these spiritually potent sites (Skar, S., 1987).

Ancient burial caves on the upper slopes as well as archaeological ruins are both revered manifestations of earlier inhabitants, a people that have gone underground to live in a world in which they carry on life just as Matapuqenos do but only upside-down (see Skar, H., n.d.; Gose, P., 1986; Bouysse-Cassagne and Harris, 1987). These subterranean spirits are called *gentiles* or pagans (Duviols, 1977: 54) and are associated with ancestor worship and past epochs. For the most part, *gentiles* live in peace with the villagers but they control the water that comes from inside the mountain to the earth's surface. As both *gentiles* and Runa are agricultural peoples, they are in constant competition over this resource. The *gentiles* expect something in return for the water the Runa use, and each household makes offerings[8] at appropriate times during the year.

Thus we find that there is an entire universe of sacred beings which meets the Matapuqenos in their everyday encounter with their surroundings. The relationship which one has with such beings is based on reci-

---

8. Harald Skar (n.d.) found that the offering supposedly claimed by the *gentiles* when they are particularly demanding is the life of a child.

procal giving of offerings and receiving protection and prosperity. It is the give and take between Runa and the animated forces in their surroundings which is crucial to maintaining a harmonious life.

Aspects of Duality in Village Religious Expression

Besides the permeation of the sacred in the everyday, there are also certain high points of religious experience through the cyclical course of time. Some of these occasions involve the entire village while others are household rituals. Both kinds of celebration are essential to the successful generation of abundance and well-being, and indicate a fruitful relationship between the villagers and their surroundings.

Such village festivities often coincide with church holy days but there is little to remind us of the classical fiestas described in the towns with their focus on church iconography and their elaborate system of fiesta sponsorship (Sallnow, 1987: 147). Instead, most of these celebrations involve the coming together first of larger family groupings, then of the inhabitants of each of the village moieties, and finally a convergence of the entire village to eat, drink, sing and dance (Skar, H., 1982: 231–41). The music, the form of the dance, the food and drink, and the location are all specific to the particular ceremony and often reflect links with a particular phase of the agricultural cycle. The feast of Santa Rosa, the village patron saint, is a typical example. Villagers meet in front of the small chapel located nearly half-way up the slope and they dance in front of the image of Santa Rosa, a statue which was bought, clothed and sent to the village by the migrant Matapuqenos living in Lima. Individual women sponsor the Santa Rosa celebration, with the responsibility being shared between female relatives who help with preparing food and drink and arrange for the hiring of musicians.

It is difficult to establish whether villagers identify Santa Rosa with Pachamama but it seems likely, at least at this time of year.[9] The celebration of her saints' day falls at a time (30 August) when villagers are waiting to begin the planting of their fields. August is also the month when Pachamama is said to be 'open'[10] (see also Allen, 1982: 179). Working the fields is delayed until the end of the month and no one

---

9. There are numerous authors who have written about the complex interrelationship between the Christian Virgin figure and Andean earth goddesses; see, for example, Garr (1972), Irarrazaval (1988) and Mariscotti de Gørlitz (1978).

10. Tristan Platt (1978: 1093) writes that the Macha of Bolivia refer to Pachamama as the Virgin during the month of August. During the rest of the year, her fertility is more important.

should marry during this time either, for it is a fruitless month, a time for waiting. The celebration of the feast day of Santa Rosa marks the end of this waiting and the planting can now begin. As noted earlier, the priest from Huancarama is invited to say a mass during Santa Rosa, and great importance is placed on the elaborateness and length of the service. The mass is the villagers' offering to Santa Rosa/Pachamama, and as such is felt to be some kind of payment for future abundance in the harvest (see also Gose, 1986: 299 for a discussion of the mass as *tinka*). The villagers feel reassured when there are many repeated prayers and blessings during the mass because as an offering, it will have greater weight.[11]

The women's celebration of Santa Rosa marks the beginning of maize planting, work carried out in pairs in which the man digs the field and the woman puts three seeds in the hole. Maize is the most valued crop grown in the valley and its seed is stored and guarded by women from one year to the next. Maize is personified as female and figures as Saramama in legends told in the village. Her partner is Taytaytrigo (Father Wheat); wheat is a crop planted on marginal lands above the village which plays only a minor role in the Matapuqenos' diet.

The calling for the rains to begin is another occasion in which the priest is often invited to hold mass in the village, the mass again serving as an offering to Pachamama in exchange for the skies to bring rain. The rains usually begin in November and anxiety mounts as time goes by if the rains do not begin. The year I witnessed the processions (1976), the rains had yet to begin in earnest in early December. People in the village were talking about a terrible drought of some earlier period which had caused many to starve. Many nights I went to sleep to the sound of beating drums and distant wailing until anxiety rose to such an extent that the village was brought together as a whole to call for the rains. The priest was invited to say mass during the day but it was during the night that the villagers congregated in force to form a long procession which wound its way up around the mountaintops. Women and children led the procession pounding on their drums and crying out in high falsetto songs in an archaic Quechua which no one could translate for me.

The planting of the maize and the coming of the rains is a time of year associated with women. They are the ones responsible for the Santa Rosa celebration and through their high-pitched singing the rains

11. It has been suggested (Randi Kaarhus, personal communication) that the emphasis on ritual repetition may be associated with the function of repetition in the Quechua language, i.e. as amplifier.

are called down to earth to nourish the young maize plants. When the dry season comes in April–May the harvest begins. The work is shared between men and women with one important exception. The women oversee the sorting and storing of the harvest of all the different crops. The storeroom or *marka* is the exclusive domain of the women of the household and when men enter there it is said to spoil the contents.

In contrast to the female time of the rains, the festivals of the dry season are male-oriented. With the harvest successfully completed, the villagers can prepare for the important celebration of San Juan (24 June). Earlier, the crosses marking the village territory were taken down from the mountain passes and carried by a group of men to mass in the church in Huancarama. It was a great test of endurance for the men carrying the heavy crosses across the mountains and when they were finally returned to their vantage points above the village, those men who had made the journey won great prestige. However, for at least the past twenty years this pilgrimage has not been made. Instead, the feast of San Juan has become the occasion on which young men and boys can demonstrate their bravado in fighting bulls and in horse racing. The emphasis on masculine prowess is found again during the Independence Day celebration of 28 July.

Certain times of the year are associated with male or female celebrations. The passing of time through these two opposite but equally important phases is essential to reproduction of the crops. As with maize and wheat, all crops are personified as either male (*tayta*/father or adult man) or female (*mama*/mother or adult female), each with its designated partner. During the evening conversations, it became a source of amusement to try to find a plant without a partner. Try as I might a second plant was always named and there was a general sense of agreement as to the appropriateness of the pairs and their ascribed gender.

Much more could surely be said about the nature of these pairings. For example, what are the characteristics demonstrated by the 'female' plants as opposed to the 'male' ones? And why should one combination be so appropriate to making a pair? What is it in the nature of the two plants of the pair that makes them complementary partners? Unfortunately, this discussion will have to be set aside in the context of the present paper. Suffice it to say that the basic principle of duality found to be so fundamental to Runa views on the creation and maintenance of the cosmos is often built on an assumption of sexuality (see Ortiz, 1982). Opposition between the rainy season and the dry or between the upper reaches of the mountain slopes as opposed to the valley (Skar, S., 1981: 39) is conceived of in terms of a sexual opposition, just as complementarity is expressed in terms of the complementarity of the conjugal pair.

As we have seen, the conjugal pair becomes a metaphor for categorising many phenomena in which the final emphasis is placed on the unity of the pair as for example in the often cited Quechua expression, everything is man/woman (or woman/man), *tukuy ama gari/warmi* (or *warmi/gari*) (Platt, 1978: 1092; Harris, 1978).

Runa Kinship

At this juncture, it would be profitable to discuss Runa kinship, a sphere of social life which is particularly relevant in the shaping of cultural notions of gender (Skar, 1981: 10). Runa kinship is bilateral (see Bolton and Mayer, 1977), with relationship to both the mother's and father's families being held as equally important. The main grouping in bilateral systems is the kindred which from the individual Matapuqenos point of view, is any consanguineal relation traced from one's grandparents (Skar, H., 1982: 167). Terminologically, Matapuqenos equate their parents' siblings with their parents, that is all one's maternal and paternal aunts are called either mother (*mamay*) or father (*tatay*). Only full siblings share identical kindreds and considering the importance of work exchanges, extended family assistance in carrying out ritual obligations, as well as family solidarity in conflicts, the strong bonds within the sibling group are the most important in a village society with weak formal leadership positions.

As is the case in most bilateral systems, both sons and daughters inherit land and animals, and strategies for countering the resultant land dispersal are focused on the choice of marriage partners. The most common pattern (c. 71 per cent) is one in which spouses are found within the same village moiety, and frequently several siblings from one family marry siblings from another (Skar, S., 1980). There are also many examples from the village in which two sisters marry two brothers, an arrangement ideal for the pooling of labour in those tasks designated specifically for men or women. For example, women pasture the animals on the upper slopes and guard the home. They do all of the cooking and much of the childcare. Men work in the valley co-operative for wages and can be away from home for a week at a time (Skar, S., 1984). However, men and women together share in the agricultural work, the produce of which is never sold for cash. While men earn wages at the co-operative, women have their own avenues for acquiring money through the sale of dairy products, poultry or their cattle and sheep.

In such family constellations, the importance of the relationship between same-sex siblings cannot be over-emphasised. Indeed, during childhood two sisters or two brothers near in age are regularly set tasks together, and often the closeness of these relationships far exceeds that of the parent/child. At a conceptual level two brothers or two sisters are identical and with both the levirate and the sororate as preferred forms of second marriage, these childhood partners gain a certain degree of individual interchangeability. The occurrence of both the levirate and the sororate emphasises the primary importance of the affinal bonds between families rather than the particular union of one man and one women.

From an individual woman's point of view, being a Runa in Matapuquio means that you are probably living in the same half of the village in which you grew up. You and your brother might be married to siblings (both actual and classificatory). If your brother's wife should die in childbirth, your brother would quite possibly marry another sister of your husband. Your fields, especially your maize lands, are in close proximity to those of your brothers and the traditional work exchanges between families are most easily arranged when your husband and his sister, (your brother's wife) have fields of similar size and location.

You and your husband together are the essential family unit and after children are born a hearth is rarely shared between households. As woman of the household, you have full responsibility for the *marka* in which all the agricultural produce and seeds are stored. You have your own lands when you enter into a conjugal relationship and it is the merging of your resources with your spouse's that forms the basis for the procreation of a new family unit just as symbolically your merging with a man is essential for your own completion as a full adult. Only within the context of this unity can you play a part in creation and recreation of society.

Linguistic Considerations

From this necessarily cursory treatment, I would like to point out what I consider to be the essential cultural content of gender for Runa in Matapuquio. The Runa have a highly complex symbolic system in which gender ideology is largely implicit or embedded. It is the unity of pairs which is the consistent focus of this symbolism (Isbell, 1976: Harris, 1978; Platt, 1978; Kaarhus, 1987). The role of symmetrical duality in Runa ideas about gender is to emphasis the unit.

This basic orientation of the unity of the pair is borne out in linguistic analyses of Quechua, a language based on the building up of suffixes to qualify the main idea. There are two suffixes to be noted in this context, -ntin and -wan and the word uklla. Both -ntin and -wan mean 'together with' but -ntin is only used in those cases in which the objects or people that are together make a single entity. In contrast, *-wan* expresses the idea that that which is together with something else does not form a single entity. Finally, the word *uklla* gives further underlining of this distinction because it expresses the anomaly of something that is alone which should be in a pair (literally, *uk-* one alone, together with the suffix *-lla* which expresses great compassion or regret; Ruis, C., n.d.: 96). Always it is the joining together which is the focus of the idea expressed (Kaarhus, 1987; Platt, 1976).

The much discussed concept of *yanatin* inspired by the work of Tristan Platt (1976, 1978) carries the argument a step further. *Yanatin* means two equal things making up a pair. When coupled with the suffix *-lla* the quality of the paired relationship is expanded to that of a mirror-image relationship, (*yanantin yanantillan: dos cosas hermanadas como guantes*, from Antonio Ricardo's dictionary of 1568; cited in Platt, 1978: 1101). Husband and wife have a *yanantin* relationship as do brother and sister (Mayer, 1977: 77); they are one and the same but different.

Catholic Notions About Women and Men

As noted above, the people of Matapuquio do not have close ties with the Roman Catholic Church but are certainly aware of its presence and turn to it first of all to gain benefit from what they perceive as potentially deriving from the efficacy of prayer and ritual blessings. These acts accord with the reciprocity between Runa and the animated forces of their natural surroundings. However, a deeper understanding of Christianity is largely lacking and I suggest that the church appears as an institution tailored to the service of the *misties* in the towns. The Christian God watches mainly over the welfare of the towns and it is the Runa gods of the landscape who care for and enter into the everyday lives of the Indians of the countryside.

From the anthropological perspective much more must be said concerning the relationship between Runa perceptions of the nature of the cosmos and the more orthodox Roman Catholic viewpoint. It must be made clear from the outset that I have no theological expertise. Brought up in a Christian tradition, my background was not Roman Catholic. Nevertheless, I suggest that anthropology affords a kind of parallel competence which allows me to identify certain broad themes of central concern to the Roman Catholic and indeed the Christian perspective in general. The following generalisations arise from conversations and shared experiences with resident missionary priests in the area who regarded anthropology as a kind of resource which could help them to resolve problems in their mission. Many of these broad themes related to what the priests identified as particular disappointments and frustrations in their work. Quite aside from conversations with the priests, numerous observations were made of situations in which the missionary presence had a high profile. Thus the following interpretation rests on my experiences of their message gleaned from various contexts.

The primary and overriding concern of the Church is that of monotheism.[12] It is over this issue that the greatest degree of subterfuge between priest and parishioner occurs. In celebrating the mass, the priest actually makes a contribution to Runa worship of the controlling forces in the landscape, perceived by them as crucial to the protection and procreation of the villagers' crops and herds. As we have seen, this worship has a male and female component but in fact the priest's offerings are most urgently required as offering to Pachamama. He is brought out of the town away from the church to the dispersed fields of the Matapuqenos. He is part of the regenerating force that animates the world – but only one aspect.

When in the presence of the priest a group of catechists were actually confronted about their worship of the mountain gods, there was a profound sense of consternation. These men represent the Church and its message in the hinterland areas yet they admitted to worshipping the protecting gods of their home villages. Even to this tutored group, the absolute idea of One God was anathema.[13] Matapuquio does not have a

12. Monotheism is the central core of Christian faith and as such poses one of the great barriers of comprehension between missionaries and non-Christians (see also Kahn, 1983; Ahmen and Hart, 1984). Ethnohistorians (Pease, 1973; Demarest, 1981) have shown us that the confrontation is a longstanding one and that many misunderstandings and misrepresentations have marked the way. The first missionaries were eager to identify the creator god of the Runa pantheon and to make of him a supreme god equivalent to their own (Duviols, 1977: 53; Urbano, 1981). Their task was to guide the indigenous populations towards a conception and final acceptance of one God which is supreme, more intelligent and powerful than all the others, and that this God created all that exists in the world (Duviols, 1977: 54). In their proselytising, this was the first step towards providing a logical motivation for disgarding all the other gods (*huacas*).

13. Marzal (1971) has a similar discussion with catechists from Cuzco about their practice of making offerings. The question which provoked the article was posed: can a Christian make such offerings and still be Christian? While I make no attempt at proposing an answer on the grounds of a similar exchange with catechists in Huancarama, it is interesting to note Marzal's views which are infused with a kind of benevolent relativism. There are many ways to finding God. This may well be the essence of how Matapuqenos view the discrepancy as well.

catechist and when I asked a priest how he thought that the villagers could retain their Roman Catholic faith he confidently replied that it was really the mothers who had the responsibility of teaching the tenets of the faith to their children.

Perhaps it was a blind response to a tactless question. Runa women are not the source of enlightened teaching about the One God. On the contrary, they are held to be the guardians fo Runa culture which they must convey to their children in unadulterated form. Many of the norms of the village underline the importance of restricting outside (polluting) influence on village women because of their socialising role. The idea of One God at the core of all Christian evangelism is far removed from women's experience of the paired regenerative forces of the animated landscape they worship. While they will attest to being Roman Catholic, for Matapuqenos this means precisely the opposite of what the priest envisages. For them it is a kind of pact by which they continue in their ways of venerating the landscape while acknowledging and according prominence to the powerful force of the Christian God.

Ambiguities in the attitudes of Runa to Christian monotheism seem to me to arise from a second broad theme implicit in the nature of the One God. Despite the obvious complexity of the issue from a theological perspective, the most evident model for introducing the Christian belief in One God is through the model of the patriarchal family.[14] The deity in this ideal family is male; indeed divinity of God is presented in terms of the obedience children show to their fathers, and wives show to their husbands. The Christian principle of service becomes enmeshed in the complicating relationships of conjugality and consanguinity.

The preponderance of the role which authority has in this patriarchical model is problematic from a Runa perspective. It is part of a coherent picture in which they are consistently in a subordinate position as regards local hierarchies, Church and State, all of which are closely associated. Until recently, acquiring official identity papers involved baptism as a first step. Many adult villagers must still approach the priest for baptism in order to acquire official recognition of their civil existence. For most village men, active contact with the Church was through the *hacienda*. Completely under the control of the *hacendado*, attendance at mass was required of the workers. Also at the village school, *misti* teachers forced their pupils to attend mass. The one significant occasion on which villagers actively choose to attend mass in

14. The trinitarian nature of the Christian God has been interpreted by Runa in terms of temporal change; God the Father as the past, the Son as the present, and the Spirit as the future (Randall, 1982).

Huancarama has always been at the New Year when their appointed leaders (*varakuna*) seek a blessing as signifying official state acceptance of their new posts.

Within the context of these hierarchically informed situations, villagers accept the authoritative model of the patriarchical family because it does reflect a real aspect of their relations with the Church and State beyond the boundaries of community. However, within the village their interaction with the divine, as it were, is couched in another communicative mode informed by the principle of reciprocity. That much of this interactive flow centres on the female creative forces of nature embodied in Pachamama and her many derivitives accentuates the difference. Male and female principles embodied in the paired deities of the landscape are the creative force of the Runa world and it is through offerings that Runa themselves can actively participate in forming that world. The act of creation is a kind of harmony between Runa and their tutelary deities.

Given the patriarchal family as model for Christian living, a third broad theme which I would identify as particularly problematic within the Roman Catholic tradition in Huancarama is that of celibacy and virginity. The fact that the priest does not live within a family but is bound to a vow of celibacy is, for most parishioners, an impossible and unnatural situation. Any light-complexioned children born in the towns or neighbouring hamlets are always the brunt of many graphic jokes about illicit sexual relations between the mother and one of the priests. That there were no religious orders for celibate women in the area exacerbates the imbalance in the situation. If the celibate priest is to stand as an example of Catholic virtue for men, there is no visible female model for women.

The absence of women in the Roman Catholic tradition in this area makes any discussion of the importance of Mary as Virgin and Mother more problematic. Nevertheless, her image does have a certain prominence in ritual processions. The theological proposition of her virginity and motherhood are hardly appreciated and indeed, as also noted elsewhere (Cáceres Olazo, 1970: 23), there is some indication that Mary takes on the role of wife of Jesus rather than as mother (Skar, H., forthcoming). Despite this she is called virgin, of course, and as object of worship she offers another example in which virginity and celibacy acquire the attribute of virtue. In the familial model presented by the priest who is the Church's representative in the parish, the proposed family is really not a family at all. The miracle of the virgin birth propounded by the celebate priest implies that the sexual connection within the family has a negative value. Runa beliefs in the sacredness of the pair and the valued creative force of sexuality, whether before marriage or not, becomes irredeemably undermined.

Conclusions

In this paper, I have presented an outline of what I consider to be the most salient features in Runa ideas about gender: the unity of the conjugal pair as an image pervading the Runa vision of the cosmos; the merging of opposites as the most important aspect in the creation of a paired unity; the emphasis on harmony as the ideal element in relations between Runa and between Runa and their animated, sacred surroundings; the maintaining of harmony through reciprocal offerings and exchanges which places an active role on Runa in the creation of prosperity; the central importance of sibling relationships in a bilateral system of kinship, particularly siblings of the same sex.

The essays in this volume attempt to analyse and assess the impact of missionaries on women; this case of a traditional Runa village, raises the problem of the incompatibility of the indigenous, and in this instance, Roman Catholic Christian beliefs. My personal view is that the key elements of monotheism, patriarchy and virginity/celibacy inherent in the Roman Catholic missionary message as I observed it pose a barrier preventing real communication between the Runa of Matapuquio and the missionary priests of Huancarama. As I have tried to argue, gender is the foundation of this division. It would seem apparent from an outsider's interpretation that the impact missionaries could have on Runa women, should a more open relationship develop, would probably be a downgrading of women and a deterioration of their position within the village. Though never directly attributed to the Church, Runa men underline the lack of respect afforded women outside the village and cite this as a negative aspect of contact with outsiders, particularly at the *hacienda*. As noted above, there are strong links between the local *hacienda* and the Church, and this association perhaps helps explain the dubious attraction the Church holds for women as they see it as a source of potential danger.

Catholic and Runa concepts which are used to differentiate men from women in terms of social worth are contradictary, not only in terms of their content but also as regards their degree of explicitness. While Catholic teachings on gender present highly complex and explicit interpretations about the opposition of good and evil, Runa notions are part of a symbolic system largely implicit or embedded in language as, for example, in the contrasting suffixes *-wan* and *-ntin* (discussed above). The Catholic notions of the male-gendered divinity, together with the negative value placed on sexuality expressed in the state of celibacy, are ideas which derive from a perceived opposition between man and woman, while the Runa conception emphasises their essential incompleteness as separate values.

In as much as the Church is an institution of prestige in the Peruvian highland context, it is a very forceful agent in transforming gender ideology, especially because its position of prestige is coupled with the promoting of the message about what gender relations in society should be. From a Runa point of view, it is the antithesis of a moral alternative for both men and women, and as such it perhaps serves them well to distance themselves from this God of the towns, this protector of the *misties*. It is the basic incompatibility of their epistemologies which may provide a partial explanation of why after some 450 years of virtual Church dominance, missionaries are still needed for proselyising work in the region. Runa have been affected by mission teaching, of course. Mass is seen as a valued element in village offerings to Pachamama during Santa Rosa when planting begins and later at a time when the rains are eagerly awaited. Runa have selected ritual elements such as prayers, incantations and the mass itself, and have placed them in the context of their own beliefs. However, it remains to be seen whether this domestication of the Church and the eclipsing of the missionary element by the gradual replacement of foreign with Peruvian priests will give scope for accommodations in the conflicting interpretations of gender.

Bibliography

Ahmen, A. S. and Hart, D. M. (1984) *Islam in Tribal Societies*, Routledge & Kegan Paul, London

Albó, Xavier (1976) 'El Ciclo Ceremonial Anual en el Mundo de los Llapuni (Bolivia)', *Allpanchis Phuturinga* 9:151–76

Allen, Catherine (1982) 'Body and Soul in Quechua Thought', *Journal of Latin American Lore* 8(2):179–96

_____ (1984) 'Patterned Time: The Mythic History of a Peruvian Community', Journal of Latin American Lore 10(2):151–73

Ardener, Shirley (ed.)(1981) *Women and Space: Ground Rules and Social Maps*, Croom Helm, London

Arguedas, José Maria (1956) 'Puquio: Una Cultura en Processo de Cambio', *Revista del Museuo Nacional* 25

Bastian, Joseph (1978) *Mountain of the Condor: Metaphor and Ritual in an Andean Ayllu*, West, St Paul, Minn.

Bolton, R. and Mayer, E. (eds) (1977) *Andean Kinship and Marriage*, American Anthropological Association, Washington DC

Bouysse-Cassagne, T. and Harris, O. (1987) 'Pacha: En Torno al Pensamiento

Aymara', in *Tres Reflexiones Sobre el Pensamiento Andino*: 11–59, HIS-BOL, La Paz

Brown, Peter (1981) *The Cult of the Saints. Its Rise and Function in Latin Christianity*, SCM Press, London

Brush, Stephen (1977) *Mountain, Field, and Family: The Economy and Human Ecology of the Andean* Valley, University of Pennsylvania Press, Philadelphia

Cáceres Olazo, M. (1970) 'Apuntes Sobre el Mundo Sobrenatural en Llavin', *Allpanchis Phuturinga* 2:23–41

Casaverde Rojas, J. (1970) 'El Mundo Sobrenatural en una Comunidad;, *Allpanchis Phuturinga* 2:121–43

Christian, William (1972) *Person and God in a Spanish Valley*, Seminar Press, London

Demarest, Arthur (1981) *Viracocha: The Nature and Antiquity of the Andean God*, Peabody Museum, Cambridge, Mass.

Doughty, Paul (1968) *Huaylas: An Andean District in Search of Progress*, Cornell University Press, Ithaca, NY

Duviols, Pierre (1977) 'Los Nombres Quechua de Viracocha, Supuesto Dios Creador de los Evangelizadores', *Allpanchis Phuturinga* 10:53–64

Garr, Thomas (1972) *Christianismo y Religion Quechua en la Prelatura Ayaviri*, Instituto de Pastoral Andina, Cusco

Geertz, Clifford (1973) *Interpretations of Culture*, Basic Books, New York

González Martinez, José Luis (1985) 'El Huanca y la Cruz: Migración y Transformación de la Mitologia Andina en las Barriadas de Lima', *America Indígena* 45(4):747–85

Gose, Peter (1986) 'Sacrifice and the Commodity Form in the Andes', *Man* (ns) 21(2):296–310

Gow, Rosalind and Condori, Bernabe (1982) *Kay Pacha*, Bartolomé de las Casas, Cusco

Gross, Daniel (1983) 'Fetishism and Functionalism: The Politial Economy of Capitalist Development in Latin America', *Comparative Studies in Society and History* 25(4):694–702

Harris, Olivia (1978) 'Complementarity and Conflict: an Andean View of Man and Women', in LaFontaine, J. (ed.), *Sex and Age as Principles of Social Organization*, Academic Books, London

Irarrazaval, Diego (1988) 'Mutación en la Indentidad Andina: Ritos y Concepciones de la Divindad', *Allpanchis Phuturinga* 31:11–85

Isbell, Billie Jean (1976) 'La Otra Mitad Essencial: Un Estudio de Complementariedad Sexual Andina', *Estudios Andinos* 5:37–56

———— (1978) *To Defend Ourselves: Ecology and Ritual in an Andean Village*, University of Texas, Austin, TX

Kahn, Miriam (1983) 'Sunday Christians, Monday Sorcerers', *Journal of Pacific History* 18(81&82):96–112

Kaarhus, Randi (1987) *Organiserende Prinsipper i Tid og Rom: Kulturell og Språklig Dualisme hos Quechua Indianerne Belyst Gjennom Konflikter i et Lokalsamfunn i Otavalo Ecuador*, Institute of Social Anthropology, Oslo

Lambert, Bernard (1977) 'Bilaterality in the Andes', in R. Bolton and E. Mayer (eds), *Andean Kinship and Marriage*: 1–27, American Anthropological Association, Washington DC

Lira, Jorge A. (1982) *Diccionario Kkechuwa–Espanol*, Bogotá: Secretaria Ejecutiva del Convenio 'Andres Bello'

Long, Norman. (ed.)(1984) *Forms of Non-Wage Labour and Rural Development*, Tavistock, London

MacCormack, Sabine (1985) 'The Heart Has Its Reasons: Predicaments of Missionary Christianity in early Colonial Peru', *Hispanic American Historical Review* 65:443–66

Mariscotti de Gørlitz, Ana Maria (1978) *Pachamama Santa Tierra Contribución al Estudio de la Religión Autóctona en los Andes Centro Merionales*, Gebr. Mann Verlag, Berlin

Marzal, Manuel (1971) *El Mundo Religioso de Urcos*, Instituto de Pastoral Andina, Cusco

———— (1983) *La Transformación Religiosa Peruana*, Pontificai Universidad Catolica del Peru, Lima

———— (1988) 'La Fiesta Patronal Andina en la Cuidad de Lima', *Allpanchis Phuturinga* 32:85–124

Mayer, E. (1977) 'Beyond the Nuclear Family', in R. Bolton and E. Mayer (eds), *Andean Kinship and Marriage*: 60–80, American Anthropological Association, Washington, DC

Mishkin, Bernard (1946) 'The Contemporary Quechua', in J. Steward (ed.), *Handbook of South American Indians*. Vol. 2:411–70, Smithsonian Institution, Washington, DC

Mission Handbook: North American Protestant Ministries Overseas (1976) MARC, Monrovia, Cal.

Neill, Stephen (1976) *A History of Christian Mission*, Penguin, Harmondsworth

Ortiz, Alejandro (1982) 'Moza: Espacio, Tiempo y Sexo en un Pueblo Andino', *Allpanchis Phuturinga* 20: 189–208

Pagden, Anthony (1982) *The Fall of Natural Man: The American Indian and the Origins of Comparative Ethnology*, Cambridge University Press, Cambridge

Pease, Franklin (1973) *El Dios Creador Andino*, Mosca Azul, Lima

———— (1981) 'Continuidad y Resistencia de lo Andina', *Allpanchis Phuturinga* 17/18:105–18

Perroud, C. and Chouvenc, J. (1970) *Diccionario Castellano–Kechwa–Castellano. Dialecto de Ayacucho*, Seminario San Alfonso, Santa Clara, Peru

Platt, Tristan (1976) *Espejos y Maiz: Temas de la Estructura Simbólica Andina*, CIPCA, La Paz

———— (1978) 'Symétries en Miroir, le Concept de Yanantin chez les Macha de Bolivie', *Annales 'Economies Sociéties Civilisations* 33(5–6): 1081–107

Randall, Robert (1982) 'Qoyllur Rit'ian Inca Fiesta of the Pleiades: Reflections on Time and Space in the Andean World', *Boletin del Instituto Francés de Estudios Andinos* 11:37–81

Rasnake, Roger (1988) *Domination and Cultural Resistance: Authority and*

Power among an Andean People, Duke University Press, London

Ruiz Cisnaros, Liz (n.d.) *Ayacucho Quechua Grammar*, manuscript

Sallnow, Michael (1983) 'Monorial Labour and Religious Ideology in the Central Andes – A Working Hypothesis', *Bulletin of Latin American Research* 2:39–56

———— (1987) *Pilgrims of the Andes: Regional Cults in Cusco*, Smithsonian Institution Press, Washington, DC

Skar, Harald (1982) *The Warm Valley People: Duality and Land Reform among the Quechua Indians of Highland Peru*, Oslo University Press, Oslo

———— (n.d.) *An Andean Cosmology*, Gothenburg: Department of Social Anthropology, University of Gothenburg, Working Paper No. 22

———— (forthcoming) 'Local Cults and the Role of the Catholic Priest', in B. Pickering (ed.), *Missionaries, Enculturation, and the Role of the Anthropologist*, Macmillan, London

Skar, Sarah Lund (1980) *Quechua Women and Agrarian Reform in the Pincos Valley: A Case from the Southern Highlands of Peru*, Mag.Art. Thesis, Oslo University

———— (1981) 'Andean Women and the Concept of Space/Time', in S. Ardener (ed.), *Women and Space: Ground Rules and Social Maps:* 35–49, Croom Helm, London

———— (1984) 'Interhousehold Cooperation in Peru's Southern Andes: A Case of Multiple Sibling Group Marriage', in N. Long (ed.), *Forms of Non-wage Labour and Rural Development:* 83–98, Tavistock, London

———— (1987) 'The Role of Urine in Andean Notions of Health and the Cosmos', in H. Skar and F. Salomon (eds), *Natives and Neighbors in South America: Anthropological Essays*: 267–94, Gothenburg Ethnographic Museum, Gothenburg

Urbano, Enrique (1981) *Wiracocha y Ayar: Hérores y Funciones en las Sociedades Andinas* Centro Bartolomé de las Casas, Cusco

Valleé, Lionel (1982) 'El Discurso Mítico de Santa Cruz Pachacuti Yamqui', *Allpanchis Phuturinga* 17:103–26

Wachtel, Nathan (1972) *The Vision of the Vanquished. The Spanish Conquest of Peru Through Indian Eyes. 1530–1570*, Harvester Press, Hassocks, Sussex

Urton, Gary (1981) *At the Crossroads of the Earth and the Sky: An Andean Cosmology*, University of Texas Press, Austin, TX

Zuidema, R. (1982) 'Catachillay: The Role of the Pleiades and of the Southern Cross and the Centauri in the Calendar of the Incas', *Annals of the New York Academy of Science* 38:203–29

13

These Catholic Sisters are all Mamas! Celibacy and the Metaphor of Maternity

Joan F. Burke

Introduction

This paper explores the impact of the Kongo culture on the expression of the Catholic sisterhood among the African members of the Sisters of Notre Dame de Namur in Lower Zaïre.[1] It suggests the consequent way in which these women perceive religious life, thereby offering to other sisters an insight into a different facet of their given call. This case study is an example of how the specific cultural context of one 'younger church' in Africa not only influences how Christianity is understood in local terms, but also demonstrates that the consequent transformation of institutions may in fact be a positive contribution to other 'older churches'.

The Churches of Africa are today very much bringing to the fore a heightened awareness of the cultural question in the larger community of Christian Churches. Since the time of St Paul, the majority of Christians have been of the so-called Western world. As a corollary, the theology that developed in the Churches was based on, and used the categories and expressions of, the philosophical tradition of the Graeco-Roman heritage. By the end of this century, however, as Walbert Bühlmann wrote, 'the Church, at home in the western world for almost 2000 years, will have shifted its centre of gravity into the Third World, where its adherents will be more numerous' (Bühlmann 1976: 20). In the conclusion of the same study, the Swiss missiologist points out the significance of this shift:

1. The Congregation first went to the region in 1894. Most of the early missionaries were Belgians.

Europe is no longer the world; the Church is no longer Church of the West .
. . . We must not stand in the way of young Churches in their search for new
experiments, new methods and a 'native' theology. To date, only a small part
of mankind has engaged in theologising: the West has had a virtual monopoly. Now the other regions of the world are meeting Christ and his message
and are beginning to make theology on the basis of their own history and
their own insights, so we must expect a springtime burst of fresh theologies
in bud. (Bühlmann, 1976: 393)

In so far as theology may be defined as 'faith reflecting on experience' (St Augustine), African sisters are creating not only a different
expression of religious life, but also contributing to the development of
a new theology to challenge and enrich existing theologies. Whereas the
dominant metaphor of the Belgian missionary sisters who had evangelised the women of Lower Zaïre was that of sisterhood, local women
have preferred a metaphor of maternity which is more consonant with
the experience and perception of their people, the matrilineal Kongo.

This case study is based on fieldwork carried out during the years
1980–8 among the sisters of Notre Dame de Namur. The Congregation
is not, strictly speaking, a missionary order. It was founded in Amiens
after the French Revolution by St Julie Billiart for the education of poor
girls. Today the sisters number 2600 and work in fifteen different countries on all five continents.

The Sisters of Notre Dame first arrived in what was then the Congo
Free State in 1894, one year after the Jesuits. The Vatican had entrusted
the latter with the evangelisation of the Lower Zaïre north of the Inkisi
River. The priests invited the sisters to join them and be responsible for
working with the women and children. From the outset, the women missionaries became involved in village education centres, health services
and basic rural development. Most of them made good use of their
being themselves daughters of Belgian farmers. As the schools began to
develop, the sisters exercised an increasing influence on the region
since education was entirely left to the missions by the colonial administration up until 1954.

Almost all of the early Sisters of Notre Dame were Belgian, with a few
Dutch, German and Irish women. As early as the 1920s, local women
asked to join them in their work and imitate them in their way of life. Several times they petitioned the Belgian Jesuit Bishop to allow them to
become sisters, but only in the late 1930s did he finally approve the opening of a novitiate for Kongo women at Lemfu. Today there are over eighty
Zaïreans among the nearly 100 Sisters of Notre Dame in the country.

The body of this paper focuses on the African expression of religious
life as observed in the 1980s, but a word should be said about the rela-

tionship between the different groups of sisters before and after the transition from a predominantly expatriate-constituted Province[2] to a Zaïrean one during the mid-1970s. I first went to Zaïre on a two month visit in 1971. It was during a period of mounting tension within the country, especially between expatriates (most Belgian) and Zaïreans. The President was preparing to announce what would become a very significant 'policy of authenticity'. This was presaged during my visit by his changing the country's name: I had gone to Congo, and I would leave Zaïre.

Among the sisters themselves there was also considerable tension. Parity between the number of Zaïrean and expatriate members had almost been reached. However, most of the posts of responsibility in the Province were still held by Belgians, including the Provincial Superior and Novice Mistress. Since almost all of the expatriate missionaries present had arrived in the country before independence in 1960, not surprisingly their ways of relating to the local population were not free from the colonial overlay of a mentality of superiority and paternalism. The examples that the Zaïrean sisters cited to me at the time included: the Belgians' condescending language in addressing or referring to the Zaïreans, their discouragement of Zaïrean sisters who wanted to pursue post-secondary and further professional training (which in fact most of the Belgians lacked), and the tight control of all finances by the expatriates. A verbal indicator of the existing tension within communities was the frequent use in conversation by members of both the respective cultural groups of the French expression, 'nous autres' (we) . . . 'vous autres' (you). Perhaps because I was an outsider and closer in age to the Zaïrean sisters – as also because I had been sent there on a fact-finding mission on behalf of the Congregation's Generalate – the Africans spoke to me very freely of how in community they were made to feel inferior to the old-time missionaries.

When I returned to live in Zaïre as a member of the Province nine years later in 1980, the situation was very much changed. As of 1976, the Provincial Superior and a year later the Mistress of Novices were Africans; and, increasingly since, so too are the local community Superiors. There was no longer the tension of the transition years that had been reflected in the French expression 'nous autres . . . vous autres'. Significantly, the common usage of the Kikongo kinship terms, such as *Yaya*, meaning 'big sister', and *Mama*, were not only used commonly by the Zaïrean sisters to address one another, but they were also freely

2. Province here refers to the semi-autonomous groupings within the Congregation which usually reflect national or linguistic boundaries.

extended to include the various expatriate members of the community. This accommodation of local kinship terminology by the sisters, even when speaking in French, suggested to me an ease of relationships among them.

The Kongo sisters are very conscious that both in the terms of their people's heritage and the tradition of the Catholic sisterhood received from the 'Belgian Mothers' of the Zaïre Province, in the kiln of their lives they are themselves firing new vessels made of African clay. They see the first Zaïrean sisters as pioneers cutting a path through an uncharted forest. As the Provincial Superior wrote in 1986 on the occasion of a Jubilee,[3]

> Today the path has been traced out and beaten down. No longer is it only a single person who is painstakingly tramping through the grass to make some headway. But rather, after a group of sixty daughters of the country have gone before, the path has become firmer and firmer under the feet. Here the trail is flat and easy to walk on; there, when it dips into the valley, it requires courage to press on (Sr Kitewo, 1986).

The sisters today are very aware that the first generation of Kongo women who joined the Congregation as path-breakers necessarily suffered in breaking the new ground. The burden of adaptation had fallen largely on them when they entered a group that was at the time in the Congo entirely Belgian in its composition. During the years since then, while the African membership has greatly increased, there has also been an important shift in Church thinking. Within the Catholic community, the Second Vatican Council in the 1960s gave great impetus to the development of a theology of 'particular churches', emphasising that each local church would have its specific expression of and response to the Christian message. Catholicity can less and less be readily identified with a uniform, 'Roman' expression of Christianity. One of the more immediately obvious signs of this shift is the replacement of Latin by the widespread use of vernacular languages for the celebration of Catholic worship.

Since 1975, there have been Zaïrean representatives at all international meetings of the Sisters of Notre Dame. Their presence and contributions to the deliberations – as also those of the sisters from the rest of Africa, Latin America and Japan - have clearly begun to have an impact on the Congregation. As the Zaïrean sisters begin to articulate and define their particular insights into the Catholic sisterhood coming from their specific experience as African women, the members of the Con-

---

3. The sisters were celebrating a twenty-fifth anniversary of the Congregation.

gregation are becoming much more aware of cultural differences that exist even in older Provinces. When delegates came together in an international gathering of the order in 1984 to finalise the revision of their Constitutions, a major concern was to write a document that respected the wide range of cultural differences existing within the membership. I would suggest that this is indicative of what will become a growing impact of the 'younger churches' on the 'older churches' – what has been called the 'reverse mission'. The evangelised are becoming themselves the evangelisers today of those who evangelised them yesterday.

An African Clay, a Different Texture

When the oldest of the Zaïrean Sisters, sister Ntieti, speaks of her early desire to become a religious, she is insistent about how there was then only one possible life conceivable for a Kongo woman:

> It belongs to women: take care of children [*kindesi*, handmaids], work in the fields, and marry in order to 'repair' [*kulonda*, remake] the clan, and that is all . . . (Reminiscences, 40th Jubilee of Profession. 2 June 1985)

Another of her novitiate companions in the early 1940s recounts how they were objects of scorn and contempt for the local population. Whenever the first Kongo sisters were seen walking along the road, people hurled biting insults at them, such as,

> Look at those sterilised cows!
> Look at those barren women who flee the labour
> pains of giving others birth! (ibid.)

And Sister Ndundu continues,

> These insults pierced our hearts;
> they are very strong words
> for an African woman [to hear]. (ibid.)

Among the matrilineal Kongo, the first and primary obligation of women is to propagate the clan (*kanda*) by bearing children (*mbongo bantu*, literally 'riches in human beings'). Consequently a sterile woman is condemned to live with a heavy burden of shame. As one proverb puts it:

> A calabash is unusable [fwa, literally, 'dead'] if
> its stopper is too tight.
> Meaning: A sterile woman is useless. (Van Roy and Daeleman, 1963: 18)

The lot of such a woman is unhappy indeed.

The importance attached to fecundity was remarked upon by the early Europeans who lived in the region at the turn of the century. John Weeks wrote,

> A barren woman . . . is ridiculed by the women of her district, and is treated with scorn by her own family, for she has failed to add her quota to the maintenance of the clan. Her name is bandied from mouth to mouth in the village song, her life is rendered intolerable by the sneers of her neighbours . . ..
> (Weeks, 1914: 107)

As Van Wing stated in his classic ethnography:

> The woman is most necessary to the clan for her productivity. It is she who gives (to the clan) the best of goods, human beings: *mbongo bantu*, 'riches in humans'. And, by her labour, it is she who ensures their well-being. She herself is the first of all 'riches' for the Kongo. (1921: 206)

The primary value of woman is perceived as her motherhood.

Towards a Matrifocal Understanding of the Sisterhood

On solemn occasions when the history of the clan (*ntangumuna*) is recounted, the most important figures besides the chiefs are their sisters, who are the 'mothers of the children' who founded the sub-lineages of the clan sections (cf. MacGaffey, 1970: 20). Kongo children receive their social identity as members of a given *kanda* (clan-section) through their mothers. It follows that, in general terms, a woman is primarily valued as a life-bearer. This valuation is not limited to mere biological reproduction. What is equally, perhaps more, significant, is that the life that the woman passes on is not seen as her own, but as that of her people.

In the Kongo cultural setting it was unimaginable to accord any positive value to celibacy, as did women religious. Without a doubt, the greatest difficulty that the local population had in accepting the Catholic sisterhood was in understanding that any woman would freely choose to commit herself to live according to a vow of chastity. It seemed hardly possible to fathom the purpose of total continence.

Many villagers, when they speak of their earlier incredulity, recount how the people were convinced that the reason why the missionary sisters returned to their countries on furlough was to have there the babies they conceived with the missionary priests. The reasoning was called into question when local women became sisters and, by contrast, were always under the scrutiny of the population. In their case, they returned to their villages for their home visits.

With the passage of time and long experience of the sisters – both expatriate and Kongo – there has been an almost complete reversal in the perception of the religious life by the population. By and large, families today do not put obstacles in the way of their daughters' entering a congregation if they so wish. This is in great contrast to the very difficult experience of the heroic, persevering women who entered religious communities in the 1930s and 1940s. Within one generation, the number of young women attracted to the Catholic sisterhood in Zaïre has increased markedly. According to a study done by Sr Mary Noberta (1955: 113), there were 870 African sisters in the combined Belgian Congo and Rwanda-Urundi in 1954. Statistics published by the Episcopal Conference of Zaïre showed that in the country there were 1891 African sisters in 1977 and 2600 by 1985.

There is no evidence that the young women wishing to become sisters look upon marriage in a disparaging way; nor do they lack the desire to be productive members of society. Rather, a different understanding of celibacy – resting upon continence alone – is very evident in the way in which the Kongo sisters themselves explain their choice of the sisterhood as their way of life. These young adults often explain their motive for becoming members of the religious congregation in terms of a maternity of a kind that makes them 'mothers for all the people'. Their choice of this alternative way of living is presented as more of an affirmation than a denial of the basic matrifocal Kongo valuation of women in terms of motherhood.

The eventual acceptance by the villagers of the celibacy of the sisters in terms of a shift in the metaphor of maternity was brought home to me in a striking way by the following illustrative incident. When I was stationed at the Lemfu Mission I overheard a conversation of a woman with her young child. It was in the late afternoon and the woman, with a filled bucket on her head, was obviously returning to the dispensary after fetching water at the stream. Most likely she was from the interior and had come to the mission seeking medical care. I was walking, seemingly unnoticed, somewhat behind the woman and her son, but within earshot. In front of them on the road was a small group of Zaïrean sisters wearing, as usual, their African wraps. The young boy asked his mother, '*Mama*, who are those women there?' She replied, 'They are *BaMama BaMaseri*.'. When he looked at her with a puzzled expression, she continued, 'They are *Mamas*, but not in the same way as I am your *mama*. *BaMama BaMaseri* are women who are Mamas for us all'.[4]

---

4. The literal translation of Mama MaSeri is 'Mother-Sister'. I would suggest, though, that the Kongo do not perceive this when they use the expression since the French 'MaSoeur' is treated more as a title/name than as a word with an intrinsic meaning as shown in the following paragraph.

It is a quite common practice in the Lower Zaïre for Catholic sisters to be addressed as '*Mama..*' This is true both of local and expatriate women. The title of address more commonly used in Belgium and the United States, 'sister', is always left in its localised French form, MaSeri (from the French 'Ma Soeur'), rather than being translated into Kikongo as *mpangi* (sister/brother). The application to the sister of the title '*Mama*', the usual form of address to a Kongo woman who has borne her people children, presumes a different perception of sisters from that of the Belgian and American sisters.[5]

The fact that most of the sisters are teachers of children, or work in the dispensary caring for the sick, strongly reinforces this perception in terms of maternity. As noted above, for the Kongo themselves, of far greater importance than physical maternity is always social maternity.[6] A proverb neatly underscores this:

> Giving birth to a child is not to care for it.
> *Meaning*: It is not enough simply to procreate,
> one must raise a child. (Van Roy and Daeleman, 1963: 64)

Since in the rural areas of Lower Zaïre the secondary schools of the sisters require that all the girls live in school, the schools do in fact become for the students their 'second village'. This arrangement is a practical necessity for those whose villages are at a great distance; in addition, lodging at school gives the girls some opportunity to study outside formal class times. In their villages, the girls would be expected to spend most of their afternoons caring for younger brothers and sisters, collecting firewood, fetching water and preparing meals for their families. Thus, educationally, most are considerably disadvantaged by comparison with boys in the village primary schools. Boys have greater opportunity to do as they like with their free time. Again, a proverb offers a good illustration of the great freedom enjoyed by the boy,

> A boy's head is like a young cassava leaf.
> *Meaning*: Boys are seen everywhere all the time. (Van Roy and Daeleman, 1963: 89)

5. Mona MacMillan and Sarah Skar pointed out in discussions that 'Mother' is commonly used as an address for Catholic Sisters in Southern Europe and Hispanic America. The latter suggested that there may be some correlation in the adopting of 'Mother' in societies of lineal descent systems which emphasise generational over the sibling relationship. This might warrant further investigation.

6. I prefer to use in this context the expression 'social maternity' rather than the term social reproduction. The former seems much closer to the KiKongo word, *bungudi*, which is a qualitative noun derived from the word *ngudi* meaning 'mother'.

As a result, the mission school becomes the 'temporary village' for the girls during term time. Every two weeks they return home to stock up on provisions for preparing their own meals at school, most often in village groups. Sometimes the mission complements their foodstuffs with the harvest of school fields. At night the students sleep in rather rudimentary dormitories on cots, or on mats on a raised slab of concrete. Some girls make mattresses with leaves stuffed into a sewn slip-cover. Schools that are too poor to have cots provide a raised slab of concrete which serves as a common bed for all.

In most of these schools a sister serves as the Directress of Boarders. Usually she is the person – much more than the Principal – looked upon by the students as their 'school mother'. As their mothers do back in their home villages, she cares for them when they are sick or grieving; she feeds them if they run out of food when she has the means; she oversees the school fields; she chides them when they are stepping out of line, and disciplines them when they are disobedient or disrespectful.

Even young teachers on the staff often relate to the Directress of Boarders as their mother. At times, they may even ask her to serve as their intermediary with the Principal who, in the school context, is more of an authority figure. Frequently the unmarried, male teachers attempt to persuade her to provide their meals since they are 'motherless' at the mission, in their own terms. At one mission where there was an expatriate sister as the Principal working with an older Zaïrean sister as the Directress of Boarders, the latter had accepted the request of the teachers to help prepare their midday meal. When the Principal learned of it, she made it clear that she was not in agreement. The Directress of Boarders retorted, 'Have you no maternal heart?'

Similarly, the unmarried nurses also have expectations that the sisters will cater for their meals when they come to work in a mission dispensary with the *BaMama BaMaseri*. The older Zaïreans are more vulnerable to these propositions than are the younger. The former certainly do extend their maternal role to include looking after the more practical, daily needs of co-workers, especially young, unattached males, who are finding it hard to adjust to looking after themselves without their mothers being close at hand: this category may also include the priests at the mission.

Hospitality and Women's Deference to Men

During the three months in 1987 that I lived in the village of Nselo carrying out a programme of interviews with women, I returned daily from my rounds in the late afternoon literally laden with gifts. Frequently, a young child had to be commissioned to accompany me and help carry the women's gifts of chickens, ears of fresh maize, bowls of *mbika* (a type of melon seed) and various kinds of fruit. Even very poor households insisted on giving me something as a token of their generosity and appreciation of my visit, especially if it was the first one. If they had no cock – the traditional gift – to offer me, they would present me with a few eggs. After an initial visit, relationships are strengthened by an exchange of gifts.

In accordance with village custom, when family members come to see a sister they usually bring something to offer to the community. The Zaïrean sisters also attach great importance to receiving visitors generously and bestowing a liberal hospitality. Besides the offering of food, the presence of community members is also important to the guests. Even if a sister is not at home when visitors come to see her, others welcome them in her name. The visitors are presented with a gift when they leave to return to the village. Usually, this is done quite discreetly. Typically, the basket that the guests gave to the hosts with a chicken or produce from their fields is given back to them containing a bit of sugar, some tea, a tin of dried milk, etc.[7] When Kongo men speak of the qualities that they want to find in their wives, they always emphasise the woman's being generous with hospitality. The welcome that their wives provide visitors gives important access to influence, as two frequently cited proverbs point out:

> There where you eat, you converse.
> Meaning: Hospitality opens the heart.

> When you eat with someone,
> the heart cannot be turned around [literally, 'twisted']. (Van Roy and Daeleman, 1963: 21)

Women themselves similarly want to be known as generous. During my interviews, I asked them how they would describe a *nkento makutu* (literally, 'woman with ears', meaning one who is worthy of respect). Young and old alike all put generous hospitality and welcome (*ntambula*, derived from the verb meaning 'offer to someone') at the top of their

---

7. The nature of goods exchanged often reflects the parties' recognising their respective different worlds. Whereas in this instance the Kongo sisters offer to villagers manufactured goods to which they have greater access when they visit family in the capital, visitors most likely will bring 'village goods', such as fruit or produce from the community fields. Similarly, at local wakes and funerals: village kin provide the participants with food and drink; city kin are expected to contribute the coffin.

list. Not infrequently this generous giving is linked with the deference to men women are expected to show.

Just as men of the village expect their wives to show generous hospitality to their guests, the priests of the parish often make similar demands on the sisters. When distinguished visitors come to the mission, it is the parish priest who usually arranges all the details of the programme for their reception. However, he invariably turns to the sisters for the preparation of the food and meals.

On a more daily basis, some priests regularly solicit the service of the sisters to prepare their cassava and bread, and perhaps even a feast-day gateau! It is not extraordinary at some missions for the clergy to come to the sisters for such mundane supplies as nails and paint, rather than stock any themselves, which they normally could do as easily. The sisters may frequently complain among themselves about such demands, but usually are accommodating and do not refuse the service. A limit was finally declared at one mission when the parish priest requested that the principal of the primary school have her girls fetch water and firewood for the rectory. In this instance, the priest addressed the sister without even considering asking the help of the students in the boys' primary school, which was much closer! The latter was run by a Zaïrean congregation of religious brothers. No reason was given why the services were requested of the girls and not of the boys; collecting wood and drawing water are more commonly the tasks of females in the villages. It is interesting to note that the archival record does show that the earlier expatriate missionary priests also turned to the sisters for domestic services. Sister Léonie de l'Assomption, wrote of 1906:

> The sisters at Kisantu do at the Mission all the wash, ironing, mending and sewing for the priests and brothers of all the mission posts of the region: Kisantu, Lemfu, Sanda, Mpese, Kipako, Ndembo. (*Congo Débuts 1894-1906*: 76)

Deference to men is most obviously shown by the sisters when priests or brothers join the community for a meal. Although all the sisters serve themselves in buffet style, they frequently bring food back to the seated men. The community may also present each priest with a bottle of beer, while they themselves drink water. At the end of the main course, visiting priests and brothers are offered a separate dessert plate although the sisters always use one plate for both the courses. Usually these special services are not offered when visiting women religious join the community at table. In one community where a priest came for a meal regularly once a week, the sisters often presented him with a particular dish expressly prepared for him. These unequal favours to male and female guests suggest that the sisters show the culturally expected deference of women to men.

By contrast, in the area of domestic arrangements, in convents there is a marked reversal of the usual male-female roles of the village. The way in which women relate to their workers, including domestic servants, suggests that there has been a clear carry-over of models dating from colonial times. A particularly striking case is the fact that the cook in the community in all of the houses of the sisters is a man. In the village, cooking is a strictly female domain.

Also, much in contrast to the more common village patterns, the sisters do not always show the usual deference expected of a woman when they speak to men working at the mission. Some may even be heard addressing male workers who are older than they are as though they were children. Hearing a woman speaking directly to a man without the usual title 'Tata', but only using his name, in a commanding voice seemed strident even to me. Towards male employees there may also be a lack of attention to such important village manners as greeting everyone on their arrival and offering them a handshake as a sign of recognition and respect. Thus, observations suggest that the worker-employer relationship in convents follows more the Belgian colonial interpretation of the subject-chief model than that of the traditional male-female model. However, sisters do seem to be much more careful in their relationships with co-workers in the professional sphere of the schools and the dispensary.

At one school where I was teaching and serving as part-time secretary, the relatively young principal came into the office one morning to express her consternation to me. She had just overheard a much younger, inexperienced sister speak to a male teacher in a condescending manner and without using any title – neither the usual French 'Professeur' nor the KiKongo 'Tata'. Before the morning was out, the principal called the sister into her office and reminded her of the importance of speaking to everyone with respect, 'just as would be worthy of a Mama in the village'. There, a 'true mother' (Mama kibeni) shows respect to all.

During my interviews in Nselo, women of all ages consistently praised a middle-aged woman named Mama Bungudi. The description of this woman given to me in one of my long chats with two grandmothers (BaNkaka), BaMama Sofi and Tifwani, who had been life-long friends, was typical:

> Look at that Mama Bungudi there. When she first came to Nselo she had only one child; now she has eight. She is just like a true mwesi Nselo [local inhabitant]. She respects everyone: men, women, children. And for that reason she herself is very respected and has great influence. (Nselo, 1 December 1987)

For the Kongo, persons merit respect when they themselves are respectful of others; the grandmothers' words show how closely women associate respect and influence with fecundity.

'Mothers for All'

It is significant that Kongo sisters themselves have come to see their chosen life as a kind of 'alternative motherhood' for the whole of the society. In a commemorative book written by the sisters in the Province on the occasion of the twenty-fifth anniversary of the first Zaïrean to enter the Congregation, they wrote:

> Chastity is the most striking characteristic of religious life in Africa because women are expected to be givers of life [to the clan]. It is to a spiritual fecundity that God calls us. Through our apostolic work, we must be true spiritual mothers. This will show itself also in how we clothe ourselves and speak . . . in all our behaviour. (*Floraison* . . . 1986: 92)

In this there is a demonstration both of how profoundly the culture has affected the understanding of religious life, and of how local sisters are affirming by their own lives the basic traditional valuing of woman primarily as mother. The Zaïrean sisters explain the celibacy of their lives as not so much a relinquishing of physical maternity for their own clan (*mama nitu*), but much more as a call to nurture and foster life for all in an unbounded, universal spiritual maternity (*mama moyo*).[8]

Unlike the first generation of Kongo religious, the young women who wish to become sisters today rarely meet with strong opposition in their families. Celibacy itself may still be a mystery for many, even family members of the sisters – and perhaps, to some extent to the sisters themselves. One of the very first Kongo women to enter the Congregation in the 1940s confided to me:

> The fact that I have chosen to live as a celibate woman religious costs me greatly even now in my later years . . . I will leave no children of my own in this world. And yet, to give myself to God and to all his people is what I do want to do with my life. I am so happy . . . (Sr Ndundu, Ngidinga, 4 December 1984)

For almost all of the sisters there is at least one person in the family who never really accepts her choice to be a religious. As one sister (born in 1955), who made her first profession of vows in 1979, explained to me,

8. *Moyo* is the Kongo word to define the life/spirit of the inner person. At death the body, *nitu*, is slipped off as an outer envelope and the person receives another body that is short and white-skinned, with red hair. Cf. Bentley (1887); Butaye (1909); Van Wing (1921: 7–10, 15).

I have one aunt, my father's sister, who asks me each time I see her, 'Isn't it long enough that you have given yourself to the Lord? It is now time that you return to us and give us some children'.

The same sister recounted to me how another (born in 1949), who had entered some years before her, had met with serious opposition from some in her family. She had to work for several years before she could enter the Congregation since her uncles obliged her to give them what they would have received as bridewealth had she married. Even in cases where one or more parents have been hesitant in the beginning, once they see that their daughters are serious in their resolve, families usually leave them to decide and do not press their objections. Much of this change in attitude is related to the people's cumulative experience of seeing religious around them and appreciating their work. Certainly, there are also families who would consider a member's becoming a Catholic sister as a mark of social prestige and hope for easy access to education and health services – not only for herself, but others in the family as well. One of the reasons for the very long probation period before the woman is allowed by the Congregation to take her final vows is to test her motivation.[9]

Precisely the religious vow of celibacy that raised such strong objections in families of young women who wished to become sisters in the first generations, because of its denying the clan the fruit of their physical maternity (*mbongo bantu*, literally 'riches in human beings'), today seems to be generally understood in terms of maternity. This is in the sense of a motherhood not limited to one family and to the propagation of one clan, but to the bearing and nurturing of life for all the People of God.

Thus, all in all, undeniably the most significant feature in the Kongo society that has influenced and actually re–formed an understanding of religious life in the local context is the important role of motherhood among the matrifocal Kongo. In the words of an elder Zaïrean sister,

Mothers of the body give us birth,
Mothers of the spirit nourish and help us to grow.

(Sr Ntieti, Ngidinga 1987)

---

9. Generally the young woman may not become a postulant in the Congregation until after she has completed a professional qualification, such as a teacher or a nurse, and worked for at least one or two years. The year of postulancy is followed by a three-year novitiate before the person may take her first vows which are made for a limited time. Only after another five years may she petition the Congregation to admit her to final vows.

And so it is that for the Zaïrean sisters maternity seems to be a very appropriate metaphor in their understanding their choice of celibacy lived in a religious community, as it is also for the Kongo people who address them as 'Mama'.

Conclusion

Reflecting on my experience of living with Kongo sisters for eight years, certainly their perception of themselves and their relationship with their people in terms of maternity affected me personally. As an American religious woman, sisterhood remains for me a central metaphor for how I understand my choice of life. It defines not only how I see my relationships with those with whom I live in community and relate to as my sisters, but also it is representative of my commitment to be for all whom I meet a sister, accepting them as my brothers and sisters. The Africans calling me 'Mama' did challenge me to reflect on how I might be for them – as for all who are my brothers and sisters – a life-bearer and particularly attuned to promoting as well the collective life of the wider community. The older Belgians and other Americans who had been in Zaïre longer than I had all seemed quite at home with the people's calling them 'Mama'. Although the Belgians would be more accustomed than the Americans, who were younger, to living in community with a hierarchical model similar to that of the Zaïre Province, by and large most of the expatriate sisters found it quite appropriate in the local Kongo context.

The intention of this essay has been to describe one case that would demonstrate the extent to which a specific cultural setting might alter and modify a Christian institution. Undeniably, Christianity has had an impact on the people of Lower Zaïre. In time, the experience of this 'young church' will inevitably have its impact on the 'older Churches' of the West. Already, within the Catholic tradition, the Vatican has formally given its approval to a distinctive rite of the Eucharist for use in Zaïre which is more consonant than the older Latin Rite with the cultural setting of the people.

Twenty years ago Pope Paul VI affirmed at a Pan-African meeting of Bishops in Kampala, Uganda:

> The expression, that is the language and mode of manifesting the Faith, may be manifold, hence it may be original, suited to the tongue, the style, the character, the genius and the culture of the one who professes this Faith. From this point of view, a certain pluralism is not only legitimate, but desirable . . . And in this sense you [Africans] may, and *you must, have an African Christianity* [emphasis mine]. Indeed you possess human values and charac-

teristic forms of culture which can rise up so as to find in Christianity, and for Christianity, a true superior fullness and prove to be capable of a richness of expression all its own, and genuinely African. (Closing discourse to All-Africa Symposium of African Bishops, 1969)

Christian communities have taken up this invitation seriously. As the anthropologist-priest Aylward Shorter has written, 'The time will come when we stop talking about translating Western Christianity into African terms, and begin talking about translating African Christian ideas into Western terms' (1975: 22).

Bibliography

Bentley, W.H. (1887), *Dictionary and Grammar of the Kongo Language as Spoken in São Salvador*, 2 vols, Baptist Missionary Society, London

Bühlmann, Walbert (1976) *The Coming of the Third Church*, St Paul Publications, Slough

Butaye, R. (1909) *Dictionnaire KiKongo-Français, Français-KiKongo*, Jules De Mester, Roulers

Floraison... (1986) See Soeurs de Notre-Dame (Province of Zaïre)

Léonie de l'Assomption (n.d.) *Congo Débuts (1894–1906)*. Manuscript in Archives of the Sisters of Notre Dame at the Mother House in Namur, Belgium

MacGaffey, W. (1970) *Custom and Government in the Lower Congo*, University of California Press, Berkeley, CA

Norberta, Mary (1955) – 'La Formation des Soeurs Indigènes en Afrique': 106–16. Offprint of an article from a journal identified only as 'UMC' (most probably *Bulletin de l'Union Missionaire du Clergé*) filed in Archives of the Sisters of Notre Dame at the Mother House in Namur, Belgium

Shorter, A. (1975) *African Christian Theology: Adaptation or Incarnation?* Geoffrey Chapman, London

Soeurs de Notre-Dame (Province of Zaïre). (1986) *Floraison de la branche Zaïroise Notre-Dame, 1961–86*, Kimwenza: unpublished internal document

Van Roy, H. and J. Daeleman (1963) *Proverbes Kongo*, Tervuren: Musée Royale de l'Afrique Centrale

Van Wing, J. (1921) *Études BaKongo: Histoire et Sociologie*, Collection: Bibliothèque Congo, no. 3. Goemaere,

———— (1959) *Étude BaKongo: Sociologie, Religion et Magie*, 2nd edition, Desclée de Brouwers, Brussels

Weeks, John. (1914) *Among the Primitive BaKongo*, Seely Service, London

Place Index

267

Name Index

Subject Index

275